ROAD & TRACK

Illustrated Automotive Dictionary

by John Dinkel

B www.BentleyPublishers.com

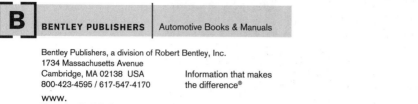

BENTLEY PUBLISHERS | Automotive Books & Manuals

Bentley Publishers, a division of Robert Bentley, Inc.
1734 Massachusetts Avenue
Cambridge, MA 02138 USA
800-423-4595 / 617-547-4170

Information that makes
the difference®

www.
BentleyPublishers
.com

Copies of this book may be purchased from selected booksellers, or directly from the publisher by mail. The publisher encourages comments from the reader of this book. These communications have been and will be considered in the preparation of this and other manuals. Please write to Bentley Publishers at the address listed at the top of this page.

Library of Congress Cataloging-in-Publication Data
Dinkel, John
    Road & track illustrated automotive dictionary / by John Dinkel.
      p. cm.
    Rev. ed. of: The road & track illustrated auto dictionary. 1st ed. c1977.
    ISBN 0-8376-0143-6 (alk. paper)
    1. Automobiles--Dictionaries. I. Title: Illustrated automotive dictionary. II. Dinkel, John. Road & track illustrated auto dictionary. III. Road & track. IV. Title.

TL9 .D56 2000
629.222'03--dc21

00-044453

Bentley Stock No. GRAD

06 05 04 03 7 6 5 4 3

The paper used in this publication is acid free and meets the requirements of the National Standard for Information Sciences-Permanence of Paper for Printed Library Materials. ∞

The Road & Track Illustrated Automotive Dictionary, by John Dinkel
© 2000 John Dinkel, Bentley Publishers

ROAD&TRACK® is a registered trademark of Hachette Filipacchi Magazines, Inc.

Manufactured in the United States of America

Front cover: Photos and illustration courtesy of Ferrari, Italy
Back cover: Photo and illustrations courtesy of Road & Track
Cover design: Mary-Margaret Mulligan

Acknowledgements

This automotive dictionary first appeared in a much abbreviated form in the pages of *Road & Track* as a series during 1975 and 1976. Much has happened in the automotive world during the past quarter century and this expanded and extensively illustrated auto dictionary is the result. It has taken nearly four years to put the more than 1,300 definitions and over 400 detailed illustrations together. Along the way I've had lots of help. On the editorial side there's been a number of editors at Bentley Publishers, but the one who has done the most to get this book into print has been Albert A. Dalia. On the illustration side, I couldn't have completed this work without major assistance from two people at the *Road & Track* library, Jim Hall and Jane Barrett. On the manufacturer side, I had help from numerous auto-related companies. Among the many were Honda, Mercedes (okay, DaimlerChrysler), Pirelli, Michelin, Ferrari, Goodyear, Porsche, Volkswagen, and Mazda. Thank you, one and all.

A special thanks to three special people: my wife Leslie and our two kids Meredith and Kevin. All three were extremely helpful in keeping me focused on writing definitions that even a non-engineer could understand and love.

In so many ways this dictionary is a work in progress. Time and technology wait for no man; new technological developments are introduced on an almost daily basis. So by the time you pick up a copy of this book, you may find it is missing the definition for some newfangled device or technology that didn't exist (or I didn't think about) when the book went to print. Not to worry. Send your comments, including missing entries (and their definitions if you have them) to Bentley Publishers at 1734 Massachusetts Ave., Cambridge, MA 02138. We'll start collecting them for inclusion in a future updated version of this dictionary.

John Dinkel

A-arm A lateral suspension locating link in the shape of the letter A. The two legs attach to the chassis by pivots and rubber bushings that allow the outboard top of the A (connected to the wheel assembly) to pivot up and down. Sometimes the A-arm is made up of two separate links. The system is widely considered to give excellent wheel-locating geometry, and it is used for the rear suspension of most racing cars and many high-performance road cars. Also called *wishbone*. Also see *unequal-length A-arms*.

ABS See *antilock braking system*.

acceleration The rate of change of velocity in relation to time; measured in ft/sec/sec or ft/sec^2.

accelerator A foot pedal linked to the throttle valve, controlling the flow of air and therefore, by means of the carburetor or fuel injection system, also the amount of fuel admitted to the engine. Also called the *throttle*.

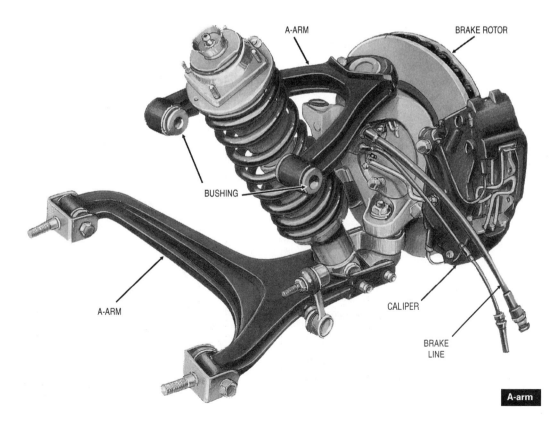

A-arm

1

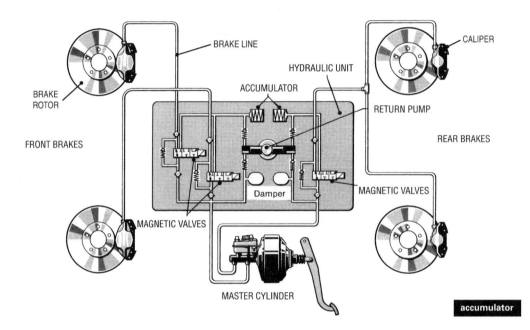

accelerator pump A carburetor device that enriches the fuel mixture for acceleration.

accelerometer A mechanical or electrical instrument for measuring and recording acceleration.

access panel See *hood*.

accumulator In a hydraulically assisted brake system, a reservoir filled with hydraulic fluid and kept under pressure during engine operation; in case of engine failure, this pressure provides reserve braking power that can stop the car several times with something approaching the degree of assistance available with the engine running.

Ackermann steering Steering geometry that allows the outside wheel to turn fewer degrees than the inside wheel to compensate for the larger circle tracked by the outside wheel. The relationship between the angles of the inner and outer wheels is not fixed; the tighter the turn, the greater the disparity between the wheels' desired turning angles.

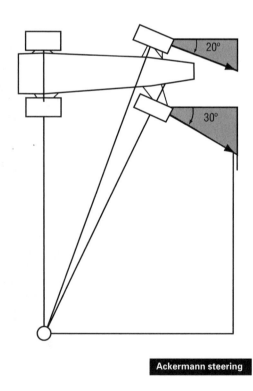

Ackermann steering

Steering geometry that does not give the ideal relationship in all types of turns results in tire scrub. Ackermann steering remains perfectly accurate only at very low speeds, before the non-linear characteristics of the tires become a factor. However, Ackermann steering minimizes scrub in the vast majority of conditions encountered by production cars, though it is a design compromise that corrects for normal driving conditions rather than for all possible turns.

active-ride suspension   See *active suspension*.

active safety   Aspects of a car's engineering that affect its accident-avoidance capabilities, especially those under driver control. Includes such factors as steering, brakes, handling, and tires — in sum, a car's total roadholding and evasive capability. Also see *passive safety*.

active suspension   A suspension system with a double-acting hydraulic actuator at each wheel, driven by a variable-rate hydraulic pump and controlled by an electronic control unit (ECU).

The ECU monitors forward speed, body attitude, lateral-versus-longitudinal velocity when cornering, wheel/hub velocity, angular displacement, and load. It also controls an onboard hydraulic power source that supplies the internal pressure necessary to counteract the external forces and optimize the vehicle's body position. The main advantage of active suspension is superior body and suspension control under all conditions, including near roll-free cornering behavior and a virtual absence of bounce and pitch. An active suspension is truly an intelligent suspension that senses outside forces and generates its own internal forces to counter them, thereby controlling body position; conventional suspensions can only react to the forces influencing them, and are thus passive systems. Generally, an active suspension will still have conventional springs to support the car's static weight when the car is at rest and the engine is off. Also known as *active-ride suspension* or *full-active suspension*.

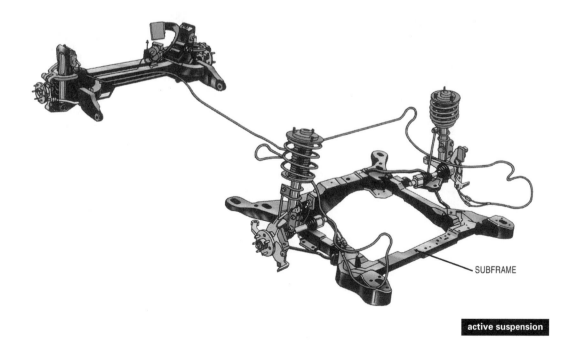

SUBFRAME

active suspension

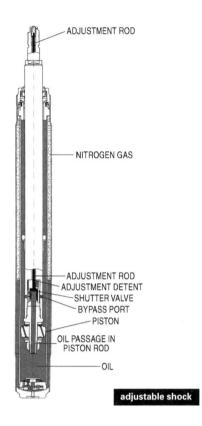

ADJUSTMENT ROD

NITROGEN GAS

ADJUSTMENT ROD
ADJUSTMENT DETENT
SHUTTER VALVE
BYPASS PORT
PISTON
OIL PASSAGE IN
PISTON ROD
OIL

adjustable shock

adaptive controls Modern electronic engine controls with the ability to "remember" major changes in environmental and operating conditions and adjust to them. An example is the adaptive feedback idle-speed control of certain engine-management systems, which shifts its adjustment range during the break-in period of a new engine and therefore needs no further attention for the car's life span, barring malfunctions.

adhesion The ability of a tire to remain in contact with a road surface without loss of traction. Also, the ability of an oil to remain in contact with a metal surface.

adiabatic engine An engine in which the heat of combustion remains within the combustion chamber and cylinder where it can be converted into power, making the engine more efficient and allowing it to operate without a cooling system.

adjustable shock A shock absorber whose jounce and rebound characteristics can be stiffened or softened, either manually or electronically, to compensate for wear or to fine-tune a suspension for rough roads, heavy loads, cornering, or racing. Manual adjustments are made on the shock absorber; some contemporary cars have shock absorbers that can be adjusted electromechanically via a switch inside the car.

advance To adjust the timing of a camshaft or distributor spark or valve operation, so that a valve opens or a spark plug fires earlier in the engine's cycle; also, the mechanism for doing this. The opposite of *retard*.

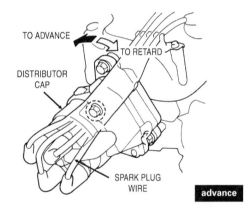

TO ADVANCE
TO RETARD
DISTRIBUTOR
CAP
SPARK PLUG
WIRE

advance

aerodynamic drag The resistance of air to the forward movement of a body such as a car. It has three sources:

Drag resistance, a function of the body's shape. Protruding objects such as mirrors, mufflers, and license plates can increase drag resistance considerably at higher speeds. Of special importance is the shape of the rear part of the body, which determines the amount of turbulence in the vehicle's wake.

Air friction on the body's external surfaces (skin). For the more or less standardized surface finish of modern passenger cars, this amounts to about 10 percent of total air resistance.

Airflow through the car for cooling or ventilation. This can reduce or increase resistance,

FRONT SPOILER

aerodynamic drag

Front impact sensors
Safety sensor
Air bag unit

The sensor sends signals to the electronic unit.
The gas generator begins to inflate the airbag.

The air bag reaches the driver's chest.

The air bag is fully inflated.

The steering column has collapsed.
The air bag begins to deflate.

airbag

depending on the function, location, and aerodynamic design of the air channels or orifices.

Aerodynamic drag, or air resistance, increases as the square of vehicle velocity; the power needed to overcome it varies as the cube of vehicle velocity. Also see *coefficient of aerodynamic drag* and *coefficient of aerodynamic lift*.

aggressive   The French now describe a car as aggressive, or refer to its aggressivity, if its structural passive safety characteristics are such that it imposes excessive injury to a pedestrian, to an occupant of another vehicle, or to another vehicle in an accident. For example, the shape of the front end and the height of the bumper of an aggressive car would tend to throw a pedestrian under the car rather than up and onto its hood. Similarly, the front end structure would be capable of penetrating another vehicle upon impact rather than crushing progressively. Also see *crush zone* and *passenger cell*.

aggressivity   See *aggressive*.

airbag   A large deflated pillow or balloon concealed in the steering-wheel hub, instrument panel, dash, door panel, or seat, designed for rapid inflation in a frontal or side impact to cushion and restrain front-seat occupants.

One or more deceleration sensors trigger inflation within milliseconds, typically by burning a solid chemical that converts to a gas that inflates the bag; the bag then deflates, also very quickly.

Airbags are an example of a passive restraint mandated for fixed percentages of cars sold in the United States by all manufacturers beginning with model year 1987. Also see *Supplemental Restraint System*.

air bleed passage   See *compensating jet*.

air capacity   See *breathing capacity*.

air cleaner   A device mounted on an engine's intake system that contains a wire mesh or paper filter to trap dust and dirt, preventing them from being drawn into the engine. Also called *air filter*.

air-cooled engine   An engine cooled by the passage of air around external cylinder fins rather than by passage of a liquid coolant through internal water jackets.

air dam, front and rear   An aerodynamic device that reduces the amount of air flowing under, and directs airflow around, a car, thus reducing its aerodynamic drag and lift.

Originally devised for racing, air dams have become a popular accessory and *de rigeur* for newer high-performance production models. Air dams are typically made of aluminum, fiberglass, or flexible plastic, the last being most practical for road use given their proximity to the ground and consequent vulnerability to scrap-

AIR DAM

air dam (front)

ing and bending. They're generally distinguished from front spoilers by being somewhat deeper. A recent development is the rear air dam, sometimes referred to as a *skirt* and generally seen with extensions of a car's rocker panels. Also see *ground effect*.

air filter   See *air cleaner*.

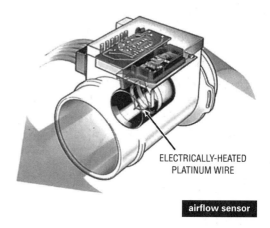

ELECTRICALLY-HEATED PLATINUM WIRE

airflow sensor

airflow sensor   The device in a fuel injection system that measures the flow of air through the intake manifold to determine the amount of fuel to be delivered; also called *mass airflow sensor*.

Bosch's mechanical K-Jetronic fuel injection system employs a mechanical sensor consisting of a plate ("flap") in the airstream, attached to a lever arm that in turn moves a plunger in the fuel distributor. The force of air on the plate moves the lever up and down, causing the plunger to open and close holes in the fuel distributor. The L-Jetronic system also uses a flap in the airstream; its movement creates voltage changes in a potentiometer (variable resistor) attached to it. These changes are relayed to the system's electronic control unit and, in turn, to the fuel distributor. Both these systems measure the volume of airflow.

In the Bosch LH-Jetronic system, the sensor is an electrically heated platinum wire. Air passing over the wire, which is part of a bridge cir-

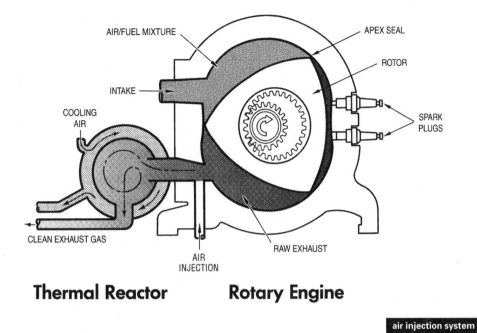

AIR/FUEL MIXTURE

APEX SEAL

ROTOR

INTAKE

SPARK
PLUGS

COOLING
AIR

CLEAN EXHAUST GAS

AIR
INJECTION

RAW EXHAUST

Thermal Reactor   Rotary Engine

air injection system

cuit, tends to cool it, thus altering its electrical resistance. An electronic amplifier detects these minute changes in resistance and regulates current to keep the wire at its original temperature. The current required is thus a measure of air mass, an even more fundamental indicator of how much fuel to supply than the volume measured by K- and L-Jetronic systems. Thus the heated wire is called an *air-mass sensor*.

air foil A device used to improve traction by increasing the aerodynamic downforce on either end of a car. In cross section, an airfoil is basically an inverted wing. Thus, instead of providing lift, as on an airplane, it causes air to push the car closer to the ground. The use of airfoils increases cornering capability and improves stability at speed, but at the expense of additional aerodynamic drag. Also called *wings*. Also see *downforce* and *ground effect*.

air-fuel mixture The blend of air and fuel supplied to an engine by the carburetor or fuel injection system.

air-fuel ratio The ratio of the mass of air to the mass of fuel supplied to an engine. The stoichiometric, or chemically correct, air-fuel ratio is the exact ratio necessary to burn all carbon and hydrogen in the fuel and produce carbon dioxide and water with no oxygen remaining.

air injection system An emission control system that injects fresh air into the exhaust ports or a thermal reactor for conversion of carbon monoxide into carbon dioxide and for combustion of unburned hydrocarbons in the exhaust gases. Also called *pulsed air injection*.

air lock See *air pocket*.

air-mass sensor See *airflow sensor*.

air pocket A quantity of air that prevents the normal flow of a liquid. Air pockets sometime occur in brake and clutch hydraulic lines, oil lines, or in the cooling system. Also see *bleed*.

air pollution Unwanted particles, mist, or gases put into the atmosphere primarily as a result of motor vehicle exhaust or the operation

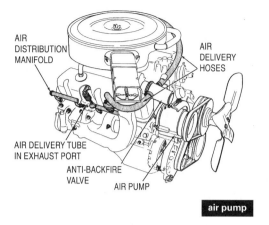

AIR DISTRIBUTION MANIFOLD

AIR DELIVERY HOSES

AIR DELIVERY TUBE IN EXHAUST PORT

ANTI-BACKFIRE VALVE

AIR PUMP

air pump

of industrial facilities. Also see *exhaust emission controls* and *exhaust emissions*.

air pump   The device that supplies the fresh air needed by an air injection system.

air resistance   See *aerodynamic drag*.

air scoop   An opening in a body panel used to duct outside air for purposes of ventilation or cooling, generally to the engine, brakes, radiator, or an oil cooler. On the hood (or the roof or rear deck of a rear- or mid-engine car) an air scoop can be used to force ambient air into the intake system. Also called *scoop*.

air scoop

air suspension   A suspension system using a type of airbag rather than metal springs to support a car and control its ride motions. Air suspension can result in excellent riding comfort over a wide range of vehicle loading because an air spring's natural frequency of vibration does not vary with load as does that of a metal spring. Air springs can be made very soft for a lightly loaded condition and their pressure automatically increased to match any increase in load, thus maintaining constant spring vibration characteristics for any load. Also called *air springing*.

air-to-air intercooler   See *intercooler*.

air-to-water intercooler   See *intercooler*.

air-valve carburetor   A carburetor in which a spring- or weight-closed air valve opens in response to engine demand. Through suitable linkage, it varies the fuel opening to give the desired mixture ratio throughout the range of operation. SU, Stromberg CD, and Keihin CV carburetors operate on this principle. Also referred to as *constant-depression, constant-vacuum,* and *variable-venturi carburetor*.

alignment   Generally refers to wheel alignment, the proper adjustment of a car's front or rear suspension for camber, toe, caster, and ride height.

all-indirect gearbox   A manual transmission in which none of the forward gears has a direct (1:1) ratio.

alloy   A metal composed of two or more elements; one or more elements is added to a pure metal to alter properties such as strength and elongation.

alloy wheel   A generic term used to describe any lightweight road wheel. The usual alloys are aluminum or magnesium, the latter material having led to the common usage of the term mag wheel, often referring to any nonsteel wheel. Alloy wheels can be cast (formed by pouring liquid metal into a mold) or forged (formed by

alloy wheels

heating the metal and then hammering or pressing it into a specific shape). Forged wheels are generally stronger than cast alloy wheels.

all-wheel drive (AWD)   A drive system in which the transmission is connected by the driving axle(s) to both the front and the rear wheels. For off-road vehicles it is usually termed *four-wheel drive* (4WD). Also see *four-wheel drive.*

all-wheel steering (AWS)   See *four-wheel steering.*

alphanumeric rating system   For tires; dating from 1968, this system is based on the load-carrying capacity of a tire rather than on a direct measurement of the section width. The capacity and size of the tire are indicated by letters ranging from A through N, with N representing the largest tire with the highest load-carrying capacity. A typical alphanumeric tire size is BR78-13, where B is the load/size relationship and R represents radial construction. If the R is missing, the tire is of bias construction. The number 78 is the aspect ratio and 13 is the wheel diameter in inches.

alternating current (AC)   Electrical current that reverses its flow in a circuit at regular intervals. The reversal typically occurs between 60 and 120 times per second, expressed as cycles per second (CPS). Compare with *direct current.* Also see *alternator.*

alternator   The part of a car's electrical system that converts mechanical energy from a drive

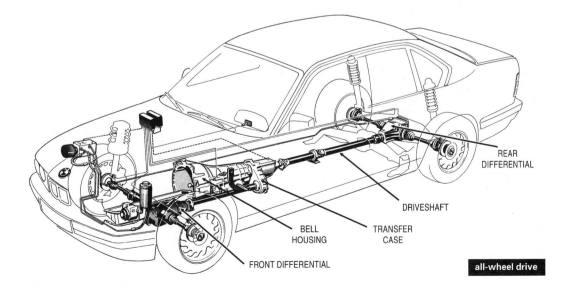

REAR DIFFERENTIAL

DRIVESHAFT

BELL HOUSING

TRANSFER CASE

FRONT DIFFERENTIAL

all-wheel drive

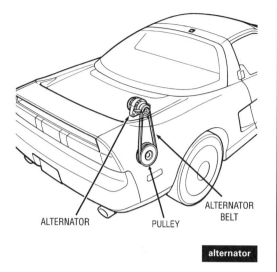

ALTERNATOR PULLEY ALTERNATOR BELT

alternator

belt into electrical energy to operate the ignition and electrical accessories and charge the battery. An alternator generates alternating current (AC) and then transforms it into the direct current (DC) used by automotive electrical systems. The alternator has replaced earlier DC generators, which are less efficient.

aluminum   A relatively soft silvery metal used where lightness is required. In cars, aluminum is always found as an alloy because in its pure form it lacks strength and rigidity and is difficult to machine. Aluminum alloys can be cast,

formed into sheets, or forged. Uses include body panels, wheels, engine blocks, radiators, transmission and differential housings, suspension members, and chassis.

ammeter   An instrument that measures the amount, or number of amperes, of current flowing in an electrical circuit.

ampere   A unit of electric current. The number of amperes is equal to the voltage divided by the resistance (in ohms) of the electrical circuit.

analog instrumentation   Gauges that use a symbolic representation, typically a pointer moving along or around a scale, to display information such as engine speed, miles per hour, oil pressure, voltage, fuel supply, or time (the "hands-and-face" clock); contrasts with digital instrumentation, in which information is expressed by numerals (digits). Traditionally, analog-gauge pointers operated by purely mechanical means such as a cable drive, but these have increasingly given way to electronic operation. Even newer are electronic graphic displays, where small liquid crystal or vacuum-fluorescent elements form a band that performs the same function as a pointer.

annular gear   A ring gear. See *ring gear* and *planetary gears*.

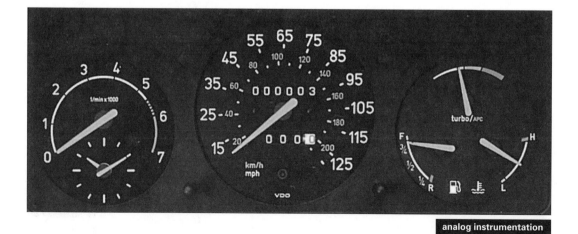

analog instrumentation

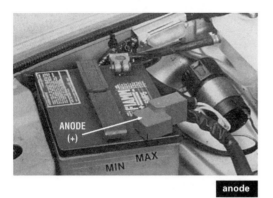

anode

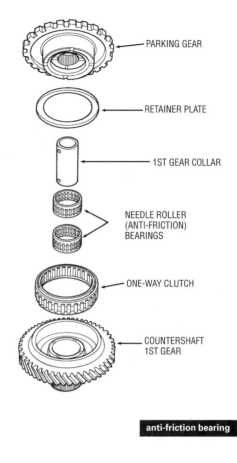

PARKING GEAR

RETAINER PLATE

1ST GEAR COLLAR

NEEDLE ROLLER
(ANTI-FRICTION)
BEARINGS

ONE-WAY CLUTCH

COUNTERSHAFT
1ST GEAR

anti-friction bearing

anode   The positively charged electrode in an electrolytic cell. An automotive battery consists of electrolytic cells. Also see *electrolyte*.

anodize   To coat or plate a metal (typically aluminum) with a protective material by electrolytic action.

anti-backfire valve   A part of the air injection system that diverts air from the air pump away from the exhaust ports for a brief time when the accelerator is first released during deceleration. This prevents fuel-rich unburned exhaust gases from mixing explosively with fresh air and causing a backfire.

anti-dive   The characteristics of a car's suspension intended to resist unwanted downward motion during braking. To achieve anti-dive reactions in a front suspension featuring unequal-length A-arms, the upper arm is angled upward toward the front and the lower arm is angled downward. The angling produces lift components in reaction to brake torque that "hold up" the front end. Also see *dive*, *lift*, and *anti-lift*.

antifreeze   Any of several substances (commonly liquids and typically ethylene glycol) mixed with water and added to a car's cooling system to lower the freezing point of the coolant and to inhibit formation of rust and other deposits that could clog the radiator and coolant passages and reduce cooling efficiency.

anti-friction bearing   Any bearing in which moving parts are in rolling contact. Also see *ball bearing*, *roller bearing*, and *needle bearing*.

anti-knock agents   Substances (such as tetraethyl lead or ethanol) added to gasoline to raise the octane number and reduce the gasoline's tendency to knock or ping. Also see *detonation*.

anti-lift   The characteristics of a car's suspension intended to resist unwanted upward motion during hard acceleration. Trailing arms and semi-trailing arms are often used in rear suspension systems because they provide strong resistance to lift. Also see *lift*, *dive*, and *anti-dive*.

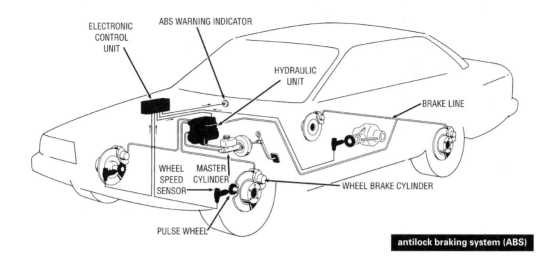

ELECTRONIC
CONTROL
UNIT

ABS WARNING INDICATOR

HYDRAULIC
UNIT

BRAKE LINE

WHEEL SPEED SENSOR

MASTER CYLINDER

WHEEL BRAKE CYLINDER

PULSE WHEEL

antilock braking system (ABS)

antilock braking system (ABS) A system that provides rapid, automatic cadence braking in response to signs of incipient wheel lockup by alternately increasing and decreasing hydraulic pressure in the brake line(s) of the affected wheel(s). This action prevents wheel lockup, thereby preserving steering control and reducing stopping distances on some road surfaces.

Under braking, an electronic control unit (ECU) receives signals from electronic sensors monitoring wheel rotation. If a wheel's rate of rotation suddenly decreases, the ECU orders a hydraulic control unit to reduce line pressure to that wheel's brake. Once the wheel resumes normal rotation, the controls restore pressure to its brake. Depending on the system, this cycle of "pumping" or cadence braking can occur up to fifteen times per second. Also see *Stop Control System.*

anti-percolation valve A carburetor vent used to prevent vapor lock by releasing hot, expanding fuel vapors. In emission-controlled engines, vapors are not released to the atmosphere but are routed into an evaporative-emission-control canister, where they are stored and then metered to the engine the next time it is started. Also see *evaporative emission control* and *vapor lock.*

anti-roll bar A transverse bar linking both sides of a suspension system; generally, a torsion bar with rubber bushings mounted on the chassis that allow it to turn freely. The bar's ends are connected to or shaped as lever arms, with attachments to the suspension linkages at each side via ball-joint links, rubber-bushed pivot links, or, on race cars, spherical rod ends called Heim joints. When both wheels take a bump equally, the wheels move the same amount without twisting the anti-roll bar. Individual wheel movement or body roll will force the bar to twist as the lever arms are variously moved, thereby adding the bar's own spring rate to that

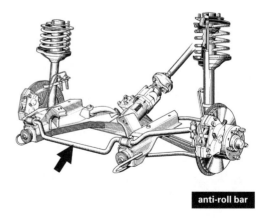

anti-roll bar

brakes, reduce the throttle opening or turbocharger boost, or perform a phased shutdown of engine cylinders until power to the wheel is sufficiently reduced that it resumes normal rotation. Also called *anti-spin, anti-slip*.

apex seal In the Wankel or rotary engine, the equivalent of a reciprocating engine's piston ring. Fitted to each of the three apexes on a rotor, the seals serve to prevent compressed-gas leakage and blowby of combustion gases, and also to release part of the heat captured by the rotor into the wall of the housing. Also called *tip seal*. Also see *Wankel engine*.

A-pillar A car's foremost roof pillars, supporting the windshield and front portion of the roof. Also called *A-post*.

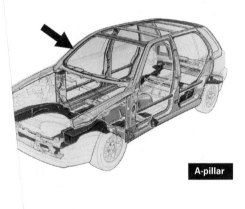

A-pillar

t See *A-pillar*.

aquaplaning A tire's tendency to ride on a layer of water instead of maintaining direct contact with the road surface. Generally more pronounced in low-profile tires with relatively large contact patches, aquaplaning can lead to loss of control. For this reason, virtually all road tires have grooves designed to channel water away from the tread. Also known as *hydroplaning*.

ARI See *Automatic Radio Information*.

armature A wire-wrapped iron or steel core forming a movable coil within the starter motor.

anti-sway bar See *anti-roll bar*.

anti-wheelspin Electronic controls that maintain vehicle traction by automatically applying the brakes and/or reducing engine power during acceleration when the system detects one or more wheels spinning. As in electronic anti-lock braking, sensors monitor wheel rotation; in this case, though, a sudden increase in a wheel's rate of rotation signals the anti-spin controls to effect gradual application of the

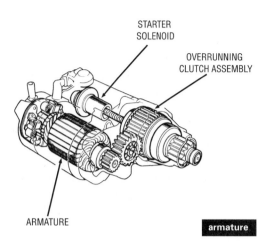

STARTER
SOLENOID

OVERRUNNING
CLUTCH ASSEMBLY

ARMATURE

armature

When it revolves in the magnetic field between the poles, an electric current is induced.

aspect ratio The ratio of a tire's cross-sectional height to its width, usually used with the expression "-series." The lower the number, the lower the tire profile. Thus, a 50-series tire (section height of 50 percent of width) has a lower profile than a 60-series tire.

asymmetrical tread

aspiration The method by which an engine breathes; used mainly to express whether the air-fuel mixture is delivered at or above atmospheric pressure. An engine without a turbocharger or a supercharger is said to be *naturally* or *normally aspirated*, while one so equipped may be said to be *hyperaspirated* or *blown*. Also see *atmospheric pressure, supercharger*, and *turbocharger*.

assisted steering See *power steering*.

asymmetrical tread A tire tread in which the shape and size of the grooves vary across its width. The purpose is to provide an optimum combination of braking, ride, handling, and wet- and dry-road characteristics.

atmosphere A unit of measure of air pressure at sea level; sometimes used for the pressure of air forced into an engine by a turbocharger or supercharger. One atmosphere equals 14.7 lbs/in.^{2} (psi) or, in the metric system, approximately 1.01 bar.

atmospheric pressure The weight of air pressing downward per unit area. The average pressure at sea level is 14.7 lbs/in.^{2} (psi).

autocross See *slalom*.

autoignition Rapid burning of the air-fuel mixture not caused by an external ignition source such as a spark, flame, or hot surface. Also see *detonation* and *dieseling*.

automatic choke See *choke*.

automatic climate control A combined heating/ventilation/air-conditioning system that automatically balances heating and cooling to maintain interior temperature at a set level. Also called *automatic temperature control*.

automatic level control See *automatic leveling*.

automatic leveling A suspension system that compensates for load variations at the front, rear, or both ends of a car, positioning it at a pre-

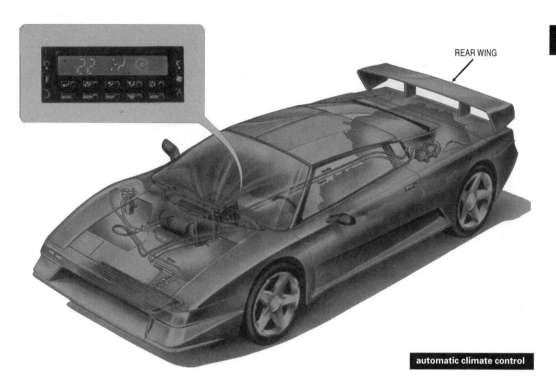

REAR WING

automatic climate control

designated level (zero pitch) regardless of load. Also called *automatic level control.*

Automatic Radio Information (ARI) A car audio system that automatically interrupts radio or cassette listening with reports on local traffic conditions so a driver can take an alternate route to avoid delays. Though national in scope, the ARI network is divided into regions, each with

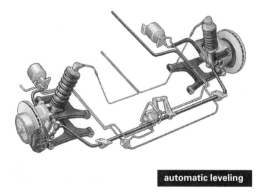

automatic leveling

its own assigned VHF frequency. First developed in Germany, ARI is now available in parts of the United States.

automatic seat belt A passive restraint device, normally a front-seat shoulder belt that fits diagonally across the wearer and is anchored at both ends, with one end feeding out from an inertia reel. When a door is closed, the belt moves into the correct position for restraining the wearer without manual fastening.

Automatic seat belts may be either mechanical or electric. The former typically mounts the inertia reel and outboard belt end on the door, with the inboard end anchored to a fixture between the seats; as the door closes, the inertia reel takes up slack in the webbing to tension the belt. In the electric type, a small motor runs the outboard end rearward along a track above the door when the door is closed (and forward when the door is opened); the inertia reel is combined with the inboard anchorage.

A

Automatic seat belts can be used in lieu of or in addition to airbags under the U.S. government mandate that specified some type of passive restraint on a fixed percentage of all cars sold in the United States beginning with model year 1987. They are simpler and therefore less expensive than airbags, and must be worn in conjunction with a manually fastened lap belt for optimum restraint.

automatic temperature control   See *automatic climate control.*

automatic transmission   A mechanism in the drivetrain with gearsets to vary the power and torque delivered to the driven wheels as a function of engine load and speed, usually incorporating a fluid coupling or torque converter to allow stopping and reversing without a foot-operated clutch. Also see *fluid coupling, infinitely variable transmission,* and *torque converter.*

autothermic piston   An aluminum piston in which steel or alloy inserts are cast to control expansion of the skirt.

auxiliary lighting   An additional driving light, fog light, or spotlight used in conjunction with normal high or low beams.

axle   A shaft on which a wheel revolves or which revolves with a wheel. Also a beam, usually solid but sometimes hollow, connecting the two wheels at one end of a car. A live axle transmits power, as in a front-engine/rear drive car. A beam or rigid or dead axle supports but does not drive the wheels, as at the rear of a front-wheel-drive car. Also see *half shaft.*

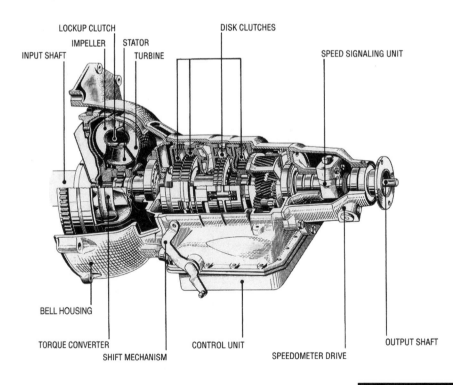

LOCKUP CLUTCH
IMPELLER   STATOR
INPUT SHAFT   TURBINE
DISK CLUTCHES
SPEED SIGNALING UNIT
BELL HOUSING
TORQUE CONVERTER
SHIFT MECHANISM
CONTROL UNIT
SPEEDOMETER DRIVE
OUTPUT SHAFT

automatic transmission

A

axle shaft See *half shaft*.

axle windup Phenomenon in which the torque being transmitted by the axle shafts to the wheels produces a reaction that rotates the live axle about its own centerline. Obviously a greater problem in cars with very high torque, axle windup can produce tramping of the rear wheels or wheel hop as the axle winds and unwinds. Also called *wheel tramp*. Also see *wheel hop*.

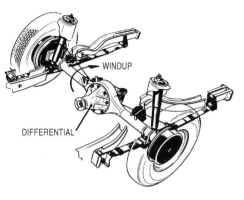

WINDUP

DIFFERENTIAL

axle windup

B

backbone frame   A lightweight frame with high torsional rigidity (resistance to axial twisting). In cross section, a rectangular box that runs along a car's longitudinal centerline; this box generally divides at the front into a V whose forward extremities are joined by a cross member to which the front suspension components are attached. At the rear, a similar triangular frame provides attachment points for the rear suspension and may enclose the final-drive housing. The design was propagated by Colin Chapman with the Lotus Elan.

backfire   Premature combustion of the air-fuel mixture exploding through an open exhaust valve and into the exhaust system, or a violent combustion in the exhaust system itself. Also, ignition of the air-fuel mixture in the intake manifold by flame from a cylinder, possibly caused by a leaking intake valve.

backing plate   See *brake backing plate.*

REAR

FRONT

backbone frame

backlash   Clearance or free play between two parts. Also, the clearance between meshing teeth in two gears that allows slight rotation of the driven gear in a direction opposite to driving rotation.

backlite   The rear window. Also see *light.*

back panel   See *fascia.*

back pressure   Any resistance to free flow in an exhaust system. Mufflers and catalytic converters cause back pressure by rerouting the

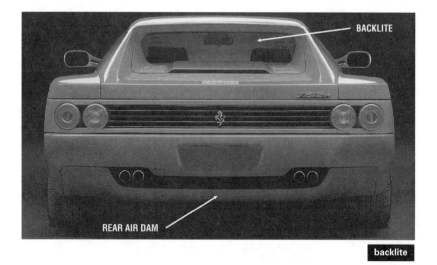

BACKLITE

REAR AIR DAM

backlite

exhaust gases for noise suppression and emission control, but an exhaust pipe alone also causes some.

backrest   See *seat back.*

backrest angle   See *seat-back angle.*

baffle   An obstruction used to change or deflect the flow of liquids or gases to prevent surging or reduce noise. Baffles may be used in the fuel tank, crankcase, muffler, and radiator. Also called *baffle plate.*

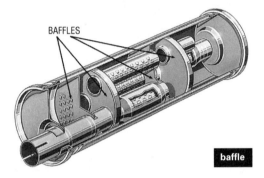

baffle

balance   The condition in which the mass of the tire and wheel are evenly distributed, resulting in minimal vibrations. Also see *balancing* and *wheel balancing.*

balance shaft   A counterweighted engine shaft, driven by the crankshaft but rotating in the opposite direction, that reduces unwanted vibration caused by an engine's inherent inertial forces. Used mainly on large-displacement four-cylinder engines with relatively high unbalanced forces, the design typically consists of two shafts turning in opposite directions, positioned on either side of the crankshaft. A single balance shaft is often used in 90-degree V-6 engines.

balancing   A process in which every reciprocating and rotating part of an engine is balanced statically and dynamically to reduce friction, wear, and vibration and to increase horsepower and reliability. Also see *balance, blueprinting* and *wheel balancing.*

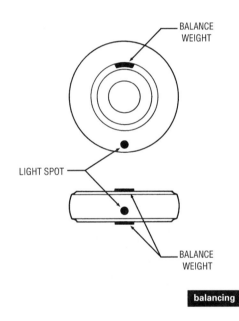

balancing

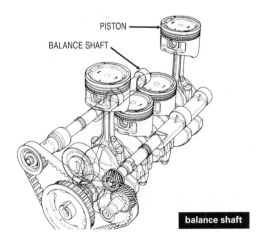

balance shaft

bald   Refers to a worn road tire that is treadless or nearly treadless and thus generally unsafe.

balking   See *lugging.*

balk ring   A friction-regulated pawl or plunger used to facilitate engagement of gears. In a manual transmission it prevents premature engagement of the gears during shifting.

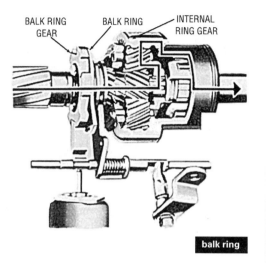

BALK RING GEAR   BALK RING   INTERNAL RING GEAR

balk ring

ball-and-nut steering   See *recirculating ball-and-nut steering*.

ball bearing   A bearing that uses steel balls inside a shell to reduce friction. Also see *bearing*.

ball joints   The ball-and-socket link that attaches the steering knuckle to the upper and lower suspension arms and the tie-rod ends to the steering arms. Ball joints act as pivots that allow the front wheels to turn for steering and compensate for changes in wheel and steering geometries that occur during jounce, rebound, and turning.

bar   A metric unit of pressure. Used for the pressure of air forced into an engine by a tur-

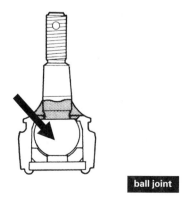

ball joint

bocharger or supercharger. One bar equals approximately 14.5 psi or 0.99 atmosphere.

barrel   The main air passage in a carburetor, where the throttle is located; for example, a four-barrel carburetor is one with four such openings and throttles. Also called *venturi*. Also see *cylinder*.

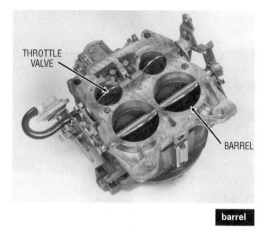

THROTTLE VALVE

BARREL

barrel

barrier crash   A procedure wherein a vehicle is driven, usually by remote control, into a wall to evaluate the vehicle's effectiveness in protecting occupants from the forces of a collision. Also used to evaluate bumpers for protection against damage. Evaluation is made with instrumented anthropomorphic dummies constructed

barrier crash

to duplicate the responses of a living person as closely as possible, though human cadavers have also been used. All new cars sold in the United States must meet federal occupant-protection criteria in a 30-mph barrier crash. The government also tests selected models for performance in a 35-mph test and publishes the results, but these play no role in certification of cars for sale. Also called *barrier test.*

barrier test   See *barrier crash.*

batch   The compound made from the materials of which rubber is constituted, i.e., the natural and synthetic rubber, load, additive, vulcanizer, sulphur, antioxidants, and accelerators. The batches used for tires are the best quality of all those employed in the rubber industry. Carbon black is the usual material used as load, which enhances the physical and chemical properties of the batch, especially abrasion resistance. Antioxidants are special substances that give a higher resistance to oxidation. Accelerators are chemical catalysts that greatly speed up the process of vulcanization.

battery   See *storage battery.*

BDC   See *bottom dead center.*

BEAD

bead

bead   Part of a tire that makes contact with and seals a tubeless tire to the rim. It is appropriately rigid to allow the anchoring of the flexible casing to the rigid metal wheel rim.

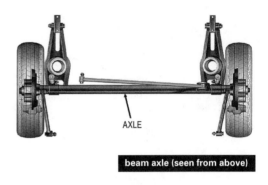

AXLE

beam axle (seen from above)

bead lockup   See *flipper.*

bead seat   The portion of the wheel rim where the bead rests.

beam axle   An axle that supports but does not drive the wheels, as at the rear of a front-wheel-drive car. Also called a *dead axle.*

bearing   The curved surface on a shaft or in a bore, or the part that permits relative motion between components with minimum wear and friction. Any component that serves as a bearing surface or surfaces. Also see *ball bearing, needle bearing, roller bearing,* and *bore.*

bearing cap   Retainers, held in place by nuts and bolts, that hold the connecting rod and the lower crankshaft bearings in place.

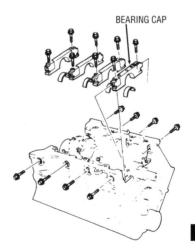

BEARING CAP

bearing cap

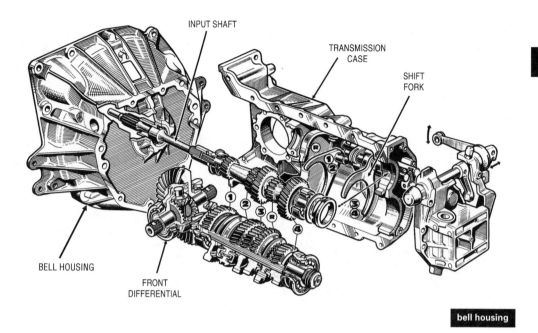

INPUT SHAFT

TRANSMISSION
CASE

SHIFT
FORK

B

BELL HOUSING

FRONT
DIFFERENTIAL

bell housing

bell housing   Bell-shaped covering for the fly-wheel and clutch of a manual transmission or the flywheel and torque converter of an automatic transmission.

belt   A reinforcing band that runs around the circumference of a tire to strengthen the tread area and/or constrain the tire under centrifugal

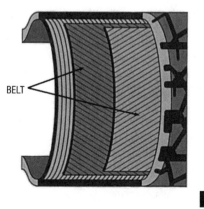

BELT

belt

force. Normally steel, but textiles and fiberglass are also used. Also see *drive belt, seat belt*.

belt line   A styling term for the line where the upper edge of a car's lower body meets the lower edge of the greenhouse.

bench seat   A car seat whose cushion runs nearly the full interior width to accommodate more than one person.

Bendix drive   Trademark for a commonly used drive on a starter motor consisting of a heli-cally grooved shaft with a pinion wheel at the end. When electricity is applied to the motor, the shaft rotates and extends, causing the pinion gear to engage the ring gear surrounding the fly-wheel. The rotation of the flywheel, and the crankshaft to which it is attached, causes the engine to turn over and fire. The rapid acceler-ation of the flywheel causes the pinion gear to disengage.

Berlina   Italian term for sedan, derived from Berlin, a form of horse-drawn coach. See *sedan*.

NACA DUCT

Berlinetta

Berlinetta   The Italian term for a coupe, frequently associated with two-seater or two-plus-two Grand Touring and sports racing cars. The Ferrari Berlinetta Boxer is one such example. Also see *coupe*.

bevel gear   A gear shaped like the wide end of a cone, used to transmit motion through an angle. Differential gears are usually bevel gears.

bezel   A ring or rim on or around the opening for a headlight, instrument, or other fix-

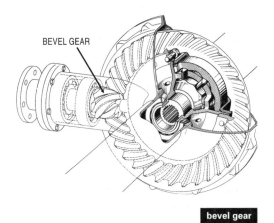

BEVEL GEAR

bevel gear

ture. It may be functional, helping to secure the fixture, or purely decorative. Some bezels are grooved to hold a transparent glass or plastic cover for dust protection, as on a speedometer or tachometer.

bhp   See *brake horsepower*.

bias angle   See *bias tire*.

bias-belted tire   A compromise design between the inexpensive bias tire and the better-handling, longer-wearing, but more expensive radial tire, having two plies of conventional fabric with about the same bias angle as the bias tire. Added to this is a two-ply belt, usually of steel, textile, or fiberglass material laid at an angle of 25–30 degrees, giving the bias-belted tire a main carcass or sidewall stiffness similar to that of the bias tire plus a belt that isn't as stiff as the radial's. The design was popular with American tire makers in the late sixties and seventies as they evolved from bias-ply to radial tire design and production.

bias-ply   See *bias tire*.

bias-ply tire   See *bias tire*.

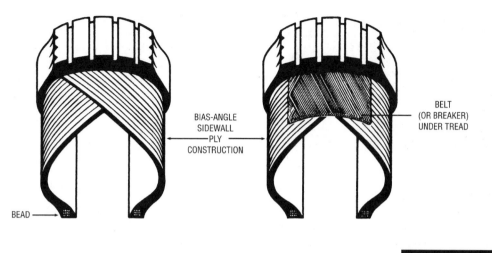

BIAS-ANGLE
SIDEWALL
PLY
CONSTRUCTION

BELT
(OR BREAKER)
UNDER TREAD

BEAD

BIAS-PLY

BELTED BIAS-PLY

bias tire; bias-belted tire

bias tire   Once the conventional automobile tire, bias tires were replaced first by bias-belted and then by radial tires and are now almost extinct on passenger cars. The cords in its plies of structural fabric are at an angle (the bias angle) to the circumferential centerline. Its carcass is constructed of adjacent layers of fabric that run continuously from bead to bead. A typical passenger-car bias tire has two plies of fabric with cords running at an angle of 30–40

degrees to the circumferential centerline. Also called *bias-ply* or *cross-ply.*

big end   The end of a connecting rod that bolts to the crankshaft. The opposite end, which attaches to the piston pin, is called the little or small end.

black box   See *electronic control module.*

bleed   To remove air bubbles or an air pocket from a brake or clutch line by opening the line to drain the air-contaminated fluid. Usually requires pumping the brake or clutch pedal to forcibly dispel the contaminated fluid, then

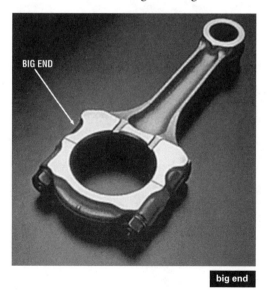

BIG END

big end

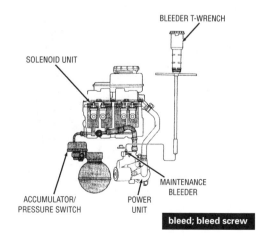

BLEEDER T-WRENCH

SOLENOID UNIT

MAINTENANCE
BLEEDER

ACCUMULATOR/
PRESSURE SWITCH

POWER
UNIT

bleed; bleed screw

blister

replenishing the brake or clutch reservoir with clean hydraulic fluid.

In a cooling system, bleeding is typically accomplished by opening a bleed screw located at the high point of the system and adding coolant until clear coolant begins to run out of the opening. The screw is then tightened to close the system.

bleeder valve   See *bleed screw.*

bleed screw   A threaded valve used to drain the cooling system or hydraulic clutch or brake lines. Also called *bleeder valve.* Also see *bleed.*

blister   A bulge in the surface of a car body, often required to provide clearance for a com-

ponent such as an air cleaner or wheel, but also frequently ornamental.

Also, small air bubbles in a coat of paint due to improper surface preparation, insufficient drying time between coats of paint, too heavy application, or incompatibility between primer and top coats.

Also, on tires, a bubble in the tread or side-wall area indicating separation caused by excessive heat.

block   See *cylinder block.*

blowby   Leakage of the compressed air-fuel mixture or the burned gases from the combustion chamber past the piston rings and into the crankcase; caused by worn piston rings, it results in power loss and oil contamination.

blower   See *supercharger* and *turbocharger.*

blown   Designates an engine equipped with a turbocharger or supercharger. Can also refer to a ruined engine.

blow-off valve   A one-way valve that opens to the atmosphere above a certain pressure to relieve excessive internal pressure. Often used in turbocharger installations to limit boost pressure

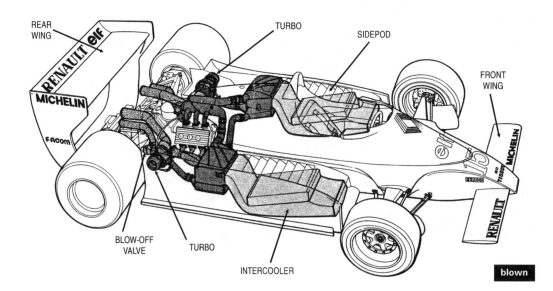

REAR WING

TURBO

SIDEPOD

FRONT WING

BLOW-OFF VALVE

TURBO

INTERCOOLER

blown

B

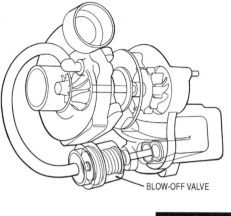

BLOW-OFF VALVE

blow-off valve

body   The external panels of a car, including the hood, fenders, doors, roof, and trunk.

body-in-white   An unpainted vehicle's basic frame/unit body structure, including sheet metal but minus any bolt-on components. Also called the *shell* or *body shell.*

body-in-white

supplied to the engine, where it is referred to as a wastegate.

blowout   The catastrophic and immediate flattening of a tire.

blueprinting   Selecting and hand-finishing engine parts to the most favorable dimensions, weights, and other specifications within allowed production tolerances.

Originally a drag racing term, referring to a practice that made an engine as good as possible while still being technically "stock" as required in certain racing classes. For example, if the engineering drawing (blueprint) specified a piston diameter of 89.00 mm ±.05 mm, and optimal engine performance is obtained with the piston at the minimum diameter, then the pistons of a blueprinted engine would be custom machined to 88.95 mm. Similarly, if the piston's weight was given as 180 grams ±1 gram, all pistons would be trimmed to 179 grams.

The blueprinted engine is as powerful, smooth, free-running, and reliable as possible within production tolerances. Also see *balancing.*

BMEP   See *brake mean effective pressure.*

boat-tailed   An open touring body whose tail is shaped like the bow of a boat. The Auburn Speedster is a famous boat-tailed design.

body lean   See *roll.*

body-on-frame construction   A type of automobile or truck construction in which the body structure is attached to a separate frame. Compare to unitized construction.

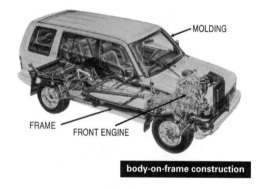

MOLDING

FRAME   FRONT ENGINE

body-on-frame construction

body roll   See *roll.*

body shell   See *body-in-white.*

body style   The configuration of a car's body. The most common types are sedan, coupe, hatchback, convertible, station wagon, and roadster. Though the design characteristics of each are generally understood, some models blend those of two or more styles and are thus difficult to classify precisely — a two-door car might be a coupe to one observer and a two-door sedan to another. Also see *van, minivan, pickup truck,* and *sport utility vehicle.*

boiling point The temperature at which a liquid changes to a gas (vaporizes). The boiling point of a liquid decreases at higher altitudes and increases under pressure. The coolant in a modern pressurized cooling system can have a boiling point as high as 260 degrees Fahrenheit.

bonded lining In drum brakes, a brake lining cemented to the shoes or bands rather than riveted.

bonnet British term for hood.

boost Pressure above atmospheric at which a turbocharger or supercharger forces air into an engine. Normal atmospheric pressure is 14.7 psi; a blower providing 10-psi boost forces air into the cylinders at an absolute pressure of 24.7 psi. Boost is sometimes measured in atmospheres, where one atmosphere equals 14.7 psi, two atmospheres 29.4 psi, and so on. In the metric system, boost is expressed in bar units, where one bar equals approximately 14.5 psi or 0.99 atmospheres. Also see *brake booster.*

boot The flexible covering used to conceal and protect the folded soft top on a convertible or cabriolet. Typically made of canvas or plastic and held in place by snap fasteners, but may be a rigid panel over a storage well.

Also, the cosmetic rubber, leather, or plastic shroud at the base of a gearshift lever. Also, the flexible protective rubber cover used to retain grease inside a constant velocity joint and to protect these joints (and steering system components) from stones, dirt, and water. In the United Kingdom, the boot is the trunk.

bore

bore The inside diameter of a hollow cylindrical object such as a bushing or bearing. In a piston engine, the diameter of a cylinder; usually measured in inches or millimeters.

As a verb, to increase the inside diameter of a cylinder or hole.

boss An extension or strengthened section of a component that holds the end of a pin or shaft; for instance, the projections within a piston for supporting the piston pin or piston-pin bushings.

bottom dead center (BDC) The position of a piston at its lowest point of travel, at the end of the intake and power strokes in a four-cycle engine.

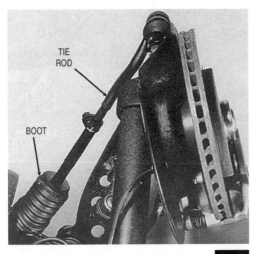

boot

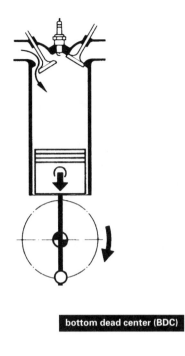

bottom dead center (BDC)

bottoming A ride motion in which an automobile suspension reaches the limit of its travel in jounce (and thus may hit its bump stops) on crossing a dip or bump. Also called *crashing through*. Also see *ride*.

bounce A condition in which a valve is not held tightly closed in its seat even though the camshaft is not opening it. Also, a condition in which the distributor points make and break contact erratically when they should remain closed.

boundary layer The thin layer of air that surrounds a body in motion and remains stationary or almost stationary relative to the body.

box Shortened form of gearbox or black box (a car's computer). Also, a vehicle's basic shape and the extent to which it comprises separate volumes. A car with a front engine compartment, a passenger compartment, and a trunk is referred to as a three-box design: three distinct volumes make up the car. A car with a front engine compartment and a passenger compartment without a separate trunk (a hatchback) is

a two-box design, and a full-size van with the engine positioned between the front seats is a one-box design. Minivans are also generally considered one-box designs, although most have separate engine compartments, because the shape of the vehicle flows in one continuous line from the front bumper to the tailgate.

boxer engine See *flat engine*.

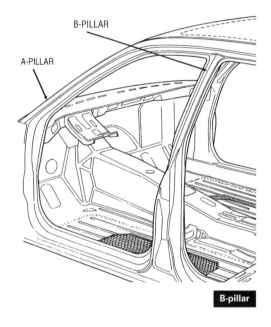

B-PILLAR

A-PILLAR

B-pillar

B-pillar The structural vertical support behind the front door, connecting the sills with the roof. Also called *B-post*; also see *hardtop*.

B-post See *B-pillar*.

brake Any mechanical device for arresting the motion of a wheel or a vehicle by means of friction; kinetic energy is converted into heat energy through the use of frictional force applied to the wheels, causing a car to slow or stop. Also see *emergency brake* and *station wagon*.

brake adjuster A toothed wheel connecting the two shoes in a drum brake. The wheel is

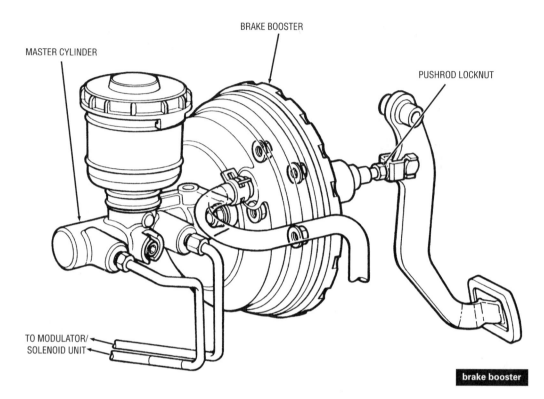

MASTER CYLINDER

BRAKE BOOSTER

PUSHROD LOCKNUT

TO MODULATOR/
SOLENOID UNIT

brake booster

rotated with a special wrench to adjust the pre-load of the linings with the brake drum.

brake anchor   In drum brakes, the pin on the brake backing plate about which the brake shoe pivots.

brake backing plate   In drum brakes, a round, nonrotating flat plate to which brake shoes and wheel cylinders are attached. Also called *backing plate*.

brake band   A cylinder-shaped band surrounding a brake drum, with an inside layer of friction material. A brake band squeezes the outside surface of the drum, whereas a brake shoe squeezes the inside surface.

brake bias   See *brake proportioning*.

brake bleeder   A valve attached to each wheel brake that can be opened and closed to bleed air from the brake lines. Also called a *bleeder valve*.

brake booster   A mechanical device (usually air-, vacuum-, or hydraulically operated) that reduces the effort normally required to stop a car. Such braking systems are commonly referred to as power-assisted, vacuum-assisted, hydraulically assisted, or power brakes. In passenger cars the boost comes from the engine intake vacuum or an engine-driven hydraulic pump. Also called a *brake servo*.

brake caliper   The basically stationary component of a disc brake that applies force from the hydraulic system to the rotor to decelerate and stop a vehicle. Also see *caliper, fixed caliper*, and *floating caliper*.

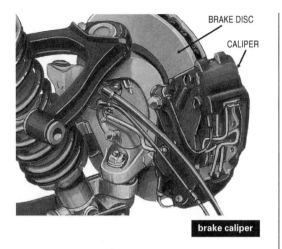

BRAKE DISC

CALIPER

brake caliper

brake cylinder   See *wheel cylinder*.

brake disc   The rotating part of a disc brake, also called a *rotor*.

brake drum   See *drum brake*.

B

brake dynamometer   A machine for measuring the torque and power produced by an engine; so called because it loads the engine by "braking" (restricting its speed) in order to measure its output.

brake fade   A condition brought about by repeated or protracted braking, resulting in reduced braking effectiveness (fading). Heat is the primary culprit, causing expansion of the brake drums and lowering the friction coefficient of the linings and pads. For this reason, the brakes of some cars are ventilated, especially front disc brakes, although a few exotic cars have used ventilated drums. Disc brakes are less prone to fade — the rotors are more effectively cooled by air moving across the brakes and in addition they can be internally vented to increase resistance to fade.

brake fluid   See *hydraulic fluid*.

brake horsepower (bhp)   The power produced by an engine, measured at the output

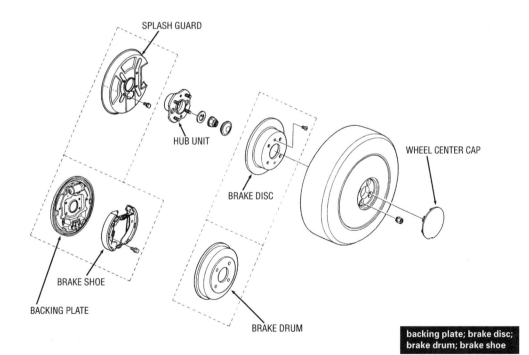

SPLASH GUARD

HUB UNIT

BRAKE DISC

WHEEL CENTER CAP

BRAKE SHOE

BACKING PLATE

BRAKE DRUM

backing plate; brake disc; brake drum; brake shoe

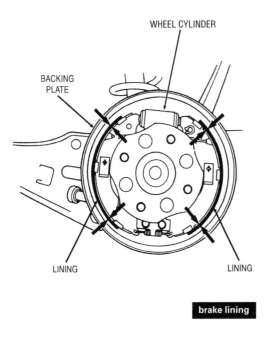

brake lining

end of its crankshaft, that is available for driving a car. Shaft power is usually measured by a brake dynamometer, hence the term.

brake lights   Red lights at the rear of a vehicle that light when the driver steps on the brake pedal and alert following traffic that the vehicle is slowing down. Also see *center high-mounted stop lamp*.

brake line   Tube or hose connecting the master cylinder to the wheel cylinders in a brake system.

brake lining   The replaceable friction material on a brake shoe that contacts a brake drum to reduce a car's speed. Most conventional linings are made of organic material. Semimetallic linings are made of steel fibers bonded together with organic resins to form a composite material that has high resistance to brake fade.

brake master cylinder   A cylinder attached to a reservoir of hydraulic fluid. An internal piston, actuated by foot pressure, produces hydraulic pressure to push fluid through the brake lines to the wheel cylinders and force brake linings or pads against a drum or disc. See illustration for *brake booster*.

brake mean effective pressure (BMEP) The average pressure inside the cylinders of an engine at a specified brake horsepower and rpm. Also see *indicated mean effective pressure*.

brake modulation   The technique by which a driver varies pedal pressure to hold a car's

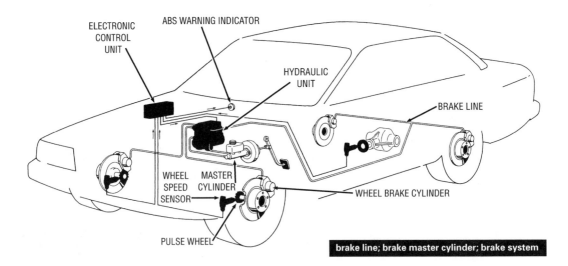

brake line; brake master cylinder; brake system

brakes on the verge of lockup. Once locked, a considerable reduction in pressure is generally required to unlock them.

brake pad   On a disc brake, the replaceable rigid backing plate and friction material that contacts the rotating disc when the brakes are applied. Sometimes referred to as a *brake puck*.

brake piston   One of two pistons found in a conventional tandem brake master cylinder. The primary piston is closest to the brake pedal. The secondary piston, actuated by fluid trapped between the two, transfers force to the brakes' hydraulic lines. Also, the pistons in the brake caliper that force the pads against the rotor.

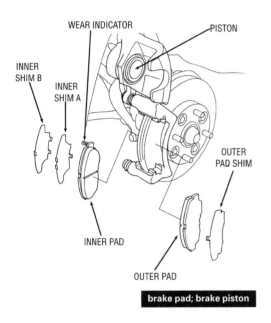

brake pad; brake piston

brake proportioning   The distribution of braking power between the front and rear wheels. For the shortest stopping distance during hard braking, the brake proportioning or bias should match the car's traction at either end.

brake proportioning valve   A valve that limits braking force to the front or rear wheels — usually as a function of pedal effort or line pres-

sure, loading of the car, or front–rear weight transfer — to prevent wheel lockup and provide maximum effective braking.

brake puck   See *brake pad.*

brake servo   See *brake booster.*

brake shoe   In drum brakes, the arc-shaped carrier to which the friction linings are mounted and that expand to force the lining against the rotating drum during braking.

brake specific fuel consumption (BSFC)   A measure of an engine's fuel efficiency during dynamometer testing. It is calculated by dividing the fuel consumed in pounds per hour by the observed horsepower.

brake system   The mechanical and hydraulic components through which pressure is applied to slow, stop, or hold a car stationary. Includes the brake pedal, the master cylinder and brake booster, hydraulic lines, the brake pads or linings, and the disc or drum brake at each wheel.

brake torquing   A technique practiced by drag racers and road testers to improve off-the-line acceleration of a car equipped with an automatic transmission. The driver prevents the car from moving by firmly depressing the brake pedal with the left foot, while applying the throttle with the right foot with the car in gear. This causes the engine rpm to rise to the torque converter's stall speed at which point the driver releases the brake pedal. This technique is particularly effective with turbocharged engines because it helps overcome turbo lag.

braking distance   The minimum linear distance required for a car to reach a complete halt from a given speed at its maximum rate of deceleration, i.e., as in an emergency or panic stop.

breaker arm   In a distributor, the movable part of a set of breaker points.

breakerless   A distributor or ignition system in which the mechanical switching device

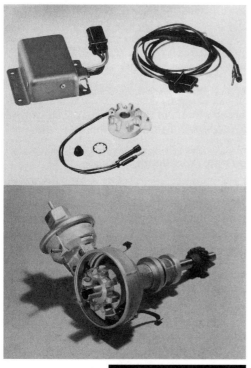

breakerless (ignition system)

breaker points

(points or contacts) is replaced by an electronic one, usually transistors. Also referred to as *contactless* or *electronic ignition.*

breaker points   In a distributor, a mechanical switch with two metal contact points that open and close; often shortened to *points.* With the points closed, energy is stored in the primary windings of the ignition coil. When they open, this energy is transferred to the secondary windings and stepped up, resulting in high voltage to fire the spark plugs. The gap between the breaker-point surfaces is critical — if the gap is too small, the timing is retarded; if too wide, the timing is advanced. Also called *contact breaker.*

break-in   The time period or number of miles during which the rough edges and friction between newly assembled moving parts and sur-

faces are gradually reduced. Generally calls for moderate load and driving speed; not nearly as critical for contemporary engines as it once was. Also called *run-in.*

breathing capacity   The volume of air that enters the cylinder during each intake stroke; also called air capacity. Because of compromises in the design of the intake manifold, the size and shape of valves, and the valve timing, the quantity of intake air actually drawn into a normally aspirated engine is usually less than that which would fill it under ideal conditions. The ratio of this actual volume to ideal volume is termed volumetric efficiency.

British thermal unit (BTU)   The amount of heat necessary to raise the temperature of one pound of water by one degree Fahrenheit.

BSFC   See *brake specific fuel consumption.*

BTU   See *British thermal unit.*

B

bucket seat

bucket seat An individual front seat providing firm lateral support, usually found in pairs; named for the early designs that resembled cutout buckets.

bucket tappet Hollow, cylindrical valve lifters, closed at one end and resembling upside-down buckets, used in some overhead-camshaft engines. The flat, closed end ("bottom of the bucket") rests against the camshaft lobe, with part of the valve spring and valve stem enclosed by the hollow cylinder.

Bugatti axle A design in which the springs pass through a tubular front axle. Though often attributed to Ettore Bugatti, the design was pioneered by Fiat on its 1922 Grand Prix car.

bulge See *blister*.

bulkhead A panel separating two compartments. For example, the front bulkhead in an automobile — sometimes referred to as the cowl, firewall, or dash panel — separates the engine compartment from the passenger compartment. The rear bulkhead separates the trunk from the passenger compartment.

bump See *jounce*.

bumper An energy-absorbing bar mounted on the front or rear of a vehicle and generally employing hydraulic shock absorbers or some kind of deformable material to protect a car from damage in low-speed impacts.

bump steer The slight turning or steering of a wheel away from its normal direction of travel as it moves through its suspension travel. At the

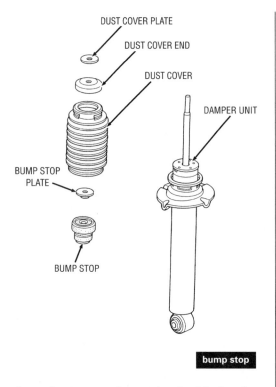

DUST COVER PLATE

DUST COVER END

DUST COVER

DAMPER UNIT

BUMP STOP PLATE

BUMP STOP

bump stop

bump stop A cushioning device, usually rubber, that limits the upward movement of suspension and wheel to prevent metal-to-metal contact that could lead to suspension damage or unpleasant ride motions. Also called *jounce bumper*, *jounce stop*, or *snubber*.

bump-thump See *wheel patter*.

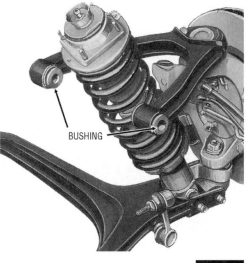

BUSHING

bushing

front, bump steer is associated with the tie-rod/linkage-arm relationship. The method of locating the rear suspension, the type of rear suspension, and the geometry of the various linkages contribute to rear bump steer.

In racing cars, bump steer is normally designed out of the suspension to make the steering and handling as precise and predictable as possible. In production cars both front and rear bump steer are usually present to some degree because of design compromises. Bump steer is not always unwanted, because suspension engineers can use it to design a small amount of understeer or oversteer into the chassis. Also called *ride steer*.

bushing A sleeve, usually removable, placed in a bore to serve as a bearing surface. Bushings often contain rubber and thus perform a cushioning as well as a bearing function.

bustleback See *notchback*.

butterfly valve See *throttle valve*.

bypass filter A type of oil filter through which only some of the oil from the oil pump flows, the remainder bypassing the filter on its way to various engine parts.

cabriolet A convertible body style, usually seating four passengers. The term is generally not used in the United States but remains the normal designation for a convertible in parts of Europe, especially France and Germany.

CAD See *computer-aided design.*

cadence braking A driving technique in which the brakes are alternately applied and released at regular intervals in quick succession so as to slow or stop a vehicle without locking its wheels and skidding. Modern antilock braking systems perform this function more effectively because their cadences are far more rapid (8–15 cycles per second) than even the best dri-

vers can manage, and because they can "pump" individual wheel brakes separately instead of only all four at once. Also see *antilock braking system* and *lockup.*

CAFE See *Corporate Average Fuel Economy.*

caliper The part of a disc brake that straddles the disc and contains the cylinder(s), piston(s), and brake pads. When the brakes are applied, brake fluid flows to the cylinders in the caliper and pushes the pistons inward, forcing the pads against the disc.

Also, a tool with two laterally adjustable legs for measuring the inside or outside diameter of

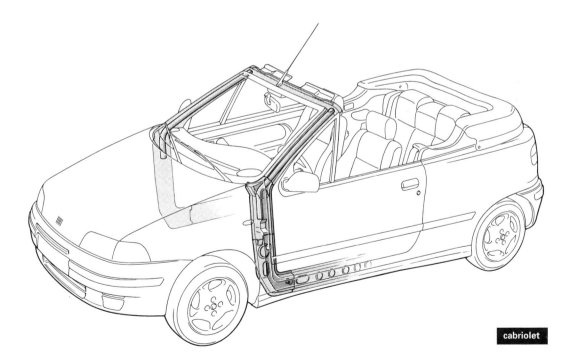

cabriolet

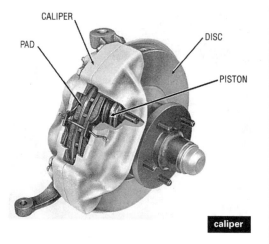

CALIPER

PAD

DISC

PISTON

caliper

a shaft or cylinder bore by contact and retaining the dimension for measurement or comparison.

Also see *fixed caliper* and *floating caliper*.

CAM   See *computer-aided manufacturing*.

cam   A rotating or sliding mechanism or a projection on a rotating shaft for imparting or receiving exact movements. A cam on a camshaft is also referred to as a lobe. The profile of each lobe determines the amount or duration of time

the valve is open. It also largely determines the valve's maximum opening or lift.

Also, a shortened form of *camshaft*.

camber   A wheel's inward or outward tilt from vertical, measured in degrees. Viewed from the front or rear, if the wheels are closer at the top than at the ground, camber is negative; if farther apart at the top, camber is positive

Also refers to a road surface or tire that is higher in the middle than at the sides; such a road or tire is said to be crowned.

camber thrust   Side (lateral) force generated when a tire rolls with camber. Camber thrust can add to or subtract from the side force a tire generates.

cam follower   A cylindrical part that rests on a camshaft lobe and is lifted by the action of the

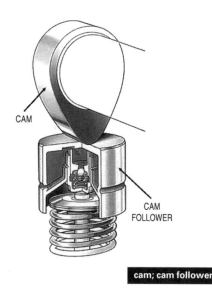

CAM

CAM FOLLOWER

cam; cam follower

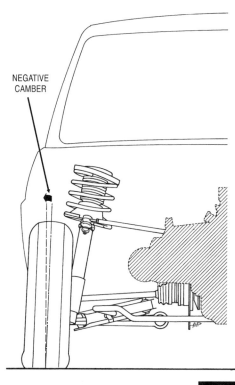

NEGATIVE CAMBER

camber

cam, opening and closing the valves in overhead-valve engines and those overhead-cam engines whose valves are not actuated by rocker arms. Also called *valve lifter* or *tappet*.

cam-ground piston   A piston whose skirt is slightly elliptical so that the widest diameter of the skirt is at right angles to the piston-pin axis. As the piston warms, it expands to become round. Such a design allows a closer fit with the cylinder, thus reducing gas blowby, cylinder scuffing, and piston slap caused by too much clearance between piston and cylinder wall.

camshaft   A shaft in the engine driven by gears, belts, or a chain from the crankshaft and containing a series of cams for opening and closing the intake and exhaust valves. Often shortened to *cam*.

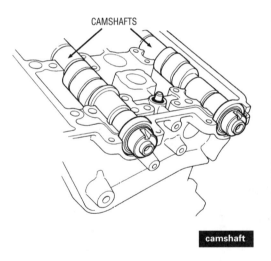

CAMSHAFTS

camshaft

cantilevered suspension   A type of suspension whose spring and shock absorber are mounted inboard, within the chassis structure. The spring and shock are at one end of a suspension arm, the wheel at the other. The arm's midpoint is pivoted from the chassis. Used mainly on racing cars.

capacitive discharge ignition (CDI)   An ignition system in which the primary power is drawn from the engine's battery into a CD power supply, where it is changed from 12 volts direct current to about 300 volts of pulsating direct current that is then stored in a capacitor. The release of this energy through the coil is governed by a silicon-controlled rectifier (SCR). When the SCR switch is closed, the voltage stored in the capacitor is supplied to the coil, which acts as a step-up transformer to boost it to around 30,000 volts for firing the spark plugs. CDI can be either all-electronic or breaker-point-controlled.

capacitor   See *condenser*. See illustration for *breaker points*.

capacity   The number of passengers a vehicle is designed to carry. Also the amount of energy (measured in ampere hours) stored by a battery, the number of gallons held in a fuel tank, and the number of quarts of oil and water held by the oil pan and cooling system, respectively. In British English, however, capacity means engine displacement.

caps   See *fascia*.

carb   A shortened form of *carburetor*.

carbon (C)   A natural element. Carbon is also a by-product of combustion, and can form deposits in the combustion chambers and on the valves and piston rings of an engine. Also see *hydrocarbons*.

carbon deposits   Residue of carbon on cylinder heads, combustion chambers, pistons, piston rings, and valves. The residue can clog mechanisms and cause combustion problems such as preignition or hesitation.

carbon dioxide (CO_2)   A colorless, odorless, nonpoisonous gas that is a component of air. Carbon dioxide is exhaled by humans and animals and is absorbed by green plants on land and in the sea.

carbon fiber   A fiber created from polymer strands which are stretched, then heated slowly while under tension to very high temperatures

carbon fiber (console trim panel)

(3000–5400 degrees Fahrenheit) to create parallel carbon strands. Carbon fibers are 92–99 percent carbon, extremely strong, and much lighter than metals. Graphite fiber, which has 99 percent carbon content, is similar; the two names are generally interchangeable.

When bound into a matrix of plastic resin by heat, vacuum, or pressure, carbon fiber forms a composite material that is very strong and light but also expensive. Because of the parallel orientation of the carbon fiber strands, carbon fiber composites have unidirectional properties and are frequently used in race car chassis (tubs) where these properties result in maximum strength and minimal weight.

carbon monoxide (CO) A colorless, odorless, highly toxic gas formed by the incomplete combustion of carbon or carbonaceous material, including gasoline. It is a major air pollutant on the basis of weight.

carburetor A device that combines vaporized fuel and air to form a combustible mixture that can be burned in an engine's cylinders. The carburetor changes the ratio of fuel and air in response to varying engine operating conditions

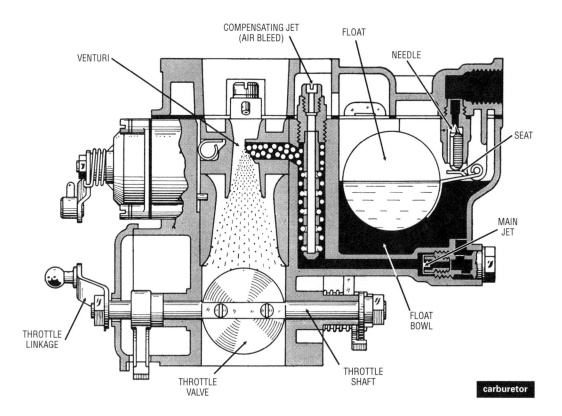

carburetor

C

such as starting, idling, cruising, and maximum power. In most current automobiles, the carburetor has been replaced by more sophisticated throttle-body injection or fuel injection. Abbreviated as *carb*.

carcass   See *casing*.

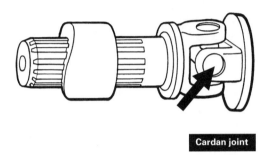

Cardan joint

Cardan joint   A universal joint with its two yokes at right angles to each other. It is named for its inventor, although it is often referred to as the Hooke joint, after Robert Hooke, who patented the conventional universal joint as it is known today in the automotive industry. Also see *universal joint*.

casing   The supporting structure of a tire. The rubber alone would not withstand the

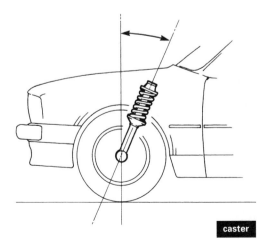

caster

forces exerted by the inflation pressure inside the tire. The casing is made of plies. Also called the *carcass*.

casing turn-up   See *flipper*.

castellated nut   See *castle nut*.

caster   The angle between a line drawn vertically through a wheel's centerline and the axis around which the wheel is steered. Caster improves a car's directional stability and on-center steering feel, but increases steering effort. Caster is considered positive when the steering axis is inclined rearward at the top.

cast iron   An alloy of iron and more than 2 percent carbon. Cast iron has long been used for engine blocks, transmission and differential cases, and exhaust manifolds because it is relatively inexpensive and easy to mold into complex shapes.

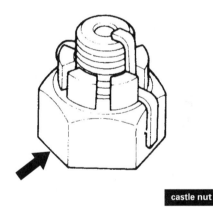

castle nut

castle nut   A nut with notches carved radially across its face to accommodate a locking pin driven through the notches and a hole in the corresponding bolt. The nut is shaped like the turret on some castles. Also called *castellated nut*.

catalyst   A substance that causes a chemical reaction to take place or to be accelerated, but which is not permanently changed by the reaction.

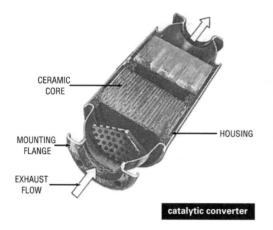

CERAMIC CORE

HOUSING

MOUNTING FLANGE

EXHAUST FLOW

catalytic converter

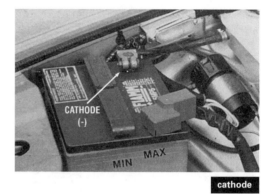

CATHODE (-)

MIN   MAX

cathode

catalytic converter An emission control device in the exhaust system, usually containing platinum or palladium as a catalyst for chemical reaction of unburned hydrocarbons and carbon monoxide. It converts them into water vapor, carbon dioxide, and other gases less toxic than untreated exhaust.

cathephoretic process A process of applying primer paint or rust inhibitor to a car's body shell. Typically, the structure is first given a small positive charge to become a cathode, then dipped in a negatively charged solution, which is the anode. The difference between the electrical charges serves to bond the solution per-

manently to the metal. Also referred to as the *electrophoretic process.*

cathode The negatively charged electrode in an electrolytic cell. Also see *anode.*

cathode-ray tube (CRT) The picture tube of a television set or the monitor of a computer. CRTs have recently appeared in cars as touch-sensitive screens by which audio and climate controls, instruments, and a trip computer may be displayed and operated. The name derives from the electron gun (cathode) that "fires" at a phosphor-coated screen (anode) in response to electrical impulses to produce an image as a series of lines (called lines of resolution) as the gun rapidly scans the screen laterally, a line at a time. CRTs are also used for guidance systems that display a vehicle's position on a map of a geographic area; as the vehicle changes direction, the map moves to guide the driver to a selected destination. Also see *navigation system.*

cavitation A condition in which a partial vacuum forms around the blades or impeller wheels of a pump, reducing the pump's output because a portion of the blade surfaces loses contact with the liquid. This can be a problem in fuel and water pumps, fluid couplings, and torque converters; when severe, it can result in erosion of pump blades and other internal surfaces.

CCV See *closed crankcase ventilation.*

Cd See *coefficient of aerodynamic drag.*

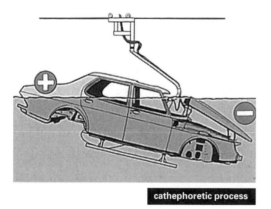

cathephoretic process

CDI   See *capacitive discharge ignition*.

center differential   A differential used to distribute power to the front and rear differentials in four-wheel-drive systems.

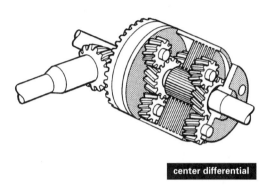

center differential

center high-mounted stop lamp (CHMSL)   A brake light positioned at or near the eye level of following drivers who, according to various studies, are apt to notice it sooner than they would the brake lights in a car's lower-mounted lamp clusters. The CHMSL is required by law on all cars sold in the United States beginning with model year 1986.

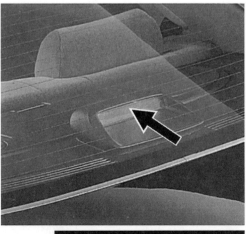

center high-mounted stop lamp (CHMSL)

center link   See *idler arm*.

center of gravity (cg)   The point at which an object's weight can be assumed to be concentrated for purposes of analysis and computations, and around which an object is in balance. An important concept because cornering, accelerative, and other forces are considered as acting on a car's center of gravity. Thus it has a great influence on body roll and other handling characteristics.

center of pressure   The aerodynamically determined point at which wind force on the side of the car is assumed to be concentrated for analytical purposes. A concept similar to the center of gravity, it is a function of the shape and aerodynamic resistance of a given car body, and thus determines the effect of side winds on a car's direction of travel. Also see *wind wander*.

center section   That portion of a wheel that comes in contact with the hub, typically having three or more bolt holes spaced evenly around a central hub centering hole, for clamping the wheel to the hub. The center section generally contains various slots or openings designed to aid brake cooling.

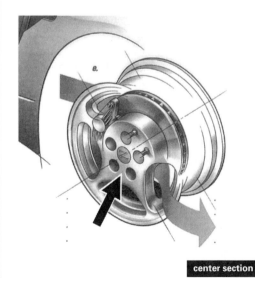

center section

43

central fuel injection See *throttle-body injection.*

central locking An electric or vacuum-operated safety system that locks and unlocks all doors, and sometimes the fuel-filler door and trunk/hatch lid, from a single point. Some systems are controlled from the driver's exterior door lock, some from the right door as well. Many systems can also be operated from inside via a dashboard or door switch or the lock button on the front doors.

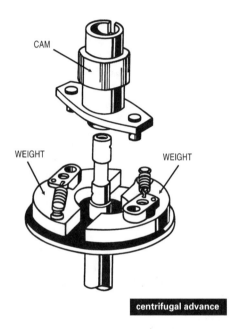

CAM

WEIGHT

WEIGHT

centrifugal advance

centrifugal advance A mechanism that varies the instant at which the spark occurs as a function of engine speed. It normally consists of two weights that rotate with the distributor shaft and move outward under centrifugal force against the tension of springs. Movement of the weights is transmitted to the breaker points or breaker plate, advancing the timing and causing the spark plugs to fire earlier.

centrifugal force The force that tends to move an object outward from a center of rota-

tion, or that an object moving in a curved path exerts on whatever is constraining it. A rock whirled on a string applies centrifugal force to the string. Equal and opposite to centripetal force. Also see *centripetal force.*

centripetal force The force needed to move an object in a curved path, and that is directed toward the center of rotation. A string attached to a whirling rock applies centripetal force to the rock. Also see *centrifugal force.*

cetane number (CN) An index that describes a diesel fuel's ignition characteristics. The higher the CN, the better the ignition quality. Cetane (normal hexadecane) is assigned an index of one hundred while another hydrocarbon, alpha-methynaphthalene, is assigned an index of zero. The cetane number is the percentage of cetane in a mixture with alpha-methynaphthalene that has the same ignition quality as the diesel fuel being rated.

Cf See *coefficient of friction.*

CFC See *chlorofluorocarbon.*

CFI Continuous fuel injection. See *fuel injection.*

chafer strip Reinforcement material, either rubber or a combination of rubber and fabric, placed around a tire's bead where the rim flange

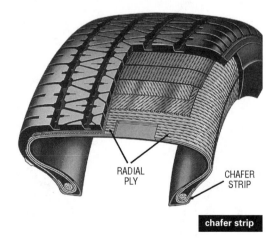

RADIAL
PLY

CHAFER
STRIP

chafer strip

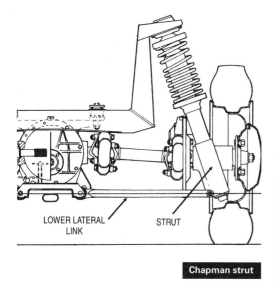

LOWER LATERAL LINK   STRUT

Chapman strut

character line

and the tire meet to prevent the rim from rubbing and damaging the tire.

Chapman strut   A type of rear suspension using a lower lateral link and a long spring/shock absorber strut to determine wheel geometry. Basically the MacPherson-strut adapted for a rear suspension by Colin Chapman, who used it on the original Lotus Elite.

character line   Any thin groove or ridge in the surface of a car body, often ornamented, that results from an intersection of planes.

charge   To pass an electrical current through a battery for keeping it in peak condition or restoring it to activity. The alternator normally performs this function, though an external battery charger might be required for a very weak battery. Can also refer to the mass of air and fuel that enters a cylinder during the intake stroke, and to filling an air-conditioning system with the proper amount of refrigerant.

chassis   The automobile frame with all operating parts, including engine, drivetrain, suspension, steering, and brakes; the car minus body, accessories, and trim. For a frameless or

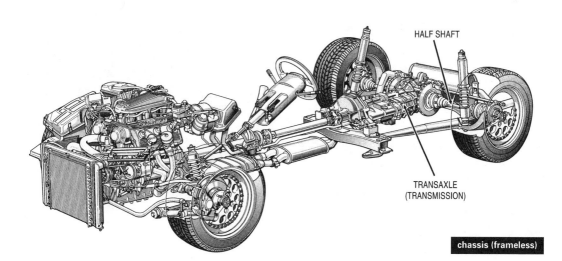

HALF SHAFT

TRANSAXLE (TRANSMISSION)

chassis (frameless)

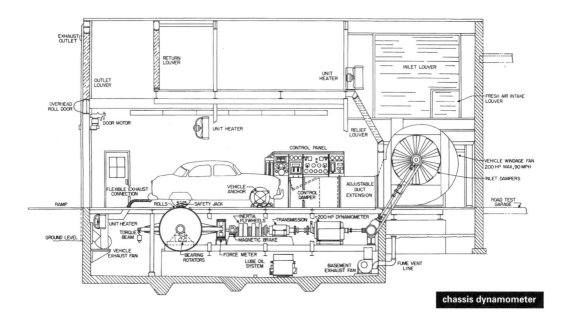

EXHAUST OUTLET
RETURN LOUVER
UNIT HEATER
INLET LOUVER
OUTLET LOUVER
FRESH AIR INTAKE LOUVER
OVERHEAD ROLL DOOR
DOOR MOTOR
UNIT HEATER
RELIEF LOUVER
CONTROL PANEL
VEHICLE WINDAGE FAN 200 HP MAX, 90 MPH
INLET DAMPERS
FLEXIBLE EXHAUST CONNECTION
VEHICLE ANCHOR
ADJUSTABLE DUCT EXTENSION
CONTROL DAMPER
ROAD TEST GARAGE
RAMP
ROLLS
SAFETY JACK
INERTIA FLYWHEELS
TRANSMISSION
200 HP DYNAMOMETER
UNIT HEATER
TORQUE BEAM
MAGNETIC BRAKE
GROUND LEVEL
VEHICLE EXHAUST FAN
BEARING ROTATORS
FORCE METER
LUBE OIL SYSTEM
BASEMENT EXHAUST FAN
FUME VENT LINE

chassis dynamometer

unitized car, merely the engine, drivetrain, suspension, and brakes. Sometimes understood as only the suspension, steering, and brakes.

chassis dynamometer   A machine for measuring the power delivered to the drive wheels of a car. Because of frictional and mechanical losses in the various drivetrain components, the measured horsepower is generally 15–20 percent less than the brake horsepower measured at the crankshaft or flywheel on an engine dynamometer.

check valve   A valve that allows passage of a liquid or gas in one direction only. Also called a *one-way valve.*

chip   Abbreviation, see *microchip.*

chlorofluorocarbon (CFC)   The chemical name for Freon -12, the refrigerant that was used in automobile air-conditioning systems. It is being phased out because it is damaging the earth's ozone layer. Also see *compressor.*

CHMSL   See *center high-mounted stop lamp.*

choke   A restriction in a carburetor throat to reduce airflow and enrich the air-fuel mixture to start and run a cold engine. A manual choke is engaged by the driver before starting and gradually released as the engine warms up. An automatic choke automatically enriches the fuel mix-

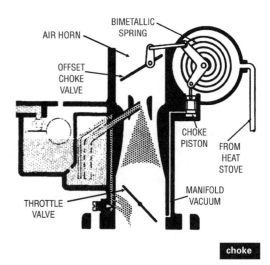

AIR HORN
BIMETALLIC SPRING
OFFSET CHOKE VALVE
CHOKE PISTON
FROM HEAT STOVE
THROTTLE VALVE
MANIFOLD VACUUM

choke

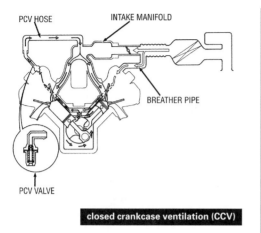

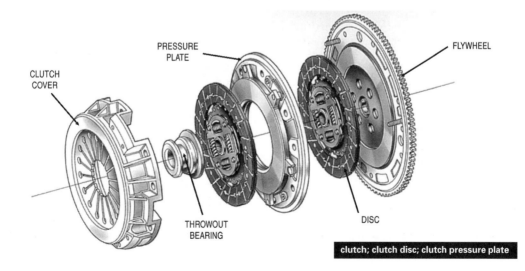

closed crankcase ventilation (CCV)

ture in accordance with engine temperature. Its operation depends primarily on the unwinding of a thermostatic (bimetallic) coil spring as heat is applied. As the spring unwinds, it causes the choke plate in the air horn to open, permitting more air to pass through the carburetor. Heat for the operation of the bimetallic spring is usually obtained from the exhaust manifold, sometimes from circulating liquid coolant.

CID Cubic inch displacement. See *displacement.*

circuit breaker A device that interrupts and protects an electrical circuit from excessive cur-

rent, and that may be reset when the circuit functions properly. Also called a *cutout.*

CI See *coefficient of aerodynamic lift.*

climate control system The system that maintains the environment inside a vehicle. It consists of the heater, air conditioner, fans, vents, ducting, and a control panel to set and adjust temperature, fan speed, and direction of airflow to heat, cool, and defrost the interior.

closed crankcase ventilation (CCV) An emission control system in which crankcase vapors are discharged into the engine intake system (usually via the intake manifold) and pass through the cylinders rather than being discharged into the atmosphere. Also called *positive crankcase ventilation.*

clutch A friction device used to connect a driving member to a driven one. A car's clutch, when engaged, connects the engine flywheel to the gearbox and thus to the remainder of the drivetrain. It allows smooth coupling and uncoupling of the engine and drivetrain by slipping as its driving and driven discs come together.

Car air conditioners have a compressor clutch, a simple electromagnetic on-off clutch that provides engagement and disengagement of

clutch; clutch disc; clutch pressure plate

the air-conditioning compressor as needed to maintain a set interior temperature.

clutch cover   See *clutch pressure plate.*

clutch disc   A rotating circular metal plate splined to the transmission input shaft with friction material on each face. The disc is located between the engine flywheel and the clutch pressure plate, and is clamped tightly between these two members when the clutch is engaged, thus transmitting power from the flywheel through the clutch and into the gearbox. Also called *friction disc.*

clutch fluid   See *hydraulic fluid.*

clutch housing   See *bell housing.*

clutch master cylinder   A cylinder attached to a reservoir of hydraulic fluid. An internal piston, actuated by foot pressure, produces hydraulic pressure to push fluid through the clutch lines to allow coupling and uncoupling of the engine and drivetrain in a vehicle equipped with a manual gearbox.

clutch pedal free travel   The distance the clutch pedal moves before its linkage begins to separate the clutch disc from the flywheel and clutch plate; also called *free play*. A small amount of free play allows for smoother clutch actuation and prevents drivers who "ride" the clutch (resting the left foot on the pedal while the clutch is engaged) from prematurely wearing out the clutch. Also see *clutch slip.*

clutch pressure plate   A metal plate that, along with the clutch cover, is bolted to the flywheel and rotates with it. When the clutch is engaged, springs between the pressure plate and the cover force the clutch disc against the flywheel and pressure plate.

clutch release bearing   See *throwout bearing.*

clutch shaft   See *drive pinion.*

clutch slip   A condition in which the friction material on each face of the clutch disc is inad-

equate to maintain the tight connection between the engine and gearbox when the clutch is engaged. When slip becomes excessive, the engine speed increases but wheel speed does not, because the slipping clutch prevents power and torque from being transmitted to the gearbox and then to the wheels. Also see *clutch* and *clutch disc.*

clutch solenoid   In some car air conditioners, a solenoid that operates a clutch on the compressor drive pulley. When the clutch is engaged, the compressor is engaged and cooling takes place.

CO   See *carbon monoxide.*

CO$_2$ See *carbon dioxide.*

coastdown   The act of coasting, i.e., letting friction reduce the velocity of an object moving along a surface in the absence of applied power or imparted motion. Sometimes used to determine a car's coefficient of aerodynamic drag.

Also refers to a procedure recommended by some manufacturers for prolonging the life of turbochargers, especially those without water-cooled bearings or housings. Typically, the engine is idled for a period of time before shutting off (especially after hard driving) to let the turbocharger oil cool somewhat. This reduces the likelihood of "coking" (formation of carbon deposits) on the unit's main bearings.

cobbled   Used by auto engineers and stylists to describe a model, prototype component, or working car assembled wholly or partly of experimental and/or borrowed elements, typically in a rough fashion.

coefficient of aerodynamic drag (Cd or Cx)   A measure of the aerodynamic efficiency of a body such as an automobile. A function of such factors as the shape of the car, its surface finish, and airflow through it for cooling or ventilation. It is measured in wind-tunnel tests or, less accurately, by coastdown. The Cd multiplied by the car's frontal area is a reliable indicator of its aerodynamic drag. For a given frontal area, the higher the drag coefficient, the greater the aerodynamic drag a car's engine must overcome at any given speed. Also see *coastdown* and *wind tunnel*.

coefficient of aerodynamic lift (Cl)   A measure of the magnitude of aerodynamic lifting forces acting on the front and rear of a car. Because these are usually unequal, separate coefficients are usually obtained and quoted. Measurement is typically made by wind-tunnel tests.

coefficient of friction (Cf)   The ratio of the frictional force between two surfaces to the perpendicular loading at their junction. The value depends primarily on the nature of the surfaces, being relatively large if the surfaces are rough and small if they are smooth.

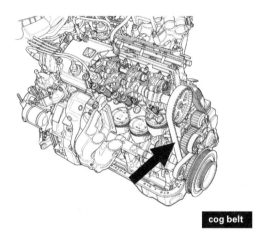

cog belt

cog belt   A toothed belt, normally of fiberglass-reinforced rubber. In cars, cog belts are primarily used to drive overhead camshafts, but are also sometimes used to drive pumps.

coil   A pulse transformer, also called the *ignition coil*, designed to step up the low "primary" voltage received from the battery or alternator to approximately 20,000 volts upon the opening and closing of the contact points. It is composed of two windings and a slot iron core. The primary winding consists of approximately two hundred turns of relatively heavy wire; the sec-

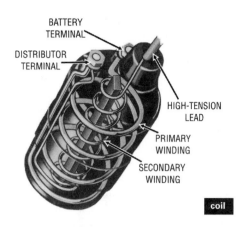

coil

ondary winding may have as many as twenty-two thousand turns of fine wire. The current through the primary winding produces a magnetic field in the coil. When the points open, the magnetic field collapses, inducing current in the coil's secondary winding. The voltage is stepped up in proportion to the ratio of secondary to primary turns, and the distributor directs this high voltage to the spark plug.

coil spring   A spiral of elastic metal (most often steel) found in varying sizes throughout a

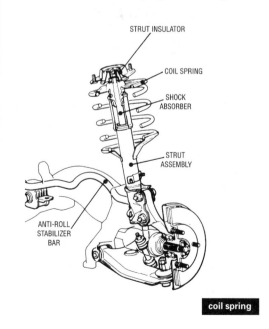

coil spring

49

car, but most notably as a springing medium in the suspension.

cold-crank rating   The minimum current (measured in amperes in the United States) a fully charged battery can deliver for 30 seconds at 0 degrees Fahrenheit without falling below 7.2 volts.

cold plug   See *heat range*.

column shift   See *floor shift*.

combustion   In an engine, the burning of the air-fuel mixture.

combustion analyser   See *exhaust gas analyser*.

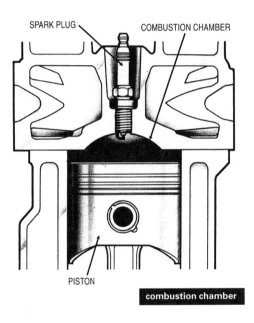

SPARK PLUG   COMBUSTION CHAMBER

PISTON

combustion chamber

combustion chamber   The volume at the top of a cylinder, in the head and/or the piston top when the piston is at top dead center, in which combustion of the air-fuel mixture begins.

compact car   By Environmental Protection Agency standards, a car enclosing 100–110 cu. ft. of passenger and luggage space.

compensating jet   A fuel tube or pipe in the carburetor, into which air is admitted through one or more holes to compensate for a tendency of the main nozzle to deliver too rich a mixture as the air velocity through the carburetor increases. Also called *air bleed passage*. See illustration for *carburetor*.

compliance   Term used to describe the "give" or resiliency designed into suspension bushings to help the suspension absorb bumps. Suspension designers achieve compliance by allowing the wheels to move slightly rearward

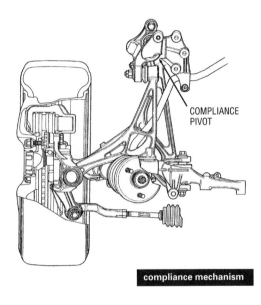

COMPLIANCE PIVOT

compliance mechanism

and up when they encounter a bump while at the same time constraining the wheels from lateral movements when cornering.

composite   A combination of different materials. Plywood is a composite of woods; the term more frequently denotes materials made up of carbon and other fibers, layered to achieve specific properties.

composite headlight   Non-sealed-beam headlight, with its shape freely chosen to permit

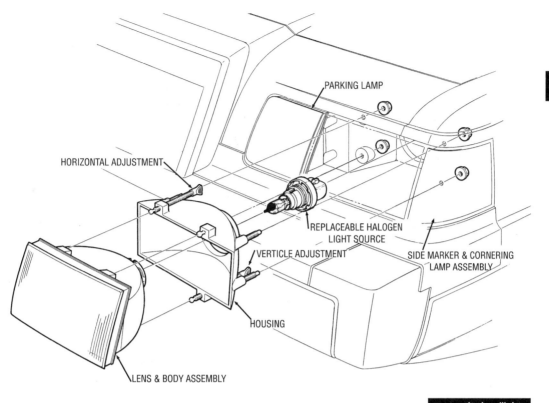

PARKING LAMP

HORIZONTAL ADJUSTMENT

REPLACEABLE HALOGEN
LIGHT SOURCE

VERTICLE ADJUSTMENT

SIDE MARKER & CORNERING
LAMP ASSEMBLY

HOUSING

LENS & BODY ASSEMBLY

composite headlight

flush mounting with a car's nose; long used in other countries, permitted in the United States by a change in regulations effective in model year 1984. Unlike conventional sealed beams, composite headlights have a separate bulb and lens that can be replaced individually if either should fail. Also see *sealed beam.*

compression See *compression stroke* and *four-stroke cycle*; also see *spring.*

compression ignition Combustion of the air-fuel mixture by the heat of compression rather than by spark. In the diesel compression-ignition engine, air is drawn into the cylinder and compressed to a temperature sufficiently high that fuel injected at the end of the compression stroke will burn.

compression ratio The extent to which the combustible gases are compressed within an engine's cylinder during the compression stroke. The ratio of the cylinder and combustion-chamber volume with the piston at bottom dead center to the volume of the combustion chamber with the piston at top dead center.

compression ring The top piston ring, forming a seal with the cylinder wall to prevent compression loss or gas blowby. Compression rings also help transfer heat from the piston into the cylinder walls and thus to the surrounding water jacket.

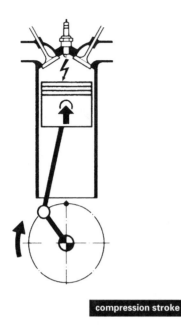

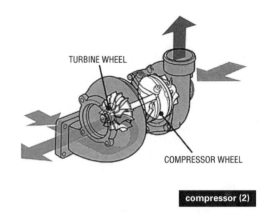

TURBINE WHEEL

COMPRESSOR WHEEL

compressor (2)

compression stroke

compression stroke   The second stroke of the four-stroke cycle, in which the piston moves upward from bottom dead center to top dead center, compressing the air-fuel mixture.

compressor   Mechanism in an air conditioner (1) that pumps vaporized refrigerant out of the evaporator, pressurizes it, and then delivers it to the condenser.

Also, a pump that compresses air delivered to an engine (2) to increase engine power. See *supercharger*.

Comprex   A type of pressure-wave supercharger; see pressure-wave supercharger.

computer-aided design (CAD)   A computer-automated system that simplifies and speeds the engineering design and drafting processes.

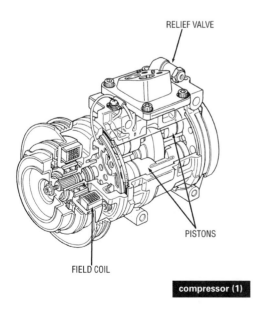

RELIEF VALVE

PISTONS

FIELD COIL

compressor (1)

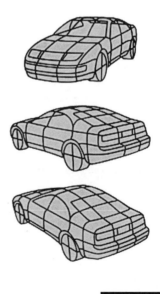

computer-aided design

computer-aided manufacturing (CAM)

computer-aided manufacturing (CAM)
The use of computers to perform tasks in the manufacturing process, as in the use of automated machinery.

condenser   In an air-conditioning system, a device for changing vapor to liquid; the component that cools the air.

In electrical circuits, a device (also called a capacitor) for temporarily collecting and storing a surge of electrical current for later discharge. In a car's ignition system, the condenser is connected across the contact points to reduce arcing by storing electricity as the distributor points open.

conductor   A material that transmits electricity.

connecting rod   The link between the piston and crankshaft, which converts the piston's rec-

connecting rod

iprocal motion to rotary motion. Often shortened to *rod* or *con rod*.

console box   A storage compartment normally located between the front seats for stowing small items such as maps, sunglasses, and spare change.

console box

constant-depression carburetor   See *air-valve carburetor*.

constant-mesh gearbox   A transmission in which the forward gears are always in mesh with one another, with the driving gears selected by small clutches that connect the various gearsets to their shafts in order to transmit power.

constant-vacuum carburetor   See *air-valve carburetor*.

constant velocity (CV) joint   A universal joint in which the driven part rotates at the same speed as the driving part, with no fluctuation in the rotational speed of the driven part as it makes a complete rotation. By contrast, in a Cardan joint the speed of the output side fluc-

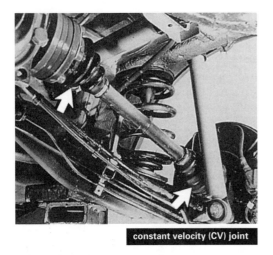

constant velocity (CV) joint

tuates cyclically. CV joints are typically used to connect the half shafts to the hubs of front-wheel-drive vehicles. Also see *Cardan joint.*

constant-volume sampling   A method of measuring exhaust emissions in which an engine's exhaust gases are collected as the car is driven through a test sequence of acceleration, deceleration, idling, and cruising on a chassis dynamometer. A quantity of air is added to the sample until a specific constant volume is obtained. Pollutant concentrations are then analyzed to determine their actual mass. Also see *chassis dynamometer.*

contact breaker   See *breaker points.*

contactless ignition   See *breakerless.*

contact patch   The area of a tire's tread in contact with the ground at any moment, i.e., with the car moving or stationary. Also called the *footprint* or *tire patch.*

contact points   See *breaker points.*

continuous fuel injection   A fuel injection system in which fuel is delivered in a steady flow. Also see *pulsed injection.*

continuously variable transmission (CVT)   See *infinitely variable transmission.*

controls   The means by which a driver operates various systems to perform functions such as heating, ventilation and air conditioning, cleaning and clearing the windshield, steering, shifting, braking, and clutching.

controls

convertible   Typically a two-door, four-seater car complete with a snug, well-fitted folding top; the definition has been extended to four-door versions as well. Convertible refers to the ability to readily convert the car from closed to open and vice versa. Strictly speaking, a convertible also has roll-down windows, as opposed to the separate side curtains of the traditional roadster. Until around 1960 the British referred to convertibles as drophead coupes, head being an English term for roof. Lately, a car is said to

convertible

be a full convertible if, when open, it has no ancillary structures above the belt line other than the windshield. Convertibles may have configurations other than open or closed, as for example a coupe that can be converted into a station wagon by exchanging one style of rear hatch for another. Also see *Targa roof* and *T-bar roof.*

coolant The mixture of water and antifreeze that draws heat from the engine and transfers it to air passing through the radiator. Oil that flows in an engine also serves to cool as well as lubricate, especially in air-cooled engines, but is not called coolant.

cooling system The system that removes heat from the engine. In a water-cooled engine it includes the radiator, fan, water pump, ther-mostat, and water jackets; in an air-cooled engine it consists of the fan and ducting.

core The interior of a hollow casting. Also, the material, often sand and usually dry, placed in a mold to form openings or give shape to a casting.

core-hole plug See *expansion plug.*

core plug See *expansion plug.*

cornering force The force on a turning vehicle's tires — the tires' ability to grip and resist side force — that keeps the vehicle on the desired arc. Also see *side force.*

cornering limit The maximum speed at which a car can negotiate a given curve.

Corporate Average Fuel Economy (CAFE) U.S. government-mandated fuel-economy standards effective in model year 1978 and applicable to all car and light-truck manufacturers selling in the United States. As calculated on the basis of EPA fuel-economy ratings, the average fuel economy of the vehicles sold in the United States by a manufacturer in a given year — its CAFE — must equal or exceed the standard for that year; manufacturers whose fleet-average economy falls below the standard are subject to a fine equal to the number of vehicles sold for the year times a specified dollar amount for each 0.1-mpg deviation. Manufacturers are also allowed credits for exceeding a given year's CAFE that may be applied to a previous or future model year. CAFE standards were relaxed during the mid-eighties fuel glut, which diminished the perception of the need for fuel conservation that prompted the law.

corrected horsepower Dynamometer output (horsepower and/or torque) of an engine adjusted or corrected to SAE standards of 60 degrees Fahrenheit and barometric pressure of 29.0 inches of mercury. The engine is tested in an "as installed" condition, meaning as it would be fitted to a car with its regular production

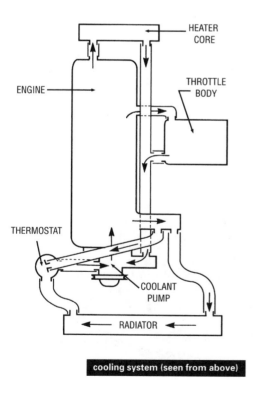

cooling system (seen from above)

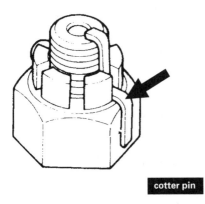

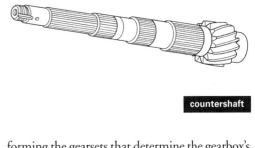

countershaft

cotter pin

intake and exhaust manifolds and with all normal accessories functioning.

cotter pin A two-pronged locking pin. It is driven through a hole in a shaft and the prongs are then separated to hold it in place. It is typically used to prevent a nut from loosening on the shaft. Also see *castle nut*.

counterbalance See *counterweight*.

countershaft The shaft in a manual gearbox that carries power by means of gears from the input shaft to the output shaft. Gears on the countershaft pair with those on the main shaft,

forming the gearsets that determine the gearbox's ratios or "speeds."

countersteer See *four-wheel steering* and *opposite lock*.

counterweight Weight added to a rotating shaft or wheel to balance normal loads on the part and offset vibration. Counterweights are used on the crankshaft and are often found on the flywheel and driveshaft. Also called *counterbalance*.

coupe A two-door closed body type, typically distinguished from a two-door sedan by a sleeker, shorter roof and longer trunk, but frequently different in other ways too. Variations include the soft-top convertible coupe (now simply convertible) and the pillarless hardtop convertible coupe (shortened to hardtop).

coupe

Coupes are generally thought of as sportier and more "personal" than two-door sedans.

courtesy light   An interior light affixed to a door to assist occupants in safely entering and exiting the vehicle at night. The definition has been extended to include lights for the glove box, ashtray, vanity mirror, for reading maps, or in the luggage or engine compartments.

cowl   The portion of a car body between the engine and passenger compartments, typically thought of as including the firewall. It usually carries the instrument panel and climate-system air plenum chamber. Stylists define it as the area bounded by the front fenders, the base of the windshield, and the rear edge of the hood. Called the *scuttle* by the British.

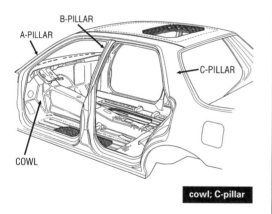

cowl; C-pillar

C-pillar   The third set of vertical roof members from the front of a car (after the A- and B-pillars), used to support the rear portion of the roof. Also called the *C-post*, or a *sail panel*, if unusually wide.

C-post   See *C-pillar*.

crankcase   The part of an engine that encloses and supports the crankshaft; in most engines, the oil pan and the lower portion of the cylinder block form the crankcase.

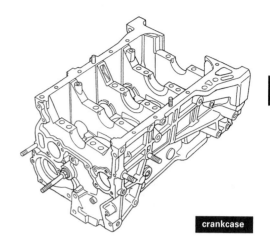

crankcase

crankpin   The bearing surface on a crankshaft to which the connecting rod is attached. Also called the *journal* or *crank throw*.

crankshaft   The engine's main shaft, so-named because of its U-shaped cranks. It delivers rotary motion taken from the reciprocating pistons and rods.

crankshaft

crank throw   See *crankpin*.

crashing through   See *bottoming*.

cross-drilled rotors   See *ventilated disc brakes*.

crossfiring   A condition in which high voltage in a spark plug wire induces current in an

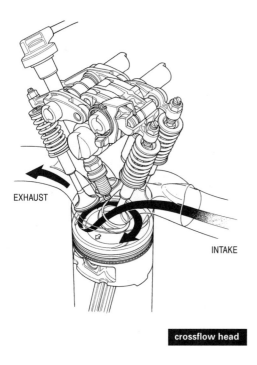

EXHAUST

INTAKE

crossflow head

adjacent wire, causing a spark plug to fire out of sequence.

crossflow head   A cylinder head in which the intake ports are located on the side opposite the exhaust ports. The resulting direct flow promotes efficient breathing and combustion.

cross member   Any automotive frame member whose primary shape is transverse. Generally attached to the main frame or body-frame structure with flexible mountings, cross

CROSS MEMBER

cross member

members typically carry suspension systems or power trains.

cross-ply tire   See *bias tire.*

crown   The top surface of a piston that forms part of the combustion chamber. Also see *camber.*

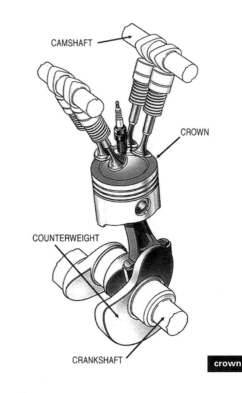

CAMSHAFT

CROWN

COUNTERWEIGHT

CRANKSHAFT

crown

CRT   See *cathode ray tube.*

cruise control   An electronic/electro-mechanical system that maintains a set car speed regardless of terrain without the driver's foot on the accelerator pedal. The basic elements are a speed sensor, a vacuum servo that varies throttle opening in response to sensor signals, and a switch that disconnects the servo whenever the brakes are applied, plus associated valves, linkages, and wiring. Most systems also include an electronic memory: the set speed is retained while braking and may be resumed afterward. Also called *speed control.*

crumple zone See *crush zone.*

crush zone Front and rear ends of a car body designed for controlled absorption of collision energy to preclude or minimize deformation of the passenger compartment. Also called *crumple zone.* Also see *passive safety.*

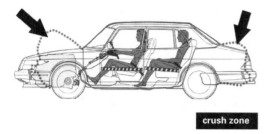

crush zone

cubic centimeter (cc) A metric measure of volume; engine displacement is typically measured in cubic inches, cubic centimeters, or liters. Multiplying cubic inches by 16.39 gives cubic centimeters; dividing cc by 1000 gives liters. Thus, 183 cubic inches equals 3000 cc, which equals 3.0 liters.

cubic inch See *cubic centimeter.*

cupping A tire wear condition caused by an unbalanced tire or faulty shock absorber; the excessive vibration causes the tread to be scooped out or "cupped" on one side of the tire.

curb-to-curb See *turning circle.*

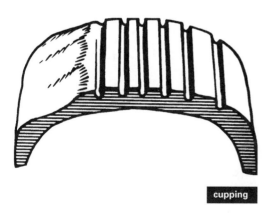

cupping

cutout

curb weight Weight of a production car that is ready for the road, with fluid reservoirs (including fuel tank) full and all normal equipment in place but without driver, passengers, or cargo.

cutout A device that interrupts an electrical circuit; often automatic. Also known as a *circuit breaker, interrupter,* or *relay.*

Also, a valve used to divert exhaust gases directly to the atmosphere instead of through a muffler.

CV joint See *constant velocity joint.*

CVT Continuously variable transmission. See *infinitely variable transmission.*

Cx See *coefficient of aerodynamic drag.*

cylinder The hollow tubular structure in an engine's cylinder block in which the piston

cylinder

travels and combustion occurs. Also referred to as the *bore* or *barrel*.

cylinder block   The lower part of an engine, usually a casting and including the cylinders and crankcase, to which other parts are attached. Also called the *engine block* or *block*.

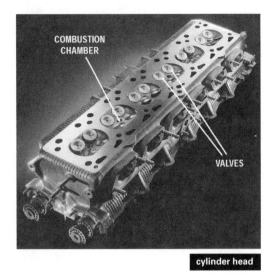

cylinder head

cylinder block

cylinder cutout   A device or system that disables the power cycles of one or more cylinders of a piston engine, usually to reduce fuel consumption.

cylinder head   That part of an engine, usually detachable, that attaches to the top of the cylin-

der block and seals the cylinders. It contains all or a portion of the combustion chambers; the water passages or air fins and oil passages for cooling and lubrication; and holds the spark plugs and, on contemporary engines, the valves.

cylinder liner   See *liner*.

cylinder pressure   The pressure in the combustion chamber at any given moment. Also see *mean effective pressure*.

damper   See *shock absorber.*

dash   See *dashboard.*

dashboard   A panel at the base of the windshield, fitted across the width of the interior, and containing gauges, switches, and instruments for vehicle operation; also called the *instrument panel* or *dash.*

dash panel   See *bulkhead.*

dashpot   A device consisting of a piston and cylinder with a restricted opening; used to slow down or delay the operation of a moving part, such as the throttle linkage.

daytime running lights (DRL)   Headlights of reduced intensity which are automatically turned on whenever a vehicle is operating with the headlamp switch in the off position, in order to make a vehicle more visible to approaching vehicles during daytime driving. This can help reduce the frequency of head-on crashes when drivers attempt to pass on two-lane roads or when driving in fog, rain, or other low-visibility conditions. With DRL on, the taillights, parking lights, and side marker lights are not usually illuminated so it is necessary to turn on the regular headlights at dusk.

db   See *decibel.*

dashboard

dead axle See *beam axle.*

deceleration Negative acceleration; the rate of change in velocity as a car slows during, for example, braking.

decelerometer An instrument for measuring deceleration.

decibel (db) The logarithmic unit used to measure sound pressure level. The logarithmic db scale was developed because the loudest sound the ear can tolerate would involve pressure it could not. Subjectively, a gain of 10 db is roughly equivalent to a doubling in amplitude. The associated dbA unit is used to measure the sound level within a car; it is determined via a sound meter having the "A" scale, which is weighted with a frequency spectrum similar to that of the human ear.

deck See *rear deck.*

deck lid See *trunk lid.*

de Dion axle A cross between independent rear suspension and a live axle, consisting of a connecting tube located by means of leaf springs or trailing arms, for example, and a chassis-mounted differential driving the wheels through universal-jointed half shafts. A de Dion system thus keeps the wheels upright just as a live axle does, but unsprung weight is reduced because the differential is separate from the axle. It also leaves room around the differential for inboard brakes, which further reduce unsprung weight.

deflection A tire's free radius minus its loaded radius. See illustration for *nominal wheel diameter.*

deflection steer Undesirable changes in the suspension and steering geometry that occur when the rubber bushings used at suspension pivots are compressed and twisted due to changing loads applied to the suspension.

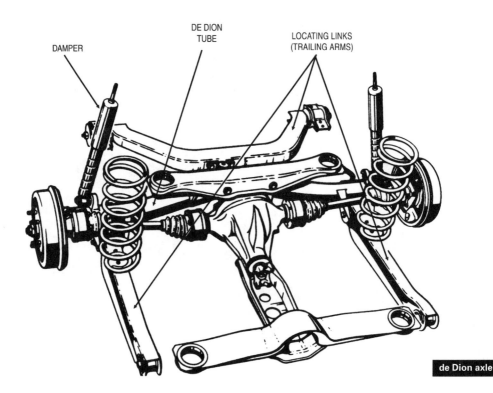

DAMPER

DE DION TUBE

LOCATING LINKS (TRAILING ARMS)

de Dion axle

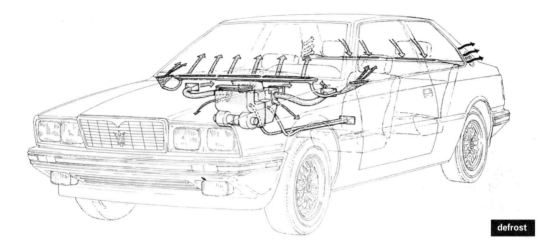

defrost

defrost A setting on a climate control system that directs hot air to the windshield and side windows to melt ice on the exterior or to clear condensation on the interior. A rear defroster usually consists of thin wires embedded in the glass of the rear window; when current passes through the glass, the wires heat and melt ice and/or clear condensation.

Department of Transportation (DOT) Part of the executive branch of the federal government, established in 1966, that sets policy for environmental safety and for all aspects of the U.S. transportation system. Also see *National Highway Traffic Safety Administration.*

detonation Excessively rapid burning of the compressed air-fuel mixture in an engine, often resulting in a noise called ping or knock. Detonation is caused by autoignition of the end gas, that part of the mixture not yet consumed in the normal flame-front reaction. It occurs when piston motion and compression raise the temperature and pressure of the end gas to the point where it autoignites. The pinging or knocking noise results from intense pressure waves in the charge that cause the cylinder walls to vibrate.

Detroit Locker Brand name of a type of differential using ratchets to lock both axle half shafts together for straight-line operation.

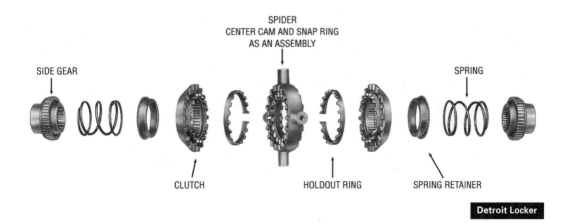

Detroit Locker

Deutsche Institüt für Normung (DIN)
German Institute for Standards. DIN horsepower, a German rating similar to SAE net horsepower (conversion factor 1.014) and used widely in Europe, is the output of an engine in metric horsepower with all normal accessories running.

de Ville French for "of town". In the coachbuilding era, the addition of "de Ville" to a body style indicated the presence of a panel over the front compartment that could be slid back or folded up, providing an opening roof. Today the term has evolved to indicate a more formal body style, as in Cadillac Sedan DeVille.

diagnostics The ability of some modern electronic devices utilizing one or more microprocessors to detect and determine the nature of a fault within itself and/or associated systems, and to display that information. Frequently called onboard diagnostics with regard to automotive engine management systems because the means for diagnosis and display are contained within the vehicle, thus eliminating the need for an external scope or other instrument. Typically, the display is integrated with some other instrument or display, for example the digital temperature readout panel of an automatic climate system.

diaphragm A stationary but flexible membrane, usually clamped at the edges and spring

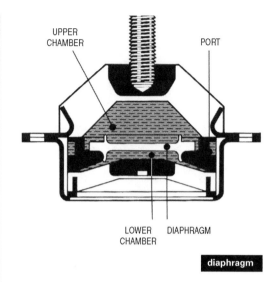

diaphragm

loaded, separating two cavities. Commonly of rubber, leather, or thin metal, and frequently used in pumps to create a pressure differential that causes a fluid to be pushed or pulled from one point to another.

diaphragm clutch See *diaphragm spring.*

diaphragm spring A type of clutch spring, shaped like a disc with tapering fingers pointed inward or like a wavy disc. In an automotive

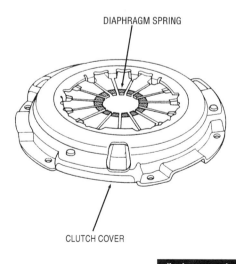

diaphragm spring

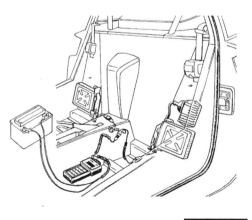

diagnostics

D

clutch, the diaphragm spring is part of the clutch pressure plate. When the clutch is engaged, this spring forces the pressure plate against the clutch disc; driver effort through the clutch linkage overcomes the spring pressure to disengage it.

dies Hardened metal blocks used to stamp or bend a piece of sheet metal into a desired shape. Also, a tool for cutting external threads, as on a bolt.

diesel engine Compression-ignition engine named for its inventor, Rudolph Diesel. See *compression ignition.*

dieseling A form of autoignition in which a gasoline engine continues to fire after the ignition has been shut off. Common in early emission-controlled engines because of the excess heat and unusually high manifold pressure that result from retarding the spark at idle. Also called *autoignition* and *run-on.*

differential A gear system that transfers power from a driveshaft or transmission to the driving axles or half shafts. It permits the outer driving wheel to turn faster than the inside wheel

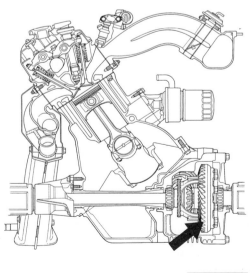

differential

when the car is turning, to prevent skidding and tire scrub.

digital instrumentation Gauges that electrically display numerals to indicate information such as engine speed, miles per hour, oil pressure, voltage, fuel supply, or time; compare to analog instrumentation. Also see *light-emitting diode* and *liquid crystal display.*

DIN See *Deutsche Institüt für Normung.*

diode An electronic device that allows current to flow mostly in one direction; usually a type of semiconductor. Also see *light-emitting diode.*

dipstick A graduated metal rod used to measure the oil level in an engine or transmission.

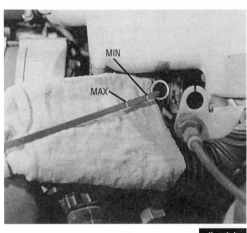

MIN

MAX

dipstick

direct current (DC) Electrical current that flows continuously in one direction; current from a car battery is one example. Compare with *alternating current.*

direct drive In automotive transmissions, the direct engagement between an engine and driveshaft, with the crankshaft and driveshaft turning at the same speed. In rear-drive cars, the transmission usually has one direct-drive (1:1) gear ratio: in five-speed transmissions, typically fourth gear.

directional tire

direct injection A fuel injection system that introduces fuel directly into the cylinder, rather than into a prechamber. Typically used for commercial diesel engines in conjunction with mechanically operated injectors, direct injection gives higher fuel efficiency than injection into a prechamber, but results in noisier engine operation. Also being investigated for gasoline engines; such engines are just beginning to come into production.

directional stability The ability of a car to be driven safely and with confidence in a straight line and at high speed without being unduly affected by pavement irregularities, crosswinds, aerodynamic lifting forces, or other external influences.

Stability is designed into the dynamic behavior of a vehicle by having larger slip angles at the front than at the rear under the action of transient side forces. When such a condition exists, a centrifugal force is produced which is opposed to the side force and, within limits, the car has intrinsic straight-line stability. However, such a car is not necessarily stable when cornering.

directional tire One with a tread pattern requiring the tire to always roll in the same direction. When the tires are rotated, a directional tire can only be switched from the front to the rear (or vice versa) on the same side of the car.

direction indicators Flashing lights at the front and rear corners of a vehicle, actuated by the driver via a stalk on the steering wheel, to alert other drivers that the vehicle is about to initiate a turn. Also called *turn signals* or *turn indicators*.

disc See *clutch disc*. Also see *disc brake*.

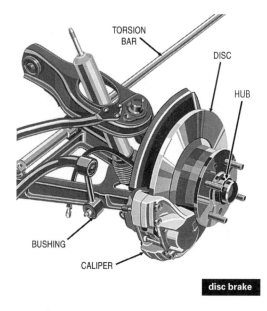

disc brake

disc brake A type of brake consisting of a flat rotor (disc) that turns with the wheel, and a stationary component called the caliper. Braking is accomplished when the caliper forces pads made of friction material against both sides of the rotating disc. Disc brakes typically provide more linear response and operate more efficiently at high temperatures than drum brakes.

discharge The flow of electrical current out of a battery; the opposite of charge.

dished piston   A piston with a depression in the crown. Also see *piston.*

displacement   The volume vacated by the piston of an engine as it moves downward in its cylinder; in multicylinder engines, the sum of these volumes for all cylinders. Displacement is the primary measure of engine size, representing the theoretical volume of air-fuel mixture that can be inducted by a cylinder on its intake stroke. Expressed in cubic inches, cubic centimeters, or liters. Also see *bore* and *stroke.*

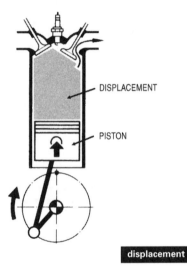

DISPLACEMENT

PISTON

displacement

distributor   A component in a conventional ignition system containing the breaker points and cam, centrifugal and vacuum advance mechanisms, and a shaft usually driven by the camshaft. The high voltage generated by the coil passes into the center terminal of the cap mounted on the top of the distributor housing. From there it passes down the rotor, and as the rotor turns it distributes the current to terminals connected by high-tension wires to the spark plugs. Also see *electronic distributor.*

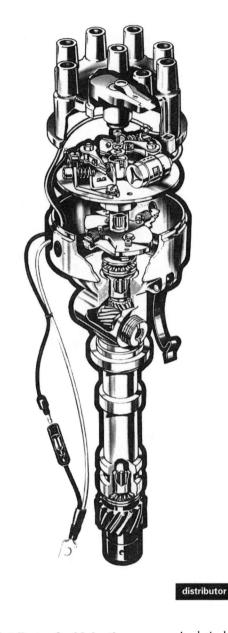

distributor

distributor fuel-injection pump   A relatively simple type of diesel-engine fuel-injection pump, which employs a single plunger and barrel to apportion fuel to the injectors at each cylinder in turn.

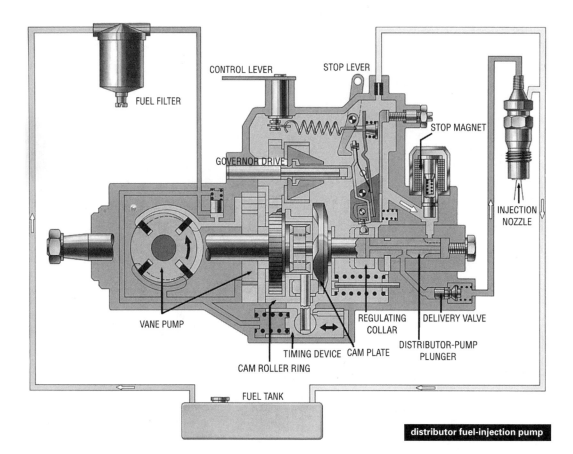

CONTROL LEVER STOP LEVER

FUEL FILTER

STOP MAGNET

GOVERNOR DRIVE

INJECTION NOZZLE

VANE PUMP

REGULATING COLLAR

DELIVERY VALVE

DISTRIBUTOR-PUMP PLUNGER

TIMING DEVICE CAM PLATE

CAM ROLLER RING

FUEL TANK

distributor fuel-injection pump

dive The nosing-down of the front end of a car during braking.

DOHC See *dual overhead cam.*

domed piston A piston with a raised crown. Also see *piston.*

DOT See *Department of Transportation.*

double A-arm See *unequal-length A-arm.*

double-clutch A driving technique, usually associated with racing, in which the driver depresses the clutch pedal, moves the shift lever out of gear and into the neutral gate, releases the clutch pedal about halfway while simultaneously using the throttle to increase engine speed,

domed piston

then depresses the clutch pedal again while shifting to the desired gear. The purpose is to minimize gear clash or grinding, especially with transmissions using unsynchronized gears. Double-clutching can be done while shifting up or down, but is usually executed using a heel-and-toe technique during downshifting. Also see *heel-and-toe* and *synchronizer.*

double cone synchronizers   A type of manual transmission gear synchronizer that uses both the inner and outer surfaces of the synchronizer cone to increase the operating area of the synchronizer, resulting in easier shifting and improved durability. Also see *synchronizer.*

double overhead cam   See *dual overhead cam.*

double wishbone   See *unequal-length A-arms.*

downdraft carburetor   A carburetor in which air flows downward through the carburetor and into the intake manifold.

downforce   Downward air pressure, generated by a car's body, that pushes the car onto the road with increasing force the faster it is driven. Downforce can be increased with aerodynamic devices such as spoilers and wings, originally developed for certain types of racing cars to enhance straight-line high-speed stability but which are also seen on some limited-production high-performance road cars. Also see *airfoil, ground effects,* and *wing.*

downshift   To change from a higher gear (numerically lower ratio) to a lower one (numerically higher ratio). Also see *kickdown.*

D-pillar   In a station wagon or minivan, the fourth or rearmost vertical roof members (after

WING

SPOILER

downforce

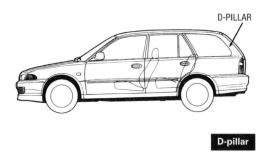

D-PILLAR

D-pillar

the A-, B-, and C-pillars) that support the rear window and the rear portion of the roof. Also called *D-post*.

D-post   See *D-pillar*.

drafting   A racing technique in which one car tucks in closely behind another (catches a tow), allowing both cars to gain straightaway speed, as their combined aerodynamic drag is actually less than their combined drag when separated by several car lengths. The lead car cuts into the air, acting as a wind break for the following car, while the latter's closeness reduces the drag-inducing turbulent flow normally generated at the rear of the first car. Also see *slipstream*. See illustration for *laminar flow*.

drag   See *aerodynamic drag*. Also, a form of racing consisting of standing-start acceleration contests for 1/8 or 1/4 mile.

drag coefficient   See *coefficient of aerodynamic drag*.

drift   See *four-wheel drift*.

drip molding   Drains that collect water from a car's roof and direct it away from the windows. Found in longitudinal pairs at the roof's edges and often extending down the A-pillars and/or rearward down the C- or D-pillars. Traditionally exposed, but hidden on many newer cars to reduce wind noise and aerodynamic drag. Also called *drip rail, rain gutter,* and *roof rail*.

drip rail   See *drip molding*.

driveability   The way an engine starts, runs at steady speeds, and responds to throttle (accelerator) changes. Specifically, it involves ease of starting, both hot and cold; the presence or absence of stumbling or hesitating on acceleration, or surging at steady speeds; the immediacy of engine response in acceleration and deceleration; and the degree to which performance and smoothness are affected by altitude and extreme ambient temperatures.

drive axle   An axle that transmits power to a drive wheel. Also see *axle* and *half shaft*.

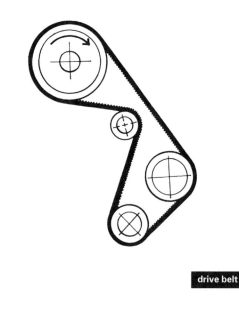

drive belt

drive belt   A continuous loop of rubber or textile material, often reinforced with steel, allowing one engine component to drive another via a pulley. In many current overhead camshaft engines the cam(s) are driven from the crankshaft via wide flat drive belts. Also called *V-belt*. Also see *fan belt, timing belt,* and *serpentine belt*.

drive-by-wire   An electronic accelerator in which there is no mechanical linkage between

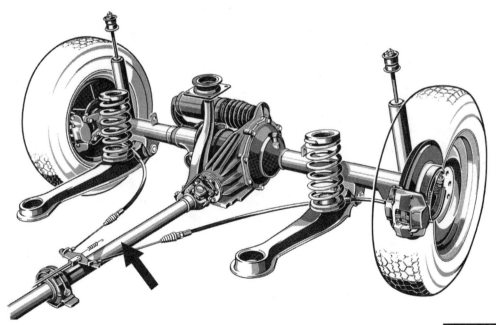

RING GEAR

DRIVE PINION

DIFFERENTIAL
CASE

AXLE

BEVEL GEAR

PINION GEAR

SHAFT

drive pinion

the accelerator pedal and the throttle valve. A position sensor on the pedal sends a signal to the power train control module, which uses an electronic motor to open and close the throttle valve. Also see *electronic accelerator*.

driveline   See *drivetrain*.

drive pinion   The shaft and gear that take power from the clutch into the gearbox. Also called the *clutch shaft*. Also, the shaft and gear that transmit power to the differential.

driveshaft   In a rear-wheel-drive or four-wheel-drive car, the long, hollow shaft with universal joints at both ends that carries power from the transmission to the differential. Runs along the car's longitudinal centerline. Also called the *propeller shaft* or *prop shaft*.

drivetrain   The power-transmitting components of a car, including manual clutch and gearbox or automatic transmission, driveshaft, universal joints, differential, axle shafts, wheels, and tires.

driveshaft

driving light

driving light   A front-mounted light that casts an intense, concentrated beam that may be as wide as that of a normal headlight but reaches farther ahead.

DRL   See *daytime running lights.*

drophead coupe   See *convertible.*

drum brake   A type of brake using a drum-shaped metal cylinder attached to the inner sur-

face of the wheel and rotating with it. When the brakes are applied, curved brake shoes with friction linings press against the drum's inner circumference to slow or stop the car.

dry gas   Gasoline with an additive such as alcohol to prevent water in the fuel from freezing in the fuel system, especially in the fuel lines, and preventing the engine from starting.

dry liner   See *liner.*

dry sump   A lubrication system in which the engine's oil supply is not contained in the crankcase (sump) but is pumped from an external container. This allows a smaller crankcase, which in turn permits the engine to be installed lower in the chassis. It also eliminates the oil starvation most conventional oiling systems suffer when subjected to extreme acceleration, braking, and cornering forces. Favored for racing cars, but also used in some high-performance road cars.

dual braking system   Designed to prevent complete loss of braking in case of hydraulic or

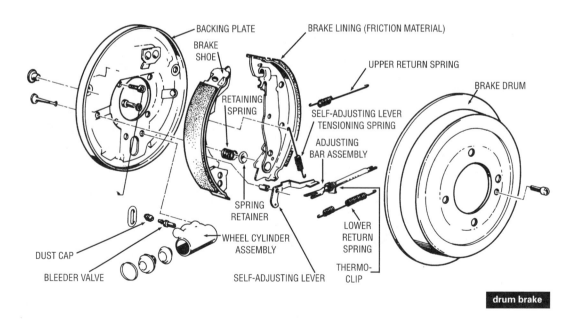

drum brake

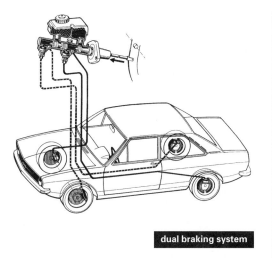

dual braking system

dual exhaust An exhaust system found on some V-engines. Most V-engines route exhaust gases from both banks of cylinders together just downstream of the exhaust manifolds. From there, the exhaust gases flow through one catalytic converter, one muffler, and one tailpipe to the atmosphere. The more expensive dual exhaust separates the exhaust flow from each of the cylinder banks to the rear of the vehicle. Doubling the components reduces exhaust back pressure and results in higher engine performance.

dual overhead cam (DOHC) An engine in which one overhead camshaft operates the intake valves and another operates the exhaust valves. Also called *twincam* engine.; DOHC vee-engines are often called quadcam engines. Also see *overhead cam.*

other brake failure, a dual braking system usually divides the four wheels into either front and rear or diagonal front/rear pairs with independent hydraulic circuits. In a few instances (Rolls-Royce, for example) three wheels are hydraulically connected in each separate system.

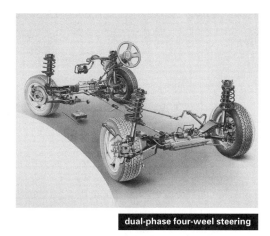

dual-phase four-weel steering

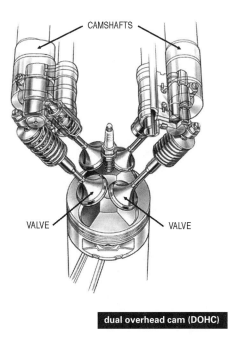

CAMSHAFTS

VALVE   VALVE

dual overhead cam (DOHC)

dual-phase four-wheel steering A system capable of steering the rear wheels either parallel with or counter to the front wheels. The Honda Prelude four-wheel-steering system is a dual-phase system. Also see *four-wheel steering.*

dual pivot Refers to a type of MacPherson strut front suspension pioneered by BMW, using two double-jointed lower control arms instead of a single arm. The system provides positive steering offset while allowing space for large brakes and wheel bearings.

dual-point   An ignition system in which two distributors or two sets of points within a single

dual-point (two distributors)

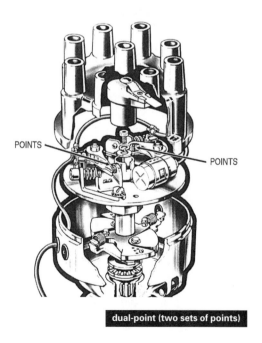

dual-point (two sets of points)

distributor are used to apportion electrical voltage among the spark plugs either for more precise spark timing or, in a few engines, to accommodate head designs with two plugs per cylinder.

dual-point injection   See *fuel injection*.

dumb irons   Referring to vintage automobiles, the forward extensions of the frame to which the half-elliptic leaf springs were typically attached. Also called *frame horns*.

durability   Literally, the length (duration) of the useful working life of a component or system. Lately, however, a synonym for long-term sturdiness as one indicator of vehicle quality, i.e., how the vehicle holds up over time and with use.

duration   The number of crankshaft degrees that a camshaft lobe holds an intake or exhaust valve open. With increasing engine speed, the actual time that the valves are open decreases.

dwell   The number of degrees of distributor rotation during which the breaker points are closed. Also called *dwell angle*.

dwell angle   See *dwell*.

Dykes ring   A compression piston ring, L-shaped in cross-section, designed to maintain contact between the combustion chamber and the ring at all engine speeds. In addition to pro-

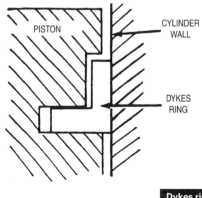

Dykes ring

viding a seal, it also helps to prevent piston-ring flutter, a phenomenon that results from the acceleration and deceleration of the piston and gas leakage behind the ring.

dynamic balancing   Balancing of a part such as a wheel or crankshaft during rotation. Lack of balance shows up as a tendency for the part to move off center, rock, or vibrate. Counterweights are then added to offset these rotational irregularities. Dynamic balancing is a more precise method of obtaining vibration-free running than static balancing.

dynamometer   A machine for measuring the horsepower and torque of an engine. An engine dynamometer measures power delivered to the flywheel; a chassis dynamometer measures power delivered to the drive wheels. Sometimes shortened to *dyno*.

dyno   See *dynamometer*.

D

east–west location See *transverse engine.*

eccentric Any rounded shape mounted off-center on a shaft and used to convert rotating to reciprocating motion through a follower which contacts the eccentric. Also called a cam. See *camshaft.*

eccentric

ECM Electronic control module or engine control module. See *electronic control module.*

ECU Electronic control unit. See *electronic control module.*

EFI Electronic fuel injection. See *fuel injection.*

EGR See *exhaust gas recirculation.*

electrical system The ignition system, starter motor, battery, alternator, voltage regulator, lights, electrical accessories, and all wiring, switches, and relays. The electrical system cranks the engine for starting, furnishes high voltage to fire the spark plugs, powers the lights, and operates the climate-control system, radio, and other amenities.

electrically controlled transmission (ECT) Transmission in which electronic circuits and microprocessors are used in place of some mechanical components.

electrode Either terminal in an electric circuit separated from the other by a gap that the current must jump; most frequently refers to the center and side electrodes of a spark plug.

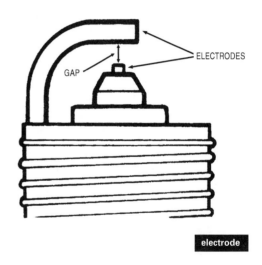

electrode

electrolyte Any solution that conducts an electric current, such as the mixture of sulfuric acid and distilled water used in automotive storage batteries. The acid enters into chemical reaction with the material on the battery plates to produce voltage and current.

electronic accelerator An electric motor rather than a mechanical linkage used to manipulate an engine's throttle for controlling air-fuel delivery and hence engine and vehicle speed in response to the accelerator pedal. It can incorporate anti-wheelspin and cruise-control functions. Also referred to as *drive-by-wire.*

electronically adjustable shock absorber
See *adjustable shock.*

electronic control module (ECM) Computerized controls for the engine or transmission and often for the interaction between the two, and for systems such as antilock braking, air bags, and traction control. Also called an *electronic control unit, engine control module, logic module,* or *black box.*

electronic distributor A component in an electronic ignition system, in which the shaft, cam, and mechanical breaker points of a conventional distributor are replaced by an electronic means of generating and distributing ignition current, such as a magnetic pulse generator and electronic trigger box. This type of distributor has important advantages over the traditional type, including the fact that the pulse gen-

erator does not wear and provides more precise control of ignition timing. Also see *distributor.*

electronic engine management A microprocessor-based system that integrates and controls both ignition and fuel-delivery systems; it may also encompass detonation control via a piezoelectric knock sensor (which signals the system to retard spark) and, in some turbocharged engines, operate a wastegate for the same purpose.

electronic fuel injection (EFI) See *fuel injection.*

electronic idle control Part of an electronic engine-management system that varies or maintains idle speed in response to input from sensors monitoring ambient temperature, coolant temperature, altitude, and similar factors. Typically includes a feedback loop, which (given steady input from other sensors) maintains a steady idle speed despite changes in engine loading, such as

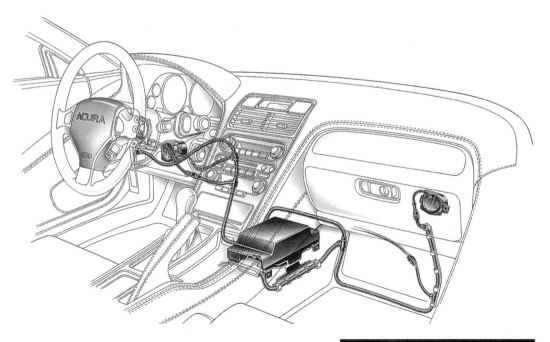

electronic control module (air bag system)

E

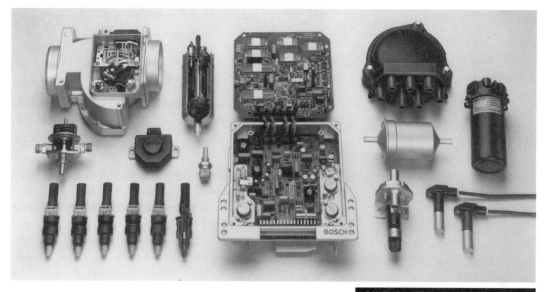

electronic engine management system

from an air-conditioning compressor cycling on and off or changing power-steering loads.

electronic ignition An ignition system using electronic switching devices to relieve or replace mechanical breaker points. There are three basic types: contact-controlled, in which the breaker points are retained but merely serve to trigger a transistor that switches the heavy primary current; magnetically controlled (also called contactless or breakerless or simply electronic), in which the points are eliminated and transistors are used as the switching device for the primary current; and capacitor-controlled (or capacitive discharge ignition), which can be either all-electronic or breaker-point controlled.

electronic temperature control See *automatic climate control*.

electronic transmission control A feature found in some automatic transmissions in which microprocessors determine and select the appropriate gear for various driving conditions via sensors monitoring the rotational speeds of the

electronic ignition

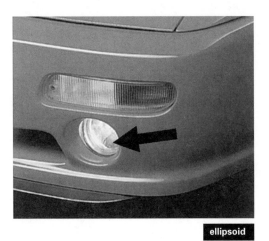

ellipsoid

engine and transmission, engine load (via intake vacuum), the positions of the transmission selector and kickdown switch, and other variables. A refinement offered by most manufacturers these days is various upshift and downshift programs,

which the driver can select for optimum economy or performance or to manually hold a gear. Some systems also include a function to reduce engine spark advance during shifting for smoother shifts and to lessen transmission wear.

electrophoretic process See *cathephoretic process.*

ellipsoid A headlight or driving light with a reflector that has a roughly flattened cylindrical shape resembling an elongated football. Deeper but smaller in diameter than conventional headlights with parabolic (dished) reflectors, it functions optically much like a slide-projector lamp, affording reduced glare and superior illumination, especially to the sides. The smaller diameter also allows it to fit flush with the lower-profile front ends of modern aerodynamic cars. Also called *polyellipsoid.*

emergency brake An independent braking system that can be used to slow or stop a car if

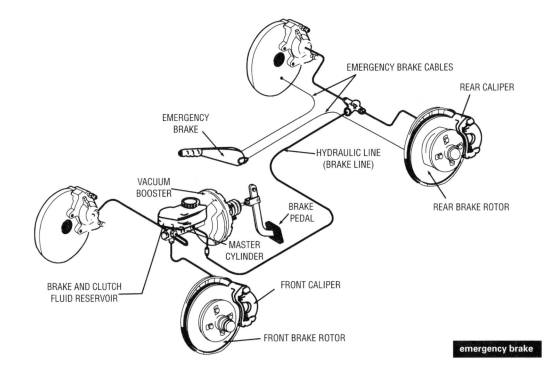

emergency brake

its primary brakes fail, or to hold the car stationary. It usually consists of a hand lever or foot pedal that actuates the front or rear brakes mechanically through a series of cables or linkages. Also called the *parking brake*.

emergency tensioning seat belt retractors   A passive safety device in which the inertia take-up reels of a three-point seat belt are triggered by the force of a collision to wind up and lock, thus removing any slack that may exist in the belt webbing and restraining the wearer.

emission controls   See *exhaust emission controls*.

encapsulation   To enclose or encase a car's engine, especially a diesel, to isolate it from the surrounding structure and minimize the amount of noise and vibration transmitted to the passenger compartment.

end gap   The distance between the ends of a piston ring when placed in a cylinder. When piston rings are installed, the end gaps should always be staggered around the piston to elim-

end gap

inate any potential leakage of the air-fuel mixture, the exhaust gases, and lubricating oil past the piston.

end gas   That part of the air-fuel mixture to burn last in the cylinder. Also see *quench area*.

end plate   See *tip plate*.

energy-absorbing bumper   Device that allows the front and rear ends of a car to absorb low-speed impacts without damage. Federal standards require protection to 2.5 mph; some carmakers provide protection to 5 mph. Also see *bumper*.

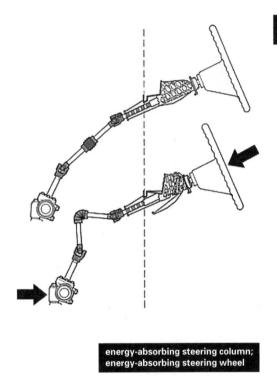

energy-absorbing steering column; energy-absorbing steering wheel

energy-absorbing steering column   A steering column and hub designed to collapse during a severe front impact to minimize rearward movement of the column and steering wheel. Also see *energy-absorbing steering wheel*.

energy-absorbing steering wheel   A steering wheel designed to yield under impact from the driver's body and reduce the risk of injury. Also see *energy-absorbing steering column*.

engine

engine   A machine that converts heat energy derived from some fuel into mechanical energy. Also see *internal combustion engine* and *motor*.

engine block   See *cylinder block*.

engine control module (ECM)   See *electronic control module*.

engine cover   See *hood*.

engine lid   See *hood*.

engine mounts   The rubber and steel supports that connect the engine and transmission to the vehicle frame. These supports absorb the twisting movements of the power train caused by engine torque and abrupt transmission shifts and also help isolate the passenger compartment from the noise and vibration produced by the power train. Hydraulic mounts, which provide better isolation and control of the power train than their conventional counterparts, have recently been developed.

engine speed   The speed at which an engine's crankshaft turns. Universally measured in revolutions per minute (rpm).

Environmental Protection Agency (EPA)   U.S. regulatory body, created in 1970, to develop and administer programs for pollution control and preservation of natural resources. Important to the automotive industry as the agency that sets standards for vehicle exhaust emissions and tests for compliance; as part of the latter, the EPA calculates the fuel economy of each year's car models in simulated city and highway driving and publishes the results as a comparative guide for consumers.

EP lubricant   See *extreme pressure lubricant*.

equalizer   In dual exhaust systems, a tube that balances pressure between the two exhaust pipes.

In sound-reproduction systems, a device used to vary the relative loudness (amplitude) of one or more portions (bands) of the frequency spectrum, thus altering the tonal "color" of a sound as heard through a speaker system. The simplest type of equalizer is a sliding or rotary tone control.

Equalization may be accomplished by one or more of four means: recording a sound so as to favor the desired quality (usually via selection and placement of microphones), providing an adjustment on the sound-reproduction instrument, using speakers designed to produce the desired tonal characteristics, and/or introducing an equalizer between the speakers and sound-reproduction device(s). Also see *graphic equalizer*.

equal-length driveshafts   On front-wheel-drive vehicles, the location of the transaxle typically requires driveshafts of differing lengths for each of the front wheels. Such a design can lead to torque steer when power is applied or the wheels are turned, problems that can be minimized by shafts of the same length. Also see *torque steer*. See illustration for *half shaft*.

ergonomics   The study of how human beings comprehend and operate machines, and how machine design affects the ease, comfort, and efficiency of their operation. In cars, the design and positioning of switches, instruments, seat, pedals, gear selector, steering wheel, and control mechanisms relative to the efficiency and comfort of the driver and passengers. Also called *human factors engineering*.

estate car   A station wagon. See *station wagon*.

E

ethanol   Short for ethyl alcohol, also known as grain alcohol, distilled from bio-mass sources (sugarcane, corn, algae, decaying organic matter). Often mixed with gasoline (typically in a 10:90 or 20:80 ratio) to form gasohol as a way to extend gasoline supplies in times of shortage, a measure that aroused interest in the United States in the early eighties. Ethanol contains less heat energy

ergonomics

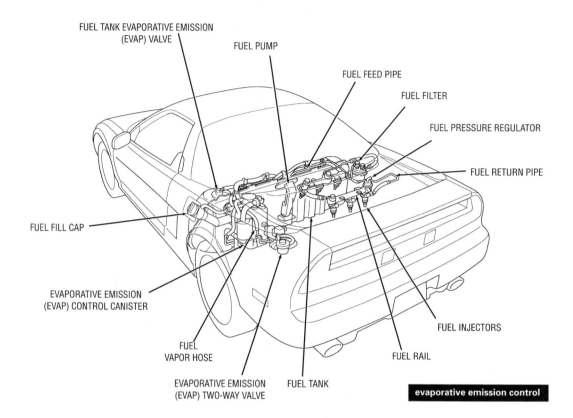

FUEL TANK EVAPORATIVE EMISSION (EVAP) VALVE

FUEL PUMP

FUEL FEED PIPE

FUEL FILTER

FUEL PRESSURE REGULATOR

FUEL RETURN PIPE

FUEL FILL CAP

EVAPORATIVE EMISSION (EVAP) CONTROL CANISTER

FUEL VAPOR HOSE

FUEL INJECTORS

EVAPORATIVE EMISSION (EVAP) TWO-WAY VALVE

FUEL TANK

FUEL RAIL

evaporative emission control

than gasoline (75,560 Btu per gallon versus 115,400 Btu) but may be used by itself to run a car with a suitably modified engine.

Ethyl Trade name for gasoline to which tetraethyl lead, ethylene dibromide, ethylene dichloride, or other octane improvers have been added. Also, a generic and now obsolete term for high-octane gasoline.

ethylene glycol See *antifreeze.*

evaporative emission control A system that prevents the escape of gasoline vapors from the fuel system into the atmosphere. Basically, a canister filled with activated charcoal and tubing that connects the canister to the fuel tank and carburetor or fuel injection system. Any vapor-filled air that leaves the fuel tank because of expansion passes through the tubing to the canister, where the vapors are captured and

stored in the charcoal. When the engine is started, the intake manifold vacuum draws fresh outside air through the canister, pulling the fuel vapor out of the charcoal and into the engine. Also termed *vapor recovery system.* Also see *exhaust emission controls.*

evaporator The device in an air conditioner in which a fluid, called the refrigerant, changes from a liquid to a vapor. This action extracts heat from the air, producing the desired cooling effect.

exhaust emission controls Systems or adjustments designed to limit noxious gases in an engine's exhaust. One approach is to reduce or eliminate the formation of harmful pollutants in the engine itself by means of effective combustion-chamber design or fuel injection; another is to destroy or otherwise alter the pollutants after they have been formed, via air injec-

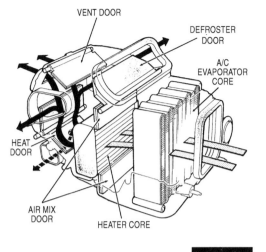

VENT DOOR

DEFROSTER
DOOR

A/C
EVAPORATOR
CORE

HEAT
DOOR

AIR MIX
DOOR

HEATER CORE

evaporator

tion systems, thermal reactors, catalytic converters, or crankcase controls that recycle fumes from the crankcase through the engine. Also called *emission controls*. Also see *evaporative emission control*.

exhaust emissions Unburned hydrocarbons (HxCx), carbon monoxide (CO), oxides of nitrogen (NOx), and other noxious gases emitted when gasoline is burned in an engine.

exhaust gas analyzer An instrument for measuring the quantity (usually in parts per million, percent, or grams per mile) and type of pollutants in an engine's exhaust. Also called a *combustion analyzer* because it can be used to determine the efficiency with which an engine is burning fuel.

exhaust gas recirculation (EGR) An exhaust emission control system in which a por-

E

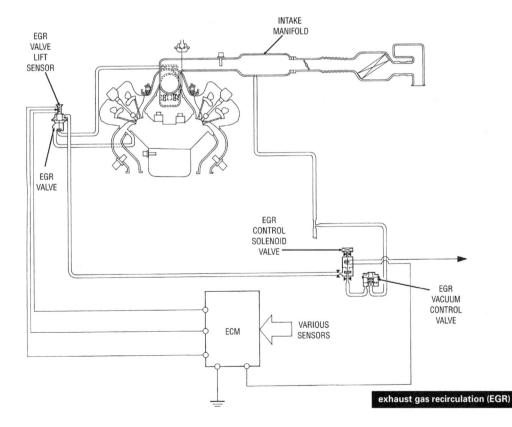

EGR
VALVE
LIFT
SENSOR

INTAKE
MANIFOLD

EGR
VALVE

EGR
CONTROL
SOLENOID
VALVE

EGR
VACUUM
CONTROL
VALVE

ECM

VARIOUS
SENSORS

exhaust gas recirculation (EGR)

exhaust header

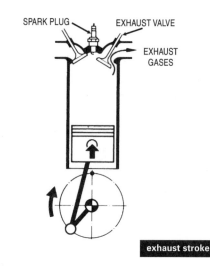

exhaust stroke

tion of the exhaust gas is picked up from the exhaust manifold, sent back to the carburetor, and reburned in the engine. Mixing exhaust gases with the fresh air-fuel mixture lowers combustion temperature and reduces the formation of oxides of nitrogen in the exhaust.

exhaust header   Similar to an exhaust manifold, but usually made of steel tubing. Generally more efficient at extracting exhaust gases than a conventional cast iron exhaust manifold, resulting in less backpressure and greater power. See *exhaust manifold.*

exhaust manifold   An assembly of tubes, usually of cast iron, that attach to an engine's cylinder head and provide paths through which burned gases from the cylinders can flow to the exhaust system.

exhaust pipe   Steel pipe that routes exhaust gases from the exhaust manifold or header to the muffler(s).

exhaust ports   Passages in the cylinder head through which gases from the exhaust valves pass to the exhaust manifold.

exhaust stroke   The upward fourth stroke of the four-stroke engine cycle, in which the piston moves from bottom dead center to top dead center, forcing the burned exhaust gases out of the cylinder.

exhaust system   The pipes, resonators, and mufflers that carry the exhaust gases from the

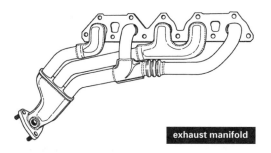

exhaust manifold

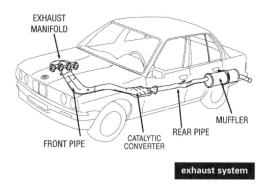

exhaust system

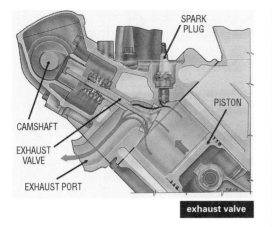

SPARK PLUG

PISTON

CAMSHAFT

EXHAUST VALVE

EXHAUST PORT

exhaust valve

exhaust manifold into the atmosphere. In modern emission-controlled gasoline engines the system also includes a catalytic converter; in stringently emission-controlled diesel engines it may include a trap oxidizer.

exhaust valve   A camshaft-driven valve in the cylinder head that opens to allow burned gases out of the cylinder and closes to form part of the combustion chamber during the compression and power strokes.

expander ring   See *expansion ring*.

expansion plug   A steel plug, slightly dished or cup-shaped, which when driven into place flattens out to fit tightly in its seat. In an engine block, expansion plugs (also called core plugs, core-hole plugs, or freeze plugs) are inserted in the holes in the casting through which the core was removed when the casting was formed. They open into cooling passages and thus provide pressure relief should the engine coolant freeze and expand.

expansion ring   A ring placed under a piston ring to increase ring pressure on the cylinder walls. Typically, an oil control ring consists of two thin rings or rails, with an expansion ring between them. The expansion ring pushes the rails up against the sides of the ring groove and out against the cylinder wall to seal and scrape oil from the wall. Also called an *expander ring*, Also see *oil control ring*.

expansion stroke   See *power stroke*.

expansion tank   In a sealed cooling system, a reservoir that connects to the radiator cap and that keeps the cooling system filled at all times. As the engine heats up, the coolant expands and a portion flows into the expansion tank. When

E

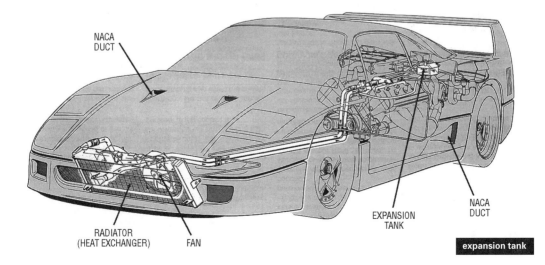

NACA DUCT

NACA DUCT

EXPANSION TANK

RADIATOR (HEAT EXCHANGER)

FAN

expansion tank

the engine reaches operating temperature, a valve in the radiator cap closes, sealing the cooling system. As the engine cools, the coolant contracts, producing a vacuum in the cooling system; the valve opens, and coolant in the expansion tank flows back into the radiator. Also called *overflow or surge tank*.

expansion valve   In an air-conditioning system, a valve located between the condenser and the evaporator that regulates the flow of liquid refrigerant to the evaporator. If cooling needs are low, the valve is almost closed; as additional cooling is required, the valve opens wider so that more refrigerant flows to the evaporator.

external combustion engine   An engine that burns its fuel outside the engine; the working fluid is entirely separated from the air-fuel mixture, the heat of combustion being transferred through the walls of a containing vessel or boiler. A steam engine is an example.

extreme pressure (EP) lubricant   A lubricant able to withstand high pressures, as between gear teeth.

fade Loss of effective braking due to heat buildup as the brakes are used constantly or repeatedly within a short time span (as in descending a steep mountain road). Drum brakes are more prone to fade than disc brakes because they dissipate heat less effectively.

fan A device with rotating curved blades designed to draw air through the radiator core of a liquid-cooled engine, especially at low speeds or idle, when the air intake through the grille is insufficient for cooling. In front-engine/rear-drive cars, the fan is usually mounted on an extension of the water-pump shaft and driven by a V-belt from a pulley mounted on the front of the crankshaft. In front-wheel-drive cars, however, the fan is electric and is located ahead of the radiator. In cars with air-cooled engines, the fan is relatively large and forces air over the engine itself.

fan belt An endless belt, typically of a rubberized material with internal steel or cord reinforcement to minimize stretching, used to transmit power from a crankshaft-driven pulley to a pulley driving the fan, alternator, or other engine accessories. It is usually V-shaped in cross section with the point of the vee fitting into a groove in the pulley. Also called V-belt. Also see *serpentine belt.*

fan clutch A thermostatically controlled device that engages/disengages the radiator cooling fan by either a viscous or electromechanical coupling. On a hot day in stop-and-go traffic or when idling, the fan clutch engages to keep air flowing through the radiator to prevent overheating. At cooler temperatures or when an adequate supply of air is being forced through the radiator by the speed of the vehicle, the clutch disengages, allowing the fan to freewheel, reducing fan noise and the load on the engine and improving fuel economy.

fan shroud A plastic, rubber, or metal covering between the fan and the radiator that directs air pulled or pushed by the fan to the radiator. Often shortened to shroud.

fascia In America, a car's front and rear exterior end panels, situated above the bumpers and sometimes made of deformable plastic matching the color of the bumper covering. Also sometimes called *caps.* The front fascia is generally below and/or ahead of the hood's forward shutline and may include headlights and/or parking lights. The rear fascia, or back panel, encompasses the taillights and, sometimes, a recess for

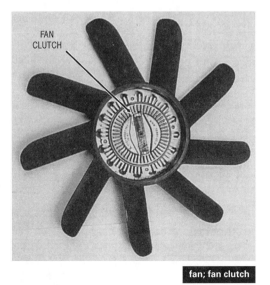

FAN CLUTCH

fan; fan clutch

FASCIA

fastback

the license plate. In British English, however, fascia means instrument panel.

fastback   A closed body style, usually a coupe but sometimes a sedan, with a roof sloped gradually in an unbroken line from the windshield to the rear edge of the car. A fastback naturally lends itself to a hatchback configuration and many have it, but not all hatchbacks are fastbacks and vice versa.

fast idle   Carburetor mechanism, normally consisting of a cam and linkage attached to the choke, that prevents a cold engine from stalling by holding the throttle partially open, causing the engine to run at a faster-than-normal speed until its coolant reaches minimum operating temperature. Modern electronic fuel injection systems accomplish fast idle with a valve that varies the engine speed according to signals from sensors monitoring coolant temperature, ambient temperature, engine load, and other factors. Also refers to a high idle speed.

fatigue   Material failure due to repeated application of stress.

feathering   Tire wear caused by excessive toe-in or toe-out, in which the tread scuffs, producing slanted wear or "feathering" on each tread ridge.

federalized version   Since 1968, a foreign-built car suitably modified so as to be legal for sale in the United States; a car that conforms to all U.S. emission and safety standards in force at the time of its manufacture, as opposed to home-market and other export versions, which typically do not.

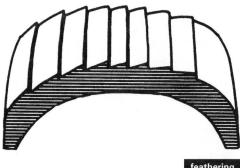

feathering

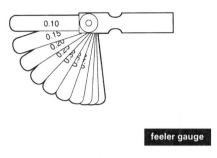

feeler gauge

federal version   A car that complies with U. S. emission standards, but not necessarily the more stringent standards required for new cars sold in California. For this reason, also called a *49-state car.* In recent years, some other states, such as New York, have been requiring cars meet certain Cailfornia standards.

Fédération Internationale de l'Automobile (FIA)   Paris-based organization, mainly concerned with regulations governing motorists traveling outside their native countries, to which most of the world's motoring organizations belong.

Fédération Internationale du Sport Automobile (FISA)   The section of the Fédération Internationale de l'Automobile that acts as the world governing body for motor sports. Previously known as the Commission Sportive Internationale (CSI), it comprises several commissions with delegates representing various sanctioning bodies (such as the Sports Car Club of America and Championship Auto Racing Teams [CART} in the United States), drivers and car builders, plus a small professional staff that carries out the commissions' decisions and advises FISA's president.

feedback mixture control   A feature of computer-controlled fuel systems in which an oxygen sensor measures the oxygen content of the engine's exhaust and feeds back a signal to the computer which, in turn, varies the air-fuel mixture to keep it close to the ratio for chemically correct combustion. Such precise control of the air-fuel ratio is critical for the proper operation of three-way catalysts.

feeler gauge   A metal strip or blade of calculated thickness for measuring the clearance between two parts. Most commonly, the tool for measuring and setting the gap between a spark plug's inner and outer electrodes.

fender   The body panel mounted over the road wheel of an automobile. Generally, pressed and formed sheet metal, but can also be plastic as in a Corvette or Saturn. Also called *quarter panel.*

F

fender

ferrous metal   Metal that contains iron.

F-head engine   An engine design, no longer used in passenger cars, with one valve or valve set in the cylinder block at the side of the piston and the other valve or valve set in the cylinder head above the piston.

FIA   See *Fédération Internationale de l'Automobile.*

fiberglass   From Fiberglas, a trade name; now generic for a flexible, nonflammable, corrosion-proof material of plastic with glass filaments. Used widely in automobiles for exterior and interior body parts, air ducts, and component covers.

fiberglass-reinforced plastic (FRP)   See *fiberglass.*

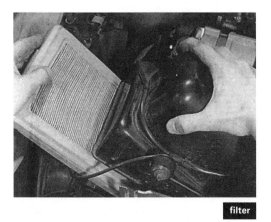

filter

final drive ratio

filter A device for removing suspended impurities or particles of foreign matter from an engine's air intake, fuel, or lubricating system.

fin A thin metal segment projecting from a surface and affording increased exposure of the surface to the air and hence greater cooling. Can also refer to wings, airfoils, and other devices on a car's exterior used to improve aerodynamic stability.

final drive ratio The ratio between the speed of the driveshaft or transmission output shaft and the speed of the drive-wheel axle shaft. It is determined by the ring-and-pinion gearing inside the differential. For example, if the driveshaft (or transmission output shaft) rotates four times for each complete turn of the differential gear, axle shafts, and wheels, the ratio is

NACA DUCT

fin

4:1. The ratio is varied by changing the number of gear teeth on the ring-and-pinion gears.

finish   The relative smoothness of a surface. Commonly used to describe the smoothness, luster, hardness, and gloss of paint on a car body. Often used with the word "fit" to describe the thoroughness and attention to detail evident in a car's assembly.

fire point   The temperature at which the vapor of a flammable liquid continues to burn. Also see *flash point.*

firewall   The partition between the engine and passenger compartments. Also see *bulkhead.*

firing order   In an engine with two or more cylinders, the sequence in which the spark is delivered to the cylinders.

FISA   See *Fédération Internationale du Sport Automobile.*

fit   The way a component aligns as one element of a structure or device relative to its intended positioning and function. Often used with the word "finish" to describe the consistency and evenness of installed body panels, exterior and interior trim, and accessories.

five-link   A system of independent rear suspension (IRS), developed by Mercedes-Benz, which uses fives links to locate each wheel. Like some other modern IRS systems, it incorporates toe control. Also see *toe control.*

fixed caliper   A caliper on a disc brake that remains stationary relative to the disc and has a piston or pistons on both sides of the disc; the pads move inward to clamp the disc from both sides. Also see *caliper.*

flame-front   The leading edge of the burning air-fuel mixture as it propagates through the combustion chamber.

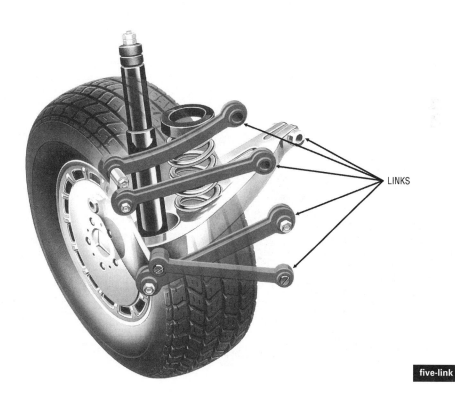

LINKS

five-link

flange Surface on a wheel rim that contacts the side of the tire bead. The different types of flange profiles are identified by a lettering system as follows: B, J, JJ, JK, K, and L. A typical wheel description would be 14 x 5J, with 14 representing the wheel diameter in inches, 5 the wheel width in inches, and J the flange profile. Also called *wheel-rim flange*.

Also, a flat plate on a pipe joint.

flash Excess material found around the parting lines of cast or forged components.

flash point The temperature at which the vapor of a flammable liquid will momentarily burst into flame (flash) but not burn continuously when an open flame is brought near. The higher an oil's flash point, the better its lubricating ability. Also see *fire point*.

flat engine An engine with two banks of cylinders situated 180 degrees opposite each other; also called a horizontally opposed engine or pancake engine. Also called a boxer engine, due to the boxlike shape of the crankcase and cylinders. The Porsche 911 six-cylinder is a well-known example.

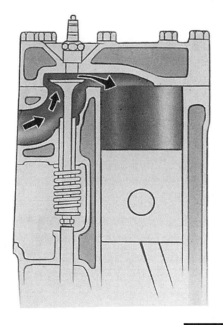

flathead

flathead An engine type, no longer used in passenger cars, with all its valves in the block on one side of the cylinder so that the head itself is flat. Also called a *side-valve* or *L-head engine* because the combustion chamber is L-shaped.

flat spot A driveability problem in which an engine momentarily hesitates during acceleration. Also, that portion of a tire tread rendered out-of-round by a car's resting in one place for a prolonged period or by braking with its wheel locked.

flipper That portion of a tire casing encircling and "flipping" around the bead. Also called the casing turn-up because of the way in which this flap of material turns-up around the bead. The flipper will vary in height; the higher it extends up the sidewall, the stiffer the sidewall and the higher the level of performance of the tire. Sometimes referred to as the bead lockup because it locks the casing around the bead to keep it from unraveling.

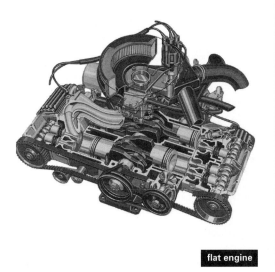

flat engine

float   A hollow device, lighter than the fluid in which it rests, used to measure a fluid level or to operate a valve controlling the entrance of fuel or another fluid. Also see *valve float*. See illustration for *carburetor*.

Also a ride motion in automobiles, a relatively slow jounce-rebound cycle such that the car seems to float momentarily off the road, usually encountered on crests or large, shallow humps. Also see *ride*.

float bowl   A chamber in the carburetor into which fuel is fed and stored until it is needed by the engine. Also see *float level*. See illustration for *carburetor*.

float connected to the needle-and-seat assembly. See illustration for *carburetor*.

flood   To pump more fuel into the combustion chambers than can be ignited by the spark plugs during a cold start, resulting in the engine refusing to start.

floorboard   The car floor under the front bulkhead; also called the toeboard.

floorpan   The mostly flat, often ribbed area that lies between a chassis' side rails. One of a car's most important structural elements (and one of the most expensive to alter), it provides a foundation for the floor as well as attachment points for components such as door posts, seats, and fender wells.

F

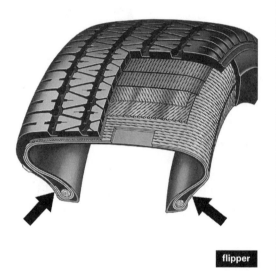

flipper

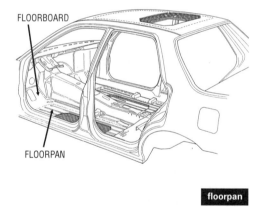

FLOORBOARD

FLOORPAN

floorpan

floating caliper   A caliper on a disc brake, with piston(s) on only one side of the rotor — generally, the caliper has only one piston. When the brakes are applied, the piston pushes the pad on one side and pulls the pad on the other to clamp the disc; the caliper moves or "floats" along a shaft. Also called a *sliding caliper*. Also see *caliper*.

float level   The predetermined height of fuel in the carburetor's bowl, usually regulated by a

floor shift   A type of transmission shift linkage in which the various gears are selected by a lever attached to or protruding through the floor rather than attached to the steering column (column shift). Also called a *stick shift*.

flow-through ventilation   A type of fresh-air system in which outside air is ducted into a car's interior (usually through adjustable openings

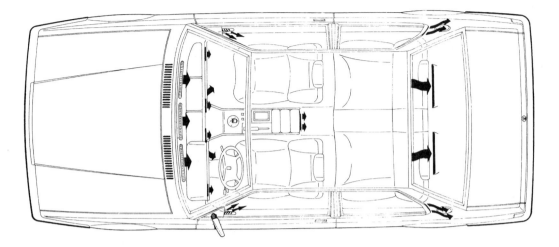

flow-through ventilation

in the dashboard), circulates, then exits through openings toward the rear of the car.

fluid coupling   Part of an automatic transmission that serves as a hydraulic clutch to transmit engine torque to the transmission gears and to cushion the flow of power. It consists of a pair of vaned rotating elements (torus members) splined to separate shafts and operating in a fluid-filled housing. The input torus or "fan" churns the hydraulic fluid and rotation is imparted to the driven member (output torus) through the hydraulic fluid. It has been replaced in virtually all modern automatic transmissions by the torque converter. See illustration for *torque converter.*

flush glass   Windshield, rear window, and side windows positioned even or nearly even with the surrounding structure so that the glass is neither recessed nor projecting. The resulting smooth contour improves aerodynamic efficiency and lessens wind noise.

flush headlight   Headlight mounted even or nearly even with the surrounding structure of a car's nose. As with flush glass, flush headlights improve the airflow over a car's body, thus reducing aerodynamic drag and wind noise.

flywheel   A heavy, toothed wheel mounted to the rear of the crankshaft; it smooths the separate power surges imparted to the crankshaft as each cylinder fires by resisting the engine's tendency to speed up at the start of the power stroke and slow down toward the end. It also serves as part of the clutch by transmitting power to the gearbox in a car with manual transmission, acts as a vibration damper and balance member for the crankshaft, and engages the teeth of the starter motor when the engine is cranked.

follower   See *cam follower.*

foot-pound   A measurement of work or energy. One foot-pound (ft-lb) equals the work done when a constant force of one pound is exerted on a body that moves a distance of one foot in the direction of the force. Not to be confused with pound-foot, a unit of torque.

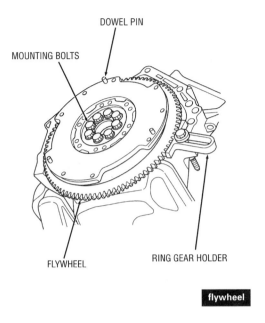

DOWEL PIN

MOUNTING BOLTS

FLYWHEEL

RING GEAR HOLDER

flywheel

footprint   See *contact patch.*

forced induction   An engine equipped with a blower to push air into the cylinders at higher than atmospheric pressure. Also see *supercharger* and *turbocharger.*

forge   A process in which molten metal is forced by either presses or hammers into die cavities. Forged metals are much stronger and more fatigue-resistant than simple cast metals and are typically used in crankshafts and suspension arms.

49-state car   See *federal version.*

fouled   A spark plug whose center and side electrodes are worn or coated with deposits so that a proper spark cannot be generated to combust the air-fuel mixture.

four-banger   An in-line four-cylinder engine, or a vehicle powered by one.

four-barrel carburetor   A carburetor with four throats or venturis.

four-bolt mains   A crankshaft main bearing cap held in place by four bolts instead of the usual two. Typically used in high-performance, racing, and other heavy-duty applications.

four-stroke cycle   The working cycle of a four-cycle engine encompasses four piston strokes, two upward and two downward. An explosion thus occurs with every other revolution of the crankshaft. The strokes are intake,

F

NORMAL

OIL-FOULED

CARBON-FOULED

fouled

97

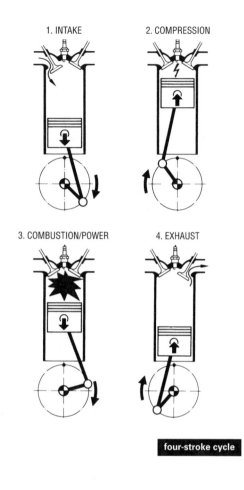

1. INTAKE 2. COMPRESSION

3. COMBUSTION/POWER 4. EXHAUST

four-wheel drift A handling term describing a car cornering with its front and rear tires sliding in a controlled manner. The driver uses both throttle and steering to keep the car on a prescribed path. Also see *neutral steer* and *slip angle*.

four-wheel drive (4WD) A drive system in which both the front and rear wheels are connected through the driveshaft and axles to the transmission, usually via a transfer case. A four-wheel-drive system is said to be full time if it is designed for permanent engagement (delivers power to both axles at all times); in a part-time system, the driver must engage four-wheel drive in conditions of marginal traction and use two-wheel drive (to the front or rear wheels) at other times. Also see *all-wheel drive*.

compression, power, and exhaust. Also called the Otto cycle, after Nikolaus August Otto, who patented the four-stroke engine in 1876.

four-valve engine An engine with two intake and two exhaust valves for each cylinder instead of one intake and one exhaust (two-valve engine). The advantage of a four-valve head is that it allows a greater total valve area within a given combustion-chamber area, thus improving the engine's breathing capacity and hence its efficiency and output.

four-valve head See *four-valve engine*.

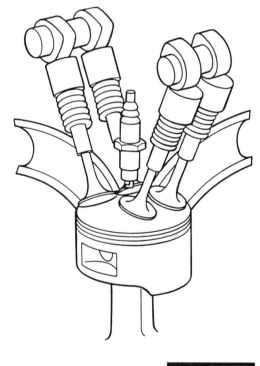

four-valve engine

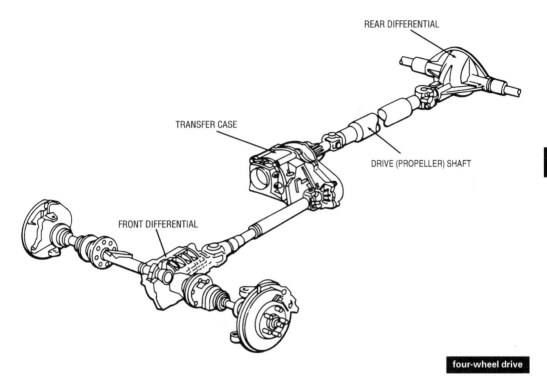

REAR DIFFERENTIAL

TRANSFER CASE

DRIVE (PROPELLER) SHAFT

FRONT DIFFERENTIAL

F

four-wheel drive

four-wheel steering (4WS) A steering system in which the rear wheels have their own steering linkage, connected mechanically and/or electronically with the front wheel linkage, and turn either parallel with or counter to the front wheels. In the parallel-steering or same-steer mode, used for most normal driving, the rear wheels turn in the same direction as the front, but at a much smaller angle, to enhance cornering stability. In the countersteering mode, the rear wheels move opposite to the front to reduce the car's turning diameter for easier parking and for enhanced low-speed responsiveness.

frame The structural load-carrying members that support a car's engine and body and are in turn supported by the suspension and wheels. In older cars and some current large American models, the frame is separate from the body; in most modern cars it is integrated with the body. See *unitized construction*.

frame horns See *dumb irons*.

free play See *clutch pedal free travel*.

free radius Radius of the tire/wheel assembly that does not deflect under load. See illustration for *nominal wheel diameter*.

freewheel A mechanical device, also known as an overrunning or one-way clutch, that engages the driving member to impart motion to a driven member in one direction only. Saabs used to be equipped with a freewheeling clutch

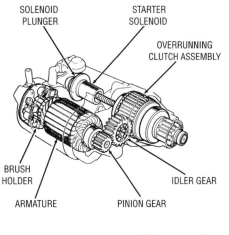

SOLENOID PLUNGER
STARTER SOLENOID
OVERRUNNING CLUTCH ASSEMBLY
BRUSH HOLDER
IDLER GEAR
ARMATURE
PINION GEAR

freewheel (starter motor)

that allowed the engine to drive the wheels but would prevent the wheels from driving the engine; thus engine braking was eliminated. A starter motor also has an overrunning clutch.

freeze plug   See *expansion plug.*

friction circle   A term used to describe the available traction of a tire, which can be used for acceleration and braking, for cornering, or for a combination of these factors. If a tire is using all its available traction to accelerate or brake (fore-aft friction), then no traction is available for cornering (lateral friction). Conversely, if the tire is cornering at its limit, then it is not capable of generating any traction for braking or accelerating unless it "steals" some of the cornering traction.

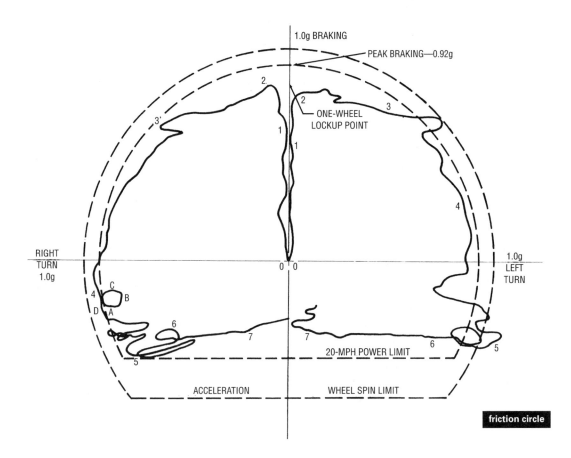

1.0g BRAKING
PEAK BRAKING—0.92g
ONE-WHEEL LOCKUP POINT
RIGHT TURN 1.0g
1.0g LEFT TURN
20-MPH POWER LIMIT
ACCELERATION
WHEEL SPIN LIMIT

friction circle

The friction circle is a graphical representation of this concept, representing the outer traction boundaries of the tire in generating cornering, braking, and acceleration forces, or a combination of these forces, at any given instant. A driver who is capable of keeping the tires at or near the boundaries of the circle at all times is going to be faster than another driver whose trace of cornering, acceleration, and braking forces falls further inside the circle because the former will be using more of the total available traction. Front-wheel-drive tuck-in and rear-drive power oversteer are two vehicle dynamics conditions that can be explained by the friction circle. Also see *tuck-in.*

friction disc See *clutch disc.*

friction drive A method of power transmission used on early cars, in which power was transmitted from a driving to a driven wheel by means of pressing one wheel against another at a right angle.

friction horsepower The amount of power consumed by an engine in driving itself. It includes the power absorbed in mechanical friction and in driving auxiliaries such as the oil pump and distributor and, in four-stroke engines, some pumping power, the energy required to compress the air-fuel mixture on the compression stroke.

friction shock absorber A mechanical, as opposed to hydraulic, device designed to dampen spring oscillations. A typical friction shock absorber of the 1920s used a sandwich arrangement of alternating flat discs of steel and friction material, the whole assembly tightened by an adjustable dished spring. Two levers forming a vee were attached by pivots to the axle and the chassis. Motion imparted to the axle and/or chassis produced relative angular movement between the steel discs and the friction discs, thus providing the damping action.

A disadvantage of this type of damper was a tendency for it to exert high initial or starting fric-

tion (also known as stiction), with more force needed to create initial movement than was required once the discs were moving. Some of the early friction shocks, such as the Andre-Hartford Telecontrol, were adjustable; the pressure on the friction discs could be varied by means of a cable controlled by a lever on the dashboard.

frontal area The combined area of a car's body as seen from the front. An important aerodynamic consideration, as less frontal area means less total air drag, which in turn reduces the "aero horsepower" a car needs to maintain a given speed. Also see *aerodynamic drag.* See illustration for *track.*

front drive See *front-wheel drive.*

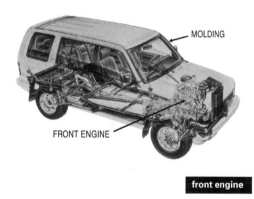

front engine

front engine Positioning of a car's engine so that its mass is concentrated mainly ahead of the front-wheel centerline. This is the conventional design for most contemporary vehicles, generally in conjunction with front-wheel drive. It results in a front weight bias and an understeering cornering behavior, which is easier for the average driver to control than an oversteering car.

front mid-engine See *mid-engine.*

front-wheel drive (FWD) A drive system in which the transmission (transaxle) is connected

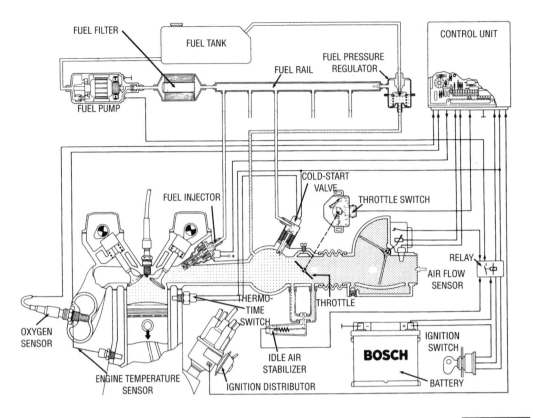

FUEL FILTER
FUEL TANK
FUEL PRESSURE
REGULATOR
FUEL RAIL
CONTROL UNIT
FUEL PUMP
COLD-START
VALVE
FUEL INJECTOR
THROTTLE SWITCH
RELAY
AIR FLOW
SENSOR
THERMO-
TIME
SWITCH
THROTTLE
OXYGEN
SENSOR
IGNITION
SWITCH
BOSCH
IDLE AIR
STABILIZER
ENGINE TEMPERATURE
SENSOR
IGNITION DISTRIBUTOR
BATTERY

fuel injection

by the driving axles to the front wheels. The engine and transaxle are usually combined into one unit. Also called *front drive.*

FRP See *fiberglass-reinforced plastic.*

fuel-air ratio See *air-fuel ratio.*

fuel consumption The amount of fuel consumed, divided by the distance driven. This measure of a car's fuel use is widely used in Europe and is expressed in liters per 100 kilometers.

fuel economy The distance driven, divided by the amount of fuel consumed. Typically expressed in miles per gallon (mpg) or kilometers per liter (km/l).

fuel filter A device installed in the fuel line, generally between the fuel pump and carbure-

tor or fuel injection system, that prevents impurities in the fuel from reaching and possibly clogging the carburetor or fuel injectors. See illustration for *fuel injection.*

fuel injection A fuel system using a pump and injectors instead of a carburetor to meter fuel.

Fundamentally, there are four types, though there are many variations. Direct injection squirts fuel directly into the combustion chambers, and is used primarily in commercial diesel engines. Prechamber injection, used on nearly all passenger-car diesel engines, injects fuel into a small chamber above the main combustion chamber. Port fuel injection, sometimes called multipoint injection, is widely used in gasoline engines and puts the fuel charge into the individual intake passages but upstream of (though

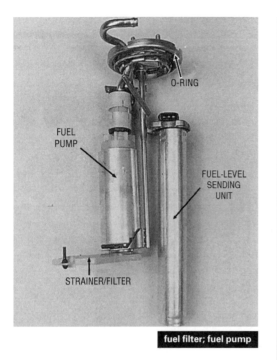

FUEL PUMP

O-RING

FUEL-LEVEL SENDING UNIT

STRAINER/FILTER

fuel filter; fuel pump

fuel injector The mechanical or electro-mechanical device that meters fuel in a fuel-injected engine. Also see *fuel injection.*

fuel line The pipe or tube through which fuel travels from the fuel tank to the fuel pump and from there to the carburetor or fuel-injector pump.

fuel pump A mechanical or electrical device that draws gasoline from the fuel tank and delivers it to the carburetor or injector pump. Mechanical pumps have a rocker arm that moves up and down on a cam on the camshaft, causing a diaphragm to move up and down and pull fuel through the pump. Electric pumps are of two basic types: A suction pump draws fuel from the tank in a manner similar to a mechanically operated pump. A pusher pump is placed in the bottom of the fuel supply tank and pushes the fuel to the carburetor or injector pump.

fuel rail A fuel line in a port fuel injection (PFI) system that feeds fuel from the injector pump to the individual injectors; in most PFI systems it resembles a rail running at or near the cylinder head.

close to) the intake valve. Throttle-body injection, also known as single- or dual-point injection, employs one or two injectors squirting into a carburetor-like device called the throttle body in gasoline engines.

Fuel delivery can be controlled mechanically or electronically and can be timed, continuous, or a combination of the two. In mechanical injection, a reciprocating pump feeds the injectors. Electronic port fuel injection employs a constant-flow pump and electromagnetic injectors to open and close each injector. Electronic injection is most frequently a timed system, in which the length of time the fuel is injected is precisely controlled (according to variables such as engine speed, manifold vacuum, and coolant temperature). Continuous injection delivers fuel in a steady flow. Sequential fuel injection is port injection timed to the opening of each injector's associated intake valve so that fuel is delivered to each cylinder in its proper firing sequence, not to part or all of the cylinders at once.

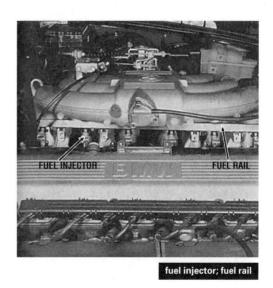

FUEL INJECTOR

FUEL RAIL

fuel injector; fuel rail

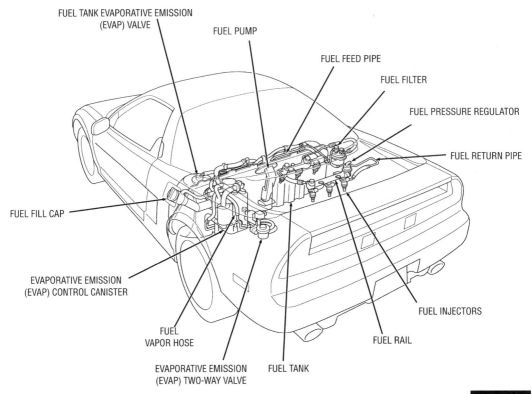

FUEL TANK EVAPORATIVE EMISSION (EVAP) VALVE

FUEL PUMP

FUEL FEED PIPE

FUEL FILTER

FUEL PRESSURE REGULATOR

FUEL RETURN PIPE

FUEL FILL CAP

EVAPORATIVE EMISSION (EVAP) CONTROL CANISTER

FUEL VAPOR HOSE

EVAPORATIVE EMISSION (EVAP) TWO-WAY VALVE

FUEL TANK

FUEL RAIL

FUEL INJECTORS

fuel system

fuel system   The system that delivers fuel to the engine, consisting of the fuel tank, fuel lines, fuel filter, fuel pump, and the carburetor or fuel injector(s) and rail(s).

fuel tank   A metal or plastic container, with a typical capacity of 8–20 gallons in a car, into which fuel is pumped and stored until needed by the engine.

full-active suspension   See *active suspension*.

full-floating axle   Drive-axle construction in which the axle shaft does not carry any weight; its sole function is propulsion. Two roller bearings support the weight of the car, which permits the axle shaft to be removed without disturbing the wheel. This design is frequently used in rac-

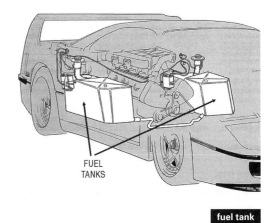

FUEL TANKS

fuel tank

ing cars so that if an axle breaks, the wheel will not fall off.

full-flow oil filter   A type of oil filter through which all the oil from the oil pump flows, without bypass.

fuse   A piece of wire that melts (or "blows") if excessive electrical current flows through it, thus protecting the circuit in which it is installed from overload.

Also to join two materials by melting them together.

fuse box   The covered housing, typically mounted under the dash and/or in the engine compartment, in which a vehicle's fuses are arranged for convenient inspection and replacement.

fusible link   A replaceable fuse placed within the wire connected to an electrical device. The link melts if the current overloads, preventing damage to the component. The link can be easily replaced without the added expense and nuisance of replacing the cable itself. Typically found in a battery cable or a cable leading to an air conditioner or other major electrical component.

fuzzy logic automatic transmission control   A feature of some newer automatic transmissions in which the electronic control module (ECM) for the transmission processes a number of inputs (such as throttle position, vehicle speed, and brake applications) and compares them with a map stored in the ECM's memory. Based on the variation between actual driving conditions and the map, the system either allows shifting or prevents it, in order to minimize gear changes. The net effect of fuzzy logic control is a reduced amount of gear hunting in up- and downhill driving. It increases operating smoothness and passenger comfort and provides optimum performance given road conditions, driving conditions, and the driver's intentions. Fuzzy logic provides the operating flexibility normally associated with a manual transmission but with the convenience of an automatic.

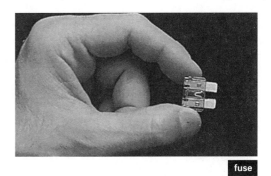

fuse

g Acceleration exerted on a body by earth's gravity. One g is equal to 32.2 ft/sec², the rate at which an object accelerates when dropped at sea level. A force of 1g equals the weight of the body at rest, 2 g's exerts a pull equivalent to twice body weight, and so on.

G-force can be used to express a car's straight-line acceleration or deceleration and, more commonly, lateral acceleration in a curve or corner. In this last context, the maximum lateral acceleration a car can achieve, measured while driving the car around a skid pad, is a useful indicator of its cornering ability. Also see *lateral acceleration*.

galvanize To apply zinc to iron or steel by dipping it in an electrically charged solution; the zinc adheres permanently to the iron or steel surface, thus protecting the underlying metal from corrosion.

gap Generally, the distance the spark must travel in jumping from the center electrode to the side electrode of a spark plug.

Also, the spacing between the points in the contact breaker fitted to a distributor.

Also used to denote the distance between adjacent body panels, such as door and fender.

gas See *gasoline*.

gas-filled shock absorber See *gas-pressure shock absorber*.

gasket Any thin, soft material installed between two metal surfaces to ensure a good seal. For example, a head gasket is placed between the cylinder head and engine block to prevent loss of combustion pressure and to keep water from leaking into the cylinders. Gaskets have traditionally been made of cork, cardboard, asbestos, or soft metal, but pliable, semi-liquid silicon-treated rubber has been used increasingly in recent years.

gasoline The liquid fuel that mixes with air to form the combustible mixture burned in most internal combustion engines. Often shortened to gas. Also see *hydrocarbon*.

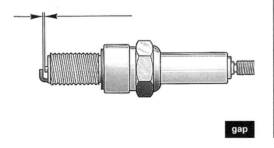

gap

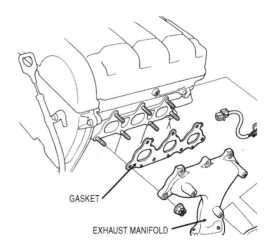

GASKET

EXHAUST MANIFOLD

gasket

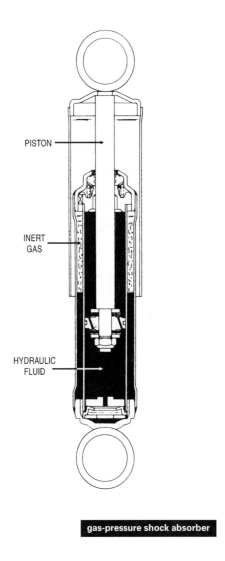

PISTON

INERT
GAS

HYDRAULIC
FLUID

gas-pressure shock absorber

gas-pressure shock absorber   A shock absorber that employs an inert gas under pressure, rather than air, to fill the space not occupied by the shock absorber's working fluid. The gas, often nitrogen, prevents the fluid from foaming, which can occur in fast driving on rough roads due to frictional heat built up by rapid movement of the shock-absorber piston. Gas-pressure shocks thus control a car's ride

motions more consistently than conventional shocks under such conditions. Also called *gas-filled shock absorber.*

gas turbine   A form of external combustion engine in which a fossil fuel is burned outside of the working chamber; hot gases are directed to turbine wheels, which drive the engine's ancillary devices and output shaft.

The basic gas turbine operates as follows: Air enters a compressor and is squeezed to a much smaller volume. It is then delivered under pressure to the combustion chamber, where fuel is introduced, mixed with the air, and burned; the quantity injected determines speed and power output. The resulting hot, high-pressure gases then proceed to a first-stage turbine (sometimes called the gas turbine or compressor turbine), which drives the compressor, and continue to the second-stage or power turbine, which delivers power to an output shaft through reduction gears. The gears are necessary because the turbines rotate at tens of thousands of rpm, not thousands as with a typical piston or Wankel rotary engine.

A gas turbine is a simple and direct way to obtain power from burning gas. It is smooth, and can run on almost any hydrocarbon fuel. But it is expensive to build, needing exotic materials able to withstand the engine's high rotational speeds and high internal temperatures (though this is being overcome by recent advances in ceramics technology); difficult to cold-start; and produces relatively high amounts of NOx. The gas turbine is also relatively poor at responding to the constantly changing demands on an automotive engine for acceleration and deceleration; hence it has been most successful in aircraft applications, where speed is constant most of the time.

gauge   An instrument that registers a quantity such as fuel supply, number of amperes, voltage, miles per hour, revolutions per minute, or oil pressure. Also see *analog instrumentation* and

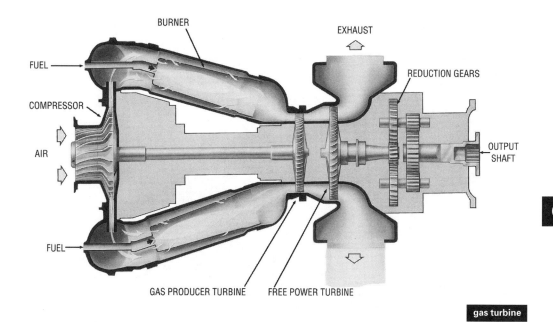

FUEL

COMPRESSOR

AIR

FUEL

BURNER

EXHAUST

REDUCTION GEARS

OUTPUT SHAFT

GAS PRODUCER TURBINE

FREE POWER TURBINE

gas turbine

G

digital instrumentation. Also, a tool for measuring clearance, thickness, or size, such as a spark plug gauge.

gauge cluster   The assortment of gauges in the dashboard.

gear   A wheel-like part with teeth or cogs cut into its rim. When the teeth of two gears mesh, one can drive (rotate) the other, thus transmitting power.

gearbox   The device in the drivetrain, consisting of an input shaft, a system of gears, and

gauge; gauge cluster

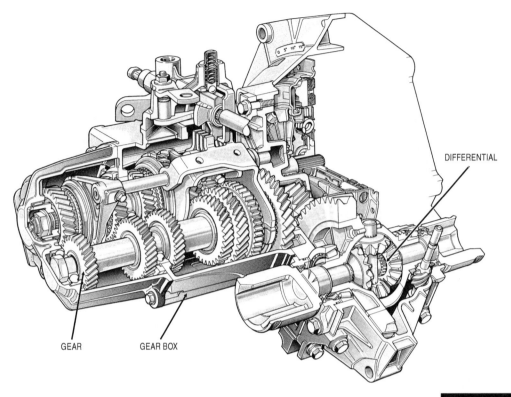

DIFFERENTIAL

GEAR   GEAR BOX

gear; gearbox

an output shaft, that multiplies engine torque for delivery to the drive wheels. A manual transmission consists of a clutch assembly plus a gearbox; an automatic transmission generally consists of a torque converter plus an automatic gearbox. Sometimes shortened to *box*.

gear lever   See *gearshift*.

gear ratio   The number of revolutions of a driving gear relative to the number of revolutions of the driven gear. For example, if a driving gear makes three revolutions while its driven gear makes one, the gear ratio is 3:1.

gearset   Two or more gears used to transmit power.

gearshift   A lever on the center tunnel or console, or on the steering column, that allows the driver to move the transmission gears into various drive positions. Some manufacturers (Chrysler, Edsel, Packard, and more recently Porsche) have offered push-button control of their automatic transmissions.

generator   The part of a car's electrical system that converts mechanical energy from a drive belt into electrical energy to operate the ignition and electrical accessories and charge the battery. The generator, which produces direct current, has been replaced by the more efficient alternator, which produces alternating current.

glaze   An extremely smooth or glossy surface polished over a long period of time. Glazing occurs on cylinder walls by the friction of the piston rings, and on the rotors on disc brakes under frequent light applications of the brake pedal. Both are unwanted conditions: cylinder glazing reduces rings' sealing efficiency, rotor glazing reduces stopping ability.

Also, a chemical compound known as rubbing compound that restores the surface smoothness and luster of a car's paint finish by stripping away a thin top layer of oxidized paint.

gearshift

Global Positioning System (GPS) A system using satellite tracking to precisely locate an object. Originally developed by the Department of Defense, the system is now available for civilians to navigate on roads, in the woods, in the air, or at sea. The system uses a satellite antenna receiver to determine location and velocity by triangulation from multiple satellites, and can be used worldwide with an accuracy of approximately 50 ft.

glove box A storage compartment located either in the dashboard on the passenger's side or in a console between the front seats for stowing small items such as the owner's manual, a flashlight, and, yes, even driving gloves.

glow plug An electrical plug, similar to a spark plug, that preheats the combustion chamber of a diesel engine to assist in cold starting, after which the plug shuts off.

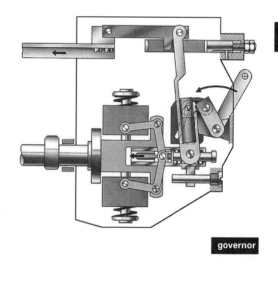

governor

governor Any part that controls the operation of another; specifically, a mechanical, hydraulic, or electrical device that limits a vehicle's velocity to something less than its true maximum, either for safety reasons or to prolong the life of the engine and drivetrain.

GPS See *Global Positioning System.*

Grand Touring See *Gran Turismo.*

Gran Turismo (GT) Italian for Grand Touring, a sport or touring car with a closed coupe body style.

Grand Turismo Omologato (GTO) Italian expression for Grand Touring cars built in high enough volume to be certified or homologated as production vehicles for racing purposes as

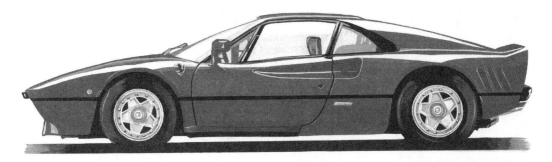

Grand Turismo Omologato

opposed to being classified as prototype or experimental racers. Also see *homologated*.

graphic equalizer　An equalizer that can be used to adjust several frequency bands via individual controls; the sliders' positions provide a visual or graphic approximation of the altered frequency spectrum, hence the name. Many automotive sound systems employ graphic equalizers for maximum variability to suit listener tastes. Also see *equalizer*.

graphite fiber　See *carbon fiber*.

greenhouse　The glassed-in area of a car body above the belt line, namely the roof, pillars, and windows.

grille　The functional and often stylish opening at the front of a vehicle through which air is routed to cool the radiator and other components.

grip　A tire's traction with the road surface.

gross horsepower　An engine's maximum output (horsepower and/or torque) as measured on a dynamometer under ideal temperature and barometric pressure conditions, with modified intake and exhaust systems and with most power-robbing accessories such as the alternator disconnected. Also see *corrected horsepower*.

gross torque　See *gross horsepower*.

ground　The negative terminal of the battery connected to the metal frame of the car and hence to the ground. By connecting one terminal of each electrically operated device to the frame, only one insulated wire is required to carry current to the device because the frame serves as a return wire.

ground clearance　The height of the lowest component on a vehicle, measured from a level surface; defines the maximum height of road hazards over which the vehicle may be driven without mechanical or structural damage.

greenhouse

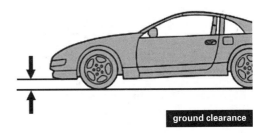

ground clearance

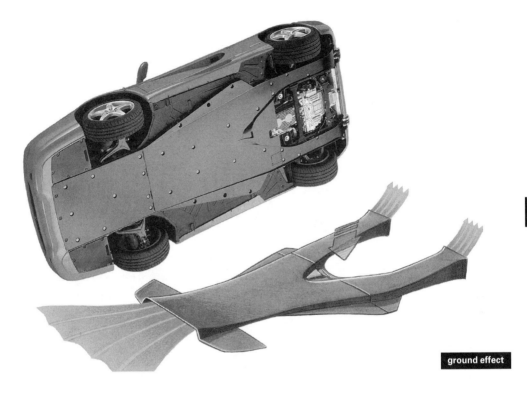

G

ground effect

ground effect   Result of the partial vacuum between the road surface and the undercarriage of an automobile; occurs primarily with racing cars and production cars fitted with air dams. The partial vacuum draws the car to the road, resulting in a significant increase in lateral acceleration and cornering speeds.

GT   See *Gran Turismo*.

GTO   See *Gran Turismo Omologato*.

guide   See *valve guide*.

gullwing   An affectionate nickname long used by enthusiasts of the Mercedes-Benz 300SL coupe, but lately applied to any car whose passenger doors are hinged to open upward and, when open, give the car the appearance of a seagull with wings spread. The most recent examples include the Bricklin SV-1 and DeLorean DMC-12.

gullwing

half shaft The rotating shaft that transmits power from the final drive unit to the drive wheels; usually refers to the two shafts that connect the road wheels to the final drive in cars with front-wheel drive or those with independent rear suspension and rear-wheel drive, as opposed to the axle shafts of a live rear axle.

Hall effect In the magnetic-pulse generator of an electronic ignition system, the generation of voltage pulses in a semiconductor layer by a speed-dependent magnetic field. The pulses are used for switching the primary ignition current on and off.

halogen See *quartz halogen.*

handling Traditional term for all aspects of a car's behavior when maneuvering or changing its direction of travel. Lateral acceleration around a skid pad and speed through a slalom course are objective measures commonly used to evaluate handling. Subjective factors include steering effort and feel; degree of body lean (roll) in corners and transient maneuvers (such as lane changes); effects of midcorner braking or throttle lift-off; and the degree of understeer or over-

hardtop

steer. Also see *neutral steer, oversteer, roll, self-aligning torque,* and *understeer.*

hardtop Term derived from the hardtop convertible models of the late forties. A closed body style without upper B-pillars; rolling down the car's side windows left an uninterrupted greenhouse opening at the juncture of the front and rear doors. In the fifties and sixties, American hardtops proliferated. Most were two- and four-door notchbacks — hardtop coupes and hardtop sedans; a few fastbacks and even a handful of pillarless station wagons were offered. Also, a rigid removable top that can be installed in place of the soft folding top on a convertible.

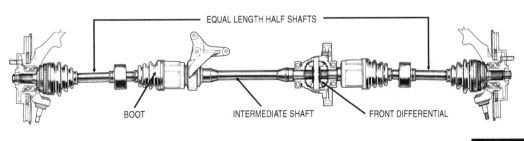

EQUAL LENGTH HALF SHAFTS

BOOT   INTERMEDIATE SHAFT   FRONT DIFFERENTIAL

half shaft

harmonic balancer   A counterbalance used to reduce the torsional or twisting vibration that occurs along the length of a rotating shaft. Frequently used on crankshafts, the balancer adds mass or inertia to the end of the crankshaft opposite the flywheel to minimize crankshaft twisting. Also called a *vibration damper*.

harmonic motion   A type of periodic motion characteristic of elastic bodies, such as the vibration of a stretched rubber band. Without shock absorbers, a car would oscillate in harmonic motion on its springs.

harshness   Any small, sharp jolt that is not filtered out of a car's ride; the opposite of compliance.

hatchback   A body style in which the conventional trunk and lid are replaced by a rear door that is generally hinged from the top and includes the rear window. Without a fixed trunk bulkhead, many hatchbacks feature a fold-down rear seat back to increase luggage capacity. Typically, hatchback sedans have a rear roof extended back to or near the end of the car.

HC   See *hydrocarbon*.

header   See *exhaust manifold*.

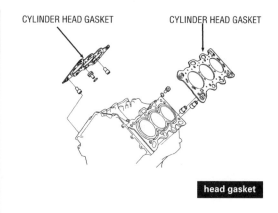

CYLINDER HEAD GASKET   CYLINDER HEAD GASKET

head gasket

head gasket   A gasket used to seal an engine's cylinder head and the block. Also see *gasket*.

headlamp   See *headlight*.

headlight   One of two or four lights mounted at the front of a vehicle and fitted with reflectors and lenses to light the road at night and in low-visibility driving conditions. Also called *headlamp*.

headliner   A vinyl or cloth covering for the inside of a car's roof, chosen to harmonize with the car's upholstery and other interior trim.

headrest   See *head restraint*.

hatchback

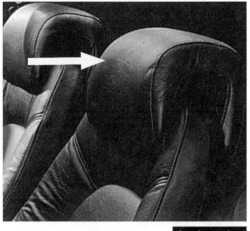

head restraint

stove on the exhaust manifold. When the engine is cold, the thermostat positions a flap so that all air going into the air cleaner passes through the heat stove. Thus hot air is supplied to the induction system soon after the engine starts. As the engine warms up, the thermostat positions the flap so that air is taken from the engine compartment and not from the heat stove.

heat exchanger   A device that transfers heat between two fluids through a separating wall. A radiator, intercooler and an oil cooler are heat exchangers that transfer heat from a liquid coolant to the atmosphere. Also see *expansion tank.*

H

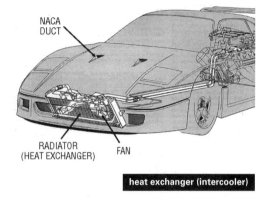

NACA DUCT

RADIATOR (HEAT EXCHANGER)   FAN

heat exchanger (intercooler)

head restraint   An extension of the seat back, either permanently affixed or adjustable for height, intended to reduce whiplash injuries in front or rear collisions by cushioning and limiting the rearward movement of the head and neck. Also called *headrest.*

heads-up display   See *head-up display.*

head-up display (HUD)   A type of electronic instrument display, borrowed from the aerospace industry, in which a lighted image of an instrument's readout, typically the road speed or engine rpm, is projected onto the inside of the windshield where it is directly in the driver's sight line. As a result, the display can be viewed without the driver having to divert his eyes from the road. Also called *heads-up display.*

heat-control valve   A thermostatically operated valve in the exhaust manifold that allows some of the exhaust gases to pass around the intake manifold when the engine is cold to preheat the fuel mixture going to the cylinders.

heated intake   An antipollution device that helps vaporize the gasoline supplied to a cold engine. The system consists of an air cleaner with a thermostat and a pipe connected to a heat

heat range   The rate at which a spark plug transfers heat from the combustion chamber to the cylinder head; commonly described by the terms hot and cold. A hot plug transfers heat slowly, causing the plug to operate at a higher temperature. A cold plug transfers heat at a faster rate, thus operating at a lower temperature. Plugs are available in different heat ranges to accommodate different engines and driving conditions. A plug must operate hot enough to stay clean (not foul), yet cold enough to prevent preignition.

heat shield   A device that prevents heat from radiating. In the engine compartment a heat shield made of a nonconducting fiber or plastic

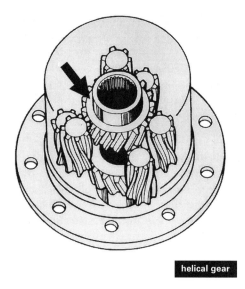

helical gear

material covered with reflective aluminum foil can be used to protect the battery, brake reservoir, or ABS piping from excessive engine heat. Heat shields are frequently installed above and below a catalytic converter to prevent excessive heat radiating through the floor and into the passenger compartment and to reduce the possibility of fire if a vehicle is parked over dry grass or brush.

heat treatment   Controlled heating and cooling of metals to change their properties. Frequently used in automotive materials to affect the hardness of suspension and engine parts.

heel-and-toe   A driving technique in which the driver places the left side or the toes of the right foot on the brake pedal and the right side or heel of the right foot on the throttle pedal so as to simultaneously brake and "blip" the throttle for a downshift. This is done to lessen the strain on the drivetrain, particularly the clutch and gearbox, and allows smoother downshifting.

Heim joint   A spherical connecting-rod end or bearing consisting of a bearing with ball and race to allow angular movement while restrict-

ing unwanted movement. Frequently found in race cars, replacing conventional rubber bushings in suspensions and throttle linkages. Heim joints provide much more precise throttle control or suspension geometry (critical to a race car) albeit at the expense of ride harshness (generally not critical in a race car). Also called *spherical rod end.*

helical gear   A gear design in which the teeth are cut at an angle to the shaft. The advantage of helical gears is that there is no chance of intermittent tooth-to-tooth operation because there are usually two teeth in engagement (mesh) at any time. The smoother working action tends to be quieter than that of straight-cut gears.

hemi   See *hemispherical combustion chamber.*

hemispherical combustion chamber   A dome-shaped combustion chamber commonly used in racing and high-performance production engines because it allows larger, less shrouded valves and straight intake and exhaust ports, resulting in high volumetric efficiency. It also has a small surface-area-to-volume ratio, which minimizes heat loss and charge cooling that can lead to high hydrocarbon emissions. Sometimes shortened to *hemi.*

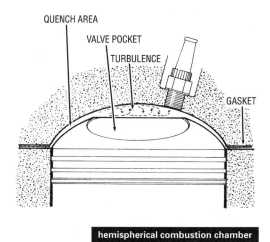

hemispherical combustion chamber

hesitation   The momentary failure of an engine to respond during acceleration; generally results from very lean air-fuel mixtures and retarded timing.

high-back seat   A car seat in which the head restraint is integral to the seat back. Also see *seat back.*

high beam   The secondary filament in a two-headlight system; in a four-light system, the high-beam headlight works in conjunction with the secondary filament of the main headlight. High beams provide additional illumination to the sides and down the road, and are normally used only when traffic is sparse.

high gear   A transmission's top or cruising gear. For example, fifth gear in a five-speed over-drive manual or fourth in the "Drive" position of a modern four-speed automatic. Also known as *top gear.*

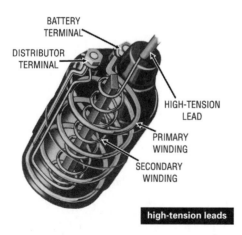

high-tension leads

high-tension leads   Wires that carry high voltage from the distributor cap to the coil and from the cap to each of the spark plugs.

high-test   Gasoline with a high octane rating.

homologated   A production car certified as eligible for one or more classes of automobile racing as defined by a governing organization.

Requirements vary with the form of competition, but typically specify engine size, horsepower, body configuration, weight, and, for some production classes, a stipulation that a minimum quantity of a model be built for public sale. Thus, the homologation special, a British term for a car designed for the requirements of a particular racing class but also built in road-going form and only in sufficient numbers to qualify it for that class. Also see *Gran Turismo Omologato.*

hone   An abrasive tool that is rotated in a bore (such as an engine cylinder) or a bushing to correct small irregularities or differences in its inner diameter.

hood   To Americans, the hinged part of a car body covering the engine (what the British call the bonnet); normally used only in reference to front-engine cars. In mid-engine cars, usually called the engine cover or access panel; in rear-engine cars, the engine lid. To the British, the hood is the folding top of a convertible, cabriolet, or roadster.

hood scoop   A duct in the hood of a car, designed to pull cooler ambient air directly into the intake system of the engine.

Hooke joint   See *Cardan joint.*

hop up   To modify a production car so that its acceleration, handling, roadholding, and performance are improved over that of an unmodified car.

horizontally opposed engine   See *flat engine.*

horsepower (HP)   A unit of measure of power or the rate at which work is done. In the United States, where work is generally expressed in ft-lb, one horsepower is equal to 550 ft-lb/sec or 33,000 ft-lb/min.

horsepower curve   See *torque curve.*

Hotchkiss drive   A type of live-axle rear suspension in which the axle is located by semi-

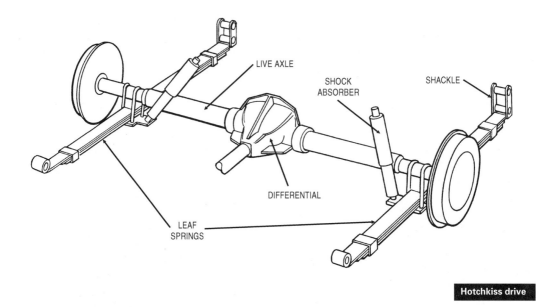

Hotchkiss drive

elliptic leaf springs. The springs, mounted longitudinally, connect to the chassis at their ends and the axle is hung from them. In this way, they not only spring the axle but also determine its freedom to move and transmit all cornering, braking, and driving forces from the axle to the body.

hot wire

hot plug See *heat range*.

hot spot An area in a combustion chamber in which localized excessive heat builds up, as around the exhaust valve, the spark plug, or carbonized combustion deposits, possibly leading to preignition.

hot wire A method of measuring the air inducted into a fuel-injected gasoline engine. A thin wire across the air intake is heated to a constant temperature by electrical current. Any change in airflow (such as when the driver pushes the accelerator down or releases it) tends to change the wire's temperature; the control system immediately corrects the temperature back to its constant value. The current required to maintain that constant value is the indicator of airflow and thus the system's basic operating signal.

Also, slang for starting a car without a key by circumventing the ignition switch/ignition system.

hub The center of a wheel or the forging or casting to which the wheel is mounted and about which it revolves.

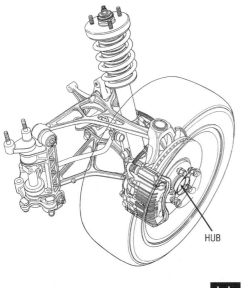

HUB

hub

hubcap A disc used to cover and protect the wheel bearings. Hubcaps have evolved into styling elements and sometimes simulate alloy wheels.

human factors engineering See *ergonomics*.

HVAC Abbreviation for a heating, ventilating, and air-conditioning system.

hydraulic Operated by the incompressibility of liquids, usually oil or water, that offer resistance when forced into a given space, and thus can transmit an applied force. Hydraulic brakes and clutches work on this principle.

hydraulic assist Hydraulic pressure, usually generated by an engine-driven pump, that reduces the driver's effort in performing certain functions. Most current power-assisted steering systems use hydraulic assist; some brake systems do, too.

hydraulic fluid The liquid used in hydraulic brake and clutch systems to transmit force: from the brake pedal to the wheel cylinders in drum

H

HVAC

121

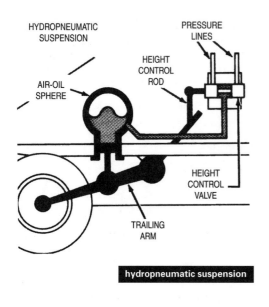

hydropneumatic suspension

brakes or to the pistons in disc brakes to force the brake shoes or pads against the rotating drums or rotors; or from the clutch pedal to the clutch slave cylinder to couple or uncouple the engine and gearbox. Hydraulic fluid has special lubricating properties and is also nonhygroscopic, meaning it will not readily absorb moisture.

hydraulic pump   A device for raising, moving or compressing fluids by means of a piston, plunger, or rotating vanes. A typical automotive application is the power steering pump. Also see *oil pump*.

hydraulic valve lifter   One that uses hydraulic oil pressure to maintain zero valve clearance (no clearance between metal parts) to reduce valve noise. This also compensates for normal wear and eliminates periodic valve adjustments. In some engines valve-clearance maintenance is accomplished by stationary hydraulically positioned pedestals, a system pioneered by Pontiac in the late seventies.

hydrocarbon (HC)   A compound composed entirely of hydrogen and carbon, such as gasoline and other petroleum products. Various hydrocarbons are produced when gasoline is burned in an engine, and these compounds constitute one of the ingredients of photochemical smog.

hydroplaning   See *aquaplaning*.

hydropneumatic suspension   A suspension system using a gas and a liquid separated by a flexible bladder as a springing medium. In the well-known Citroen system, the springing unit is a metal sphere whose top portion contains an inert gas. Incompressible fluid (oil) is carried in the lower part of the sphere. In response to changes in vehicle loading, the suspension system alters the gas pressure, which in turn exerts pressure on the liquid to keep the car at standard height.

hyperaspirated   See *aspiration*.

hypoid gear   A type of spiral-bevel gear in which the drive pinion is located below the center of the ring gear, thus allowing the driveshaft and a car's floor to be lower to the ground.

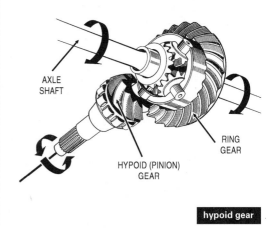

hypoid gear

I-beam suspension See *monobeam suspension.*

icing A condition in which ice forms at the edge of the carburetor throttle plate, restricting the flow of the air-fuel mixture when the throttle plate is at or near the idle position, thus causing the engine to stall. The ice formation results from rapid fuel vaporization that can lower the mixture's temperature and cause moisture in the air to freeze. Icing is most likely to occur when ambient air temperature is 28–55° Fahrenheit and relative humidity 65–100 percent, and before the engine has reached operating temperature.

ideal air-fuel ratio See *stoichiometric ratio.*

idiot light See *warning light.*

idle circuit The carburetor system that supplies fuel to the engine at idle and low speeds. Above about 15 mph, the idle circuit gradually passes out of operation and fuel is then supplied by the main metering system. Also called the *low-speed circuit.*

idler arm One of the connecting levers in parallel, relay-type steering linkage. The steering gearbox is attached to a pitman arm, which converts rotary motion to lateral motion. The pitman arm generally connects to a transverse center link, which connects to the idler arm on the opposite side of the car. The ends of the center link connect to two adjustable tie rods that transmit the lateral movement of the center link to the steering arms at each steering knuckle. See illustration for *steering box.*

idler gear A gear interposed between two other gears to reverse the direction of rotation of the output gear.

REVERSE IDLER GEAR
SHAFT ASSEMBLY

idler gear

idle speed The engine speed with the throttle closed and the transmission in neutral.

I-4 In-line four-cylinder engine. See *in-line engine.*

IFS Independent front suspension. See *independent suspension.*

ignition See *ignition system.*

ignition advance See *advance.*

ignition coil See *coil.*

ignition cutout See *rev limiter.*

ignition points See *breaker points.*

ignition retard See *retard.*

ignition switch A switch, generally on the steering column or the dash, that connects and disconnects the ignition system from the battery

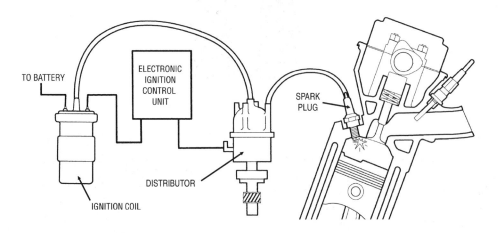

TO BATTERY

ELECTRONIC
IGNITION
CONTROL
UNIT

SPARK
PLUG

DISTRIBUTOR

IGNITION COIL

ignition system

and starter motor so the engine can be started and stopped as desired.

ignition system The system that provides spark to ignite the air-fuel mixture in the combustion chamber, consisting of the battery, coil, distributor, condenser, ignition switch, spark plugs, and related wiring.

ignition timing The timing or firing of the spark plug relative to piston top dead center and expressed in degrees of crankshaft rotation.

I-head engine See *overhead valve engine.*

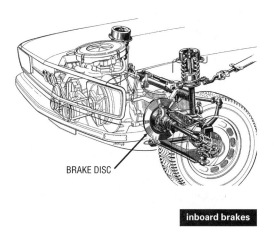

BRAKE DISC

inboard brakes

IMEP See *indicated mean effective pressure.*

impeller A rotating wheel with vanes, used in pumps to drive and circulate a fluid. Examples are found in the fluid coupling or torque converter of an automatic transmission, and in the water pump.

inboard brakes Brake discs or drums and associated components located near the centerline of the car and acting directly on the axle half shafts rather than on the wheels. Usually found only at the rear and generally attached to the differential housing. However, some Formula One cars have had inboard front disc brakes, as did the original Audi 100. The primary advantage of inboard brakes is reduced unsprung weight. Also see *outboard brakes.*

independent suspension Front or rear suspension in which each pair of wheels is sprung independently of the other, so that a disturbance affecting one wheel has no effect on the opposite one. Independent front suspension (IFS) is universal in passenger cars, having long since replaced beam-axle front suspension. The advantages of independent rear suspension (IRS), which is not yet quite universal, over a rigid rear axle include reduced unsprung weight, improved ride and handling on rough surfaces, and room

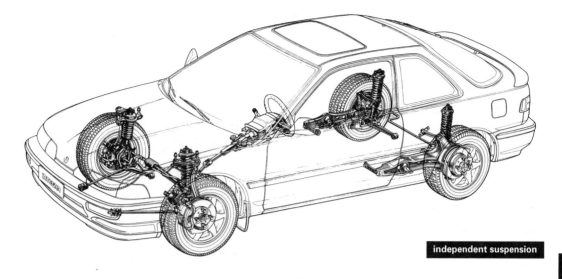

independent suspension

I

for a larger trunk, as there is no need to allow space for the vertical motion of a differential.

indicated horsepower The theoretical engine output (horsepower and torque) produced within the cylinders of an engine, calculated from the indicated mean effective pressure. It is higher than the brake horsepower and torque because it does not include the frictional losses that occur by the time the power/torque reach the crankshaft, where the brake horsepower is measured.

indicated mean effective pressure (IMEP) The average of the pressures developed inside a cylinder during one complete cycle — intake, compression, power, and exhaust — of a four-stroke engine. It is used as the basis for calculating indicated horsepower and torque.

indicated torque See *indicated horsepower.*

induction coil See *coil.*

induction stroke See *intake stroke.*

induction system The system that delivers the air-fuel mixture to the cylinders. Includes the carburetor or fuel injection system, intake manifold, intake ports, and intake valves.

inertia The tendency of objects to remain motionless if at rest or to continue in the same direction if already in motion. Effort is thus required to start a body moving or to retard it, stop it, or change its direction once it is in motion. Also see *moment of inertia.*

inertia reel The mechanism in a seat belt that causes the lap and/or shoulder straps to lock securely when the car exceeds a specified

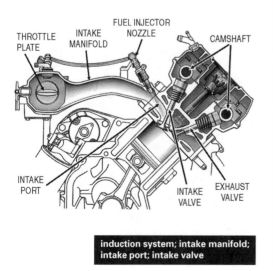

induction system; intake manifold; intake port; intake valve

deceleration rate or the reel itself exceeds a specified angular acceleration.

inertia switch A resettable switch designed to turn a component off as a function of vehicle deceleration. A fuel pump controlled by an inertia switch will shut off the flow of fuel at a level of deceleration associated with severe impact or if the vehicle rolls over. Inertia switches are also used on some seat belts to sense vehicle deceleration or the motion of the occupant and prevent the belt from spooling out when a predetermined level of deceleration is exceeded.

infinitely variable transmission A transmission in which the ratios continuously vary or are "stepless," as opposed to the fixed ratios in conventional automatic and manual transmissions. An infinitely variable transmission typically has a mechanism of belts and pulleys that alters the transmission ratio as a function of accelerator position and speed. With this arrangement, it is possible to keep the throttle at a fixed high position for most steady driving conditions, thereby loading the engine sufficiently to assure high efficiency and a consequent improvement in fuel economy. Also called *continuously variable transmission*.

inflation pressure The pressure of the air inside a tire; the higher pressure exerts greater force on each unit of surface than the force exerted by the atmosphere. In conjunction with the tire casing's ability to undergo distortion, this results in the load being borne resiliently so as to absorb impact and shocks from uneven road surfaces. Tire manufacturers fix the proper inflation pressure according to the weight of the car.

injected An engine equipped with fuel injection.

injector See *fuel injector*.

in-line engine An engine with all its cylinders in a row. Also called straight, as in straight eight or straight four.

in-line fuel-injection pump A fuel-injection pump in which a small camshaft operates a row of plungers, one for each engine cylinder, that

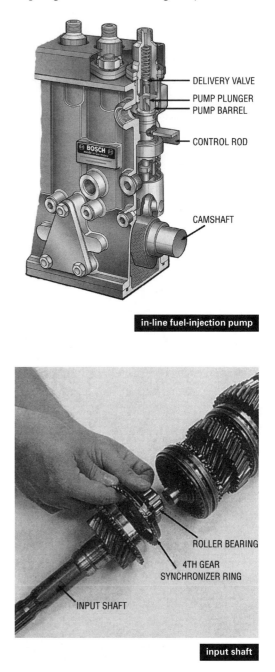

in-line fuel-injection pump

input shaft

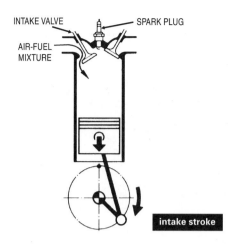

INTAKE VALVE · SPARK PLUG

AIR-FUEL MIXTURE

intake stroke

open and close orifices through which fuel is delivered to the individual injectors.

input shaft A shaft carrying a driving gear. In a transmission, for example, the shaft that receives power from the engine and transmits it to the gears.

insert For bearings, a replacement shell-type bearing made to extremely close tolerances and generally used for main and connecting-rod bearings.

For valves, replaceable valve seats made of hard, heat-resistant metal and screwed or shrunk into the cylinder head.

inside diameter See *rim diameter.*

instrument See *gauge.*

instrument cluster See *gauge cluster.*

instrument panel See *dashboard.*

intake manifold The assembly of tubes, usually of cast iron, aluminum, or plastic, through which the air-fuel mixture flows to the intake ports. In an engine with manifold fuel injection, the intake manifold carries air and fuel; with port fuel injection, it carries air only.

intake ports The passages in the cylinder head through which the air-fuel mixture flows from the intake manifold to the intake valves.

intake stroke The first stroke of the four-stroke cycle, during which the piston moves downward from top dead center to bottom dead center, creating a partial vacuum that draws the air-fuel mixture into the cylinder. Also called *induction stroke.*

intake valve A camshaft-driven valve in the cylinder head that opens to allow the air-fuel charge into the cylinder and closes to form part of the combustion chamber during the compression and power strokes. See *poppet valve.*

integral valve seat A valve seat machined into the cylinder head as opposed to one which is inserted into the head. Integral valve seats in a cast iron head can be locally heat-treated or hardened to increase their durability. Also see *insert.*

I

intercooler A small heat exchanger, similar to the radiator used in an engine's cooling system, that reduces the temperature of air delivered to an engine by a turbocharger or supercharger; the denser air-fuel mixture that results is more explosive when burned, which increases engine power. The reduced temperature also allows other power-increasing measures such as a higher compression ratio or more aggressive spark timing to be incorporated into an intercooled engine. An air-to-air intercooler uses air as the cooling medium; an air-to-water intercooler uses water.

interior noise The intensity (amplitude) of all sound heard inside a moving car, typically excluding that produced by the heating/air conditioning system or an audio system; usually measured in decibels (db) on the "A" weighing scale of a sound meter, thus expressed as dbA. Interior noise stems from the power train (intake hiss and exhaust boom from the engine, whining of transmission or differential gears), the road (dependent on road surface and relative roughness as well as the tires' size and tread design), and the car's shape and acoustical properties (the former determining the degree to which air is heard rushing over and around the car at speed, the latter perhaps amplifying the

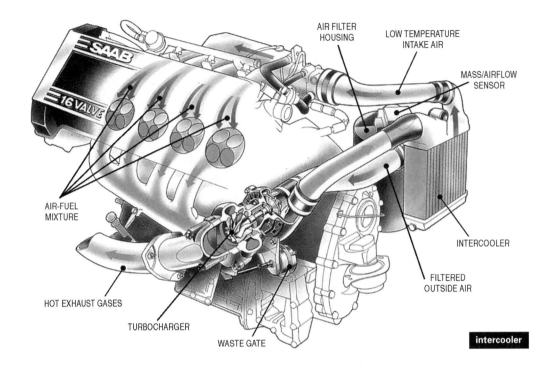

AIR FILTER HOUSING

LOW TEMPERATURE INTAKE AIR

MASS/AIRFLOW SENSOR

SAAB

16 VALVE

AIR-FUEL MIXTURE

INTERCOOLER

HOT EXHAUST GASES

FILTERED OUTSIDE AIR

TURBOCHARGER

WASTE GATE

intercooler

exhaust note or road noise into a body "boom"). Interior noise is reduced by design factors that include sound insulation and isolating sources of vibration.

intermediate gear Any transmission gear between low and high. For example, in a four-speed transmission, second and third are the intermediate gears.

internal combustion engine (ICE) An engine in which fuel burns within cylinders or some other enclosed space, and the power of this combustion is converted directly into mechanical work. The working fluid consists of products of combustion of the air-fuel mixture itself. The Mazda rotary and Ferrari V-12, although quite different in design, are both internal combustion engines. Compare to *external combustion engine*.

interrupter See *cutout*.

involute gear teeth Gear teeth of slightly rounded profile that engage mating teeth under rolling, rather than sliding, friction, thus reducing power loss and wear. Nearly all gears used in automobiles have involute teeth.

IRS Independent rear suspension. See *independent suspension*.

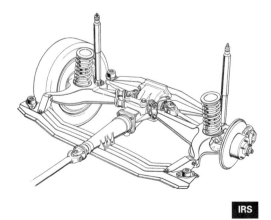

IRS

jack A hydraulic or mechanical device used to raise a car, primarily for changing a wheel or tire.

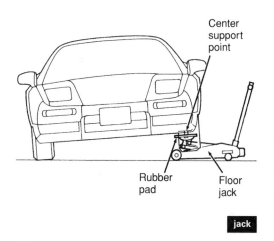

Center support point

Rubber pad

Floor jack

jack

jacking A characteristic of a swing-axle rear suspension in which a cornering force acting on the suspension tends to lift the car through the solidly mounted differential, forcing the outboard wheel to "jack" or tuck under the car. Extreme jacking forces can cause a car to overturn.

jack stand Adjustable pyramid-shaped support, usually of steel, used in pairs or groups of four to raise a car off the ground for purposes of maintenance and/or storage.

Japanese Industrial Standard (JIS) Provides net ratings of engine horsepower and torque of Japanese and other Asian cars; roughly equivalent to those obtained by the SAE and DIN measurement methods.

jet A calibrated nozzle in a carburetor through which fuel is drawn and mixed with air. A carburetor normally contains several jets — idle, main, power — to provide the proper combustible mixture for all conditions of engine load and speed. See illustration for *carburetor*.

jounce The upward movement of a car's wheels and suspension when acted on by a bump; the downward reaction to this movement is called *rebound*.

jounce bumper See *bump stop*.

jounce stop See *bump stop*.

journal That part of a shaft or axle in actual contact with a bearing.

judder Low-frequency vibrations in the brakes or clutch experienced when the brake or clutch pedal is depressed. Usually a result of imbalance, wear, or warping of the flywheel, clutch disc/pressure plate, or the brake rotors.

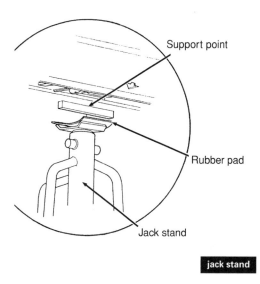

Support point

Rubber pad

Jack stand

jack stand

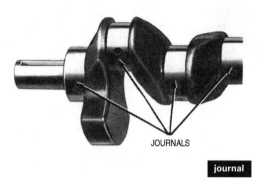

JOURNALS

journal

jumper cables A set of heavy-gauge insulated electrical wires used to start a car with an external battery. The cables are fitted at each end with one positive and one negative terminal, typically large spring-loaded clips for gripping the terminals of both batteries.

jump start Starting the engine of a car with a discharged or weak battery by attaching cables from the weak battery to a charged or helper battery.

Kamm tail   Body design named after the German aerodynamicist Dr. Wunibald Kamm, who conceived the sharply cutoff tail design found on many racing and road cars. A perfectly streamlined tail would have a conical shape and be impractically long. Kamm showed that the law of diminishing returns begins to operate after the tail's cross-sectional area tapers to about 50 percent of the maximum.

K-band   A radar frequency designated by the Federal Communications Commission solely for monitoring traffic.

keepers   Tapered, keylike, split locking collars used in pairs to hold the valve retainer in place on a valve stem.

KE-Jetronic   A modified form of K-Jetronic fuel injection developed and produced by Bosch, in which electronic controls are used in conjunction with a mechanical flap to determine fuel delivery. KE-Jetronic applies electronic controls to such functions as cold starting, mixture enrichment during warm-up, and feedback from the exhaust oxygen sensor.

Kevlar   A strong, light, flexible, abrasion-resistant, and expensive synthetic fiber that can be combined with a plastic resin to produce an efficient composite material. Kevlar is sometimes used as a belt material in ultra-high-performance tires and for race car body panels.

key   A small block inserted between a shaft and a gear or hub to lock them together so that they rotate as a single unit. A key fits into a milled slot, known as a keyway, cut into both the shaft and the mating part.

keyway   See *key*.

kickback   The tendency of a steering wheel to move or "kick" in the driver's hands as the result of road shock transmitted to it through the steering linkage; also called steering fight.
   Also, the rapid pulsation or chatter felt through the brake pedal as an antilock braking system modulates the hydraulic pressure of one or more brake lines.

kickdown   In an automatic transmission, an accelerator-linked device that allows the driver

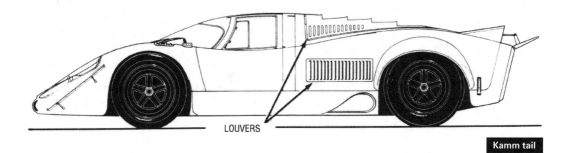

LOUVERS

Kamm tail

131

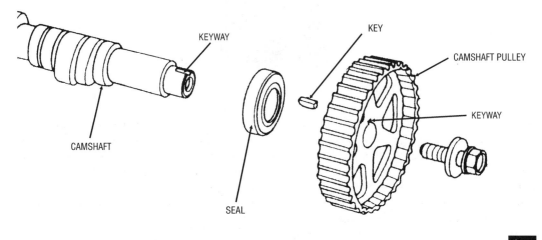

KEYWAY

CAMSHAFT

SEAL

KEY

CAMSHAFT PULLEY

KEYWAY

key

to select a lower gear for hill climbing or increased acceleration by depressing the throttle pedal. It accomplishes automatically the equivalent of downshifting a manual transmission. Also see *downshift*.

kickdown switch   See *downshift and kickdown*.

kickup   The shaping of a fender, side rail, or other structure into an upwardly concave shape for purposes of clearance between components or for aesthetic style.

kingpin   In solid-axle and some early independent front suspensions, the nearly vertical pin in the end of the axle around which the stub axle (or spindle) and wheel pivot. Replaced by ball joints in modern front suspensions. Also see *ball joints*.

kingpin inclination   The angle formed by a line drawn through the longitudinal axis of the kingpin and a vertical line through the centerline of the tire. Also called *steering-axis inclination*.

K-Jetronic   A type of gasoline-engine fuel injection developed and produced by Bosch, which meters fuel to the engine mechanically

and continuously on the basis of the position of a flap in the intake airstream. The greater the airflow, the more the flap is deflected from its resting position; in turn, the deflection causes the flow of fuel to be increased.

knee bar   A passive safety device, part of a supplemental restraint system; an impact-absorbing padded panel beneath the dashboard that prevents occupants from "submarining" beneath

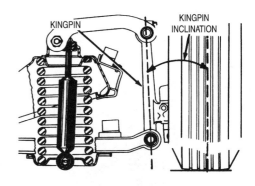

KINGPIN

KINGPIN
INCLINATION

kingpin; kingpin inclination

knee bar

the instrument panel during a crash. Also called *knee bolster*.

knee bolster   See *knee bar*.

knock   A general term used to describe loose or worn mechanical parts such as bearings. Also, a synonym for *detonation*.

knock sensor   In modern electronic engine-management systems, especially those in which electronic ignition and fuel injection are integrated, a device that detects actual or incipient detonation and signals the system's central processing unit to make appropriate adjustments (typically, retarding the spark) to restore smooth engine running and forestall the damage that would result from prolonged knocking. Knock

K

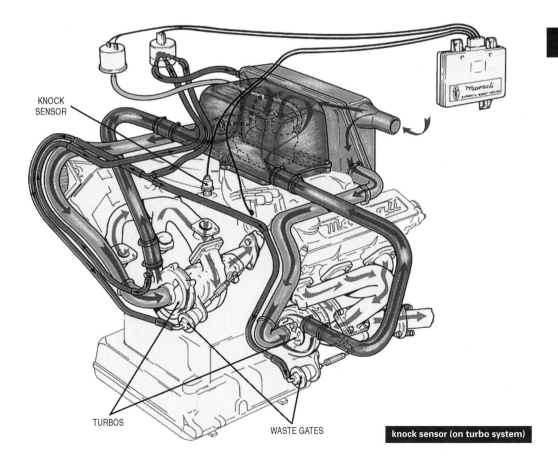

KNOCK SENSOR

TURBOS

WASTE GATES

knock sensor (on turbo system)

sensors allow use of a higher compression ratio, greater turbocharger boost, and/or more advanced ignition timing than would otherwise be possible, thus increasing engine efficiency in a variety of operating conditions. Most knock sensors are mounted on the engine block and detect the sharp vibration set off by knock, generating by piezoelectric means an electrical signal.

knuckle   See *steering knuckle.*

L-head engine   See *flathead*.

L-Jetronic   A Bosch-developed gasoline-engine fuel injection system in which fuel is metered to the engine by electronically controlling the amount of time that the fuel injectors are open. Also known as a *pulsed injection system*.

ladder frame   A chassis constructed with two heavy-section longitudinal members connected by smaller transverse members. Comparatively heavy and generally lacking in torsional rigidity, the design is now uncommon, except in trucks and some SUVs.

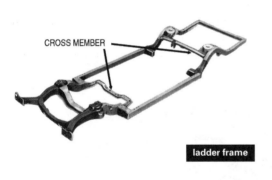

CROSS MEMBER

ladder frame

laminar flow   Smooth airflow over a surface, such as an automobile body.

Also, inside an engine, the smooth flow of the air-fuel mixture through the intake manifold and ports. In laminar flow all portions of the airstream are essentially parallel, and their relative velocities are fairly constant.

laminated glass   A thin layer of rubbery plastic sandwiched between two sheets of glass. Laminated windshields are required on cars sold in the United States. It is safer than toughened

(tempered) glass because damage, unless extensive, is localized and generally won't seriously impair vision. When struck by a large blunt object, a laminated windshield bows without puncturing, and its plastic interlayer holds the glass and prevents it from splintering. Also see *safety glass*.

lash   Clearance or play between two parts. Also see *valve clearance*.

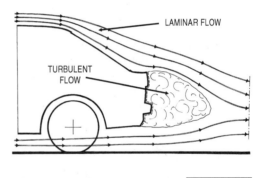

LAMINAR FLOW

TURBULENT FLOW

laminar flow

lateral acceleration   The sideways acceleration, measured in g's, of an object in curvilinear motion. As a car traverses a curve, centrifugal force acts on it and tries to pull it outward. To counteract this, the tires develop an equal and opposite force acting against the road.

Lateral acceleration of cars is usually measured on a skid pad. A car is driven around a large circle (generally 100 ft to 300 ft in diameter) as fast as it will go without sliding off the circle. By knowing the circumference of the circle and the

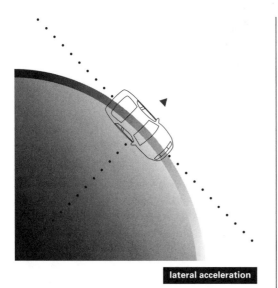

lateral acceleration

time required to negotiate the circle, the steady-state lateral acceleration can be calculated.

lateral arm   A suspension arm often used as the bottom locating link with MacPherson strut or Chapman strut suspensions, and positioned perpendicular to the vehicle's longitudinal cen-

terline. Also called *lateral link,* and *transverse arm* or *link.* Also see *MacPherson strut* and *Chapman strut.*

lateral link   See *lateral arm.*

lateral runout   Side-to-side wobbling of a wheel as it rotates. Also see *shimmy.*

lateral support   The ability of a car seat to restrain the natural sideways movements exerted on an occupant by the car's cornering forces. A relatively high degree of restraint is characteristic of front "sports" seats found in many modern cars, especially performance models capable of high lateral acceleration. Such seats are often deeply bucketed, upholstered in cloth, and have prominent longitudinal bolsters (wings) on the cushion and/or backrest, which are sometimes laterally adjustable.

LCD   See *liquid crystal display.*

lead-free gasoline   Gasoline without tetraethyl lead or any other lead compound added to increase its octane rating and thus reduce its knock or detonation tendencies; also

lateral support

known as unleaded. The elimination of such additives was one reason compression ratios, and thus specific outputs, were reduced on many production engines during the seventies. That trend has since been reversed by increasingly sophisticated electronic controls and the widespread availability of higher-octane (premium) unleaded gasoline. Health authorities now generally agree that the lead emitted in automotive exhaust constitutes a health hazard, and many industrial countries have enacted laws that reduce the amount of lead that can be added to gasoline.

leading arm A suspension component to which a wheel or, in non-independent suspension, a rigid axle is attached and that swings in a plane parallel to the car's longitudinal axis from a pivot at its rearward end. The wheel is thus ahead of, or leads, the arm's fixed pivot point.

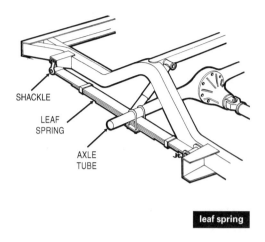

leaf spring

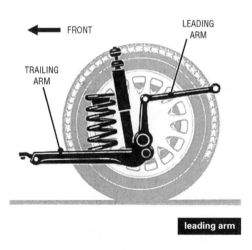

leading arm

leaf spring A spring composed of one or more long, slightly curved flexible steel or fiberglass plates. A number of plates (leaves) of diminishing lengths are mounted on top of one another and clamped together. When used with a live rear axle, at least one end of the spring is attached to the car frame by a shackle to allow for changes in the spring's length as it flexes, and

the center is fixed to the axle. Chevrolet pioneered the use of a fiberglass/epoxy leaf spring at the rear of the 1981 Corvette and added a transverse single-leaf spring to the front in 1984.

lean An air-fuel mixture that has more air than is needed for normal engine running; the opposite of rich. Caused by maladjustment and/or malfunction of one or more fuel-system components. May inhibit starting, and usually results in erratic engine behavior during driving. Also see *driveability, hesitation, rich, stumble,* and *surge.*

lean surge See *surge.*

LED See *light-emitting diode.*

lever-arm shock absorber A type of shock absorber used on many British cars as late as the 1970s, comprised of a piston acted upon by a lever arm attached to the hub or axle.

Lexan Trade name for a transparent, shatterproof, heat-resistant plastic commonly used for rear windows and windshields (rules permitting) of race cars.

LH-Jetronic A refinement of Bosch's L-Jetronic fuel injection system, the main difference being the use of an air-mass sensor instead of an air-flow sensor.

lift The tendency of the rear end of a car to rise during braking; also see *dive*.

Also, the tendency of the front end of a rear-drive car to rise during hard acceleration. Also see *squat, coefficient of aerodynamic lift,* and *cam*.

liftback A fastback body style incorporating a hatchback. Also see *hatchback* and *fastback*.

lifter See *cam follower*.

liftgate A top-hinged tailgate. Also see *tailgate*.

lift-throttle oversteer See *trailing-throttle oversteer*.

light Vintage term used to describe a car's side or door window. Four-light signified a body with two windows per side. The rear window was frequently referred to as the backlight or backlite.

light-actuated pickup A sensor that reacts to light; used in some ignition systems to replace the points in the distributor, much like a magnetic pickup.

light alloy Commonly, an alloy made with a high proportion of aluminum or magnesium; more generally, any alloy composed largely of lightweight metals.

light-emitting diode (LED) A semiconductor diode that emits light when a current flows through it. LEDs can emit infrared, red, orange, yellow, or green light.

limited-slip differential A differential in which cone or disc clutches or a viscous fluid lock the two independent axle shafts together, forcing both wheels to transmit drive torque regardless of the traction available to them. It also allows a limited amount of rotational difference between the two shafts to accommodate the differential action.

limousine Strictly speaking, a chauffeur-driven car, typically with a long wheelbase, in which passengers sit in the rear and are separated from the driver by a glass pane that lowers into a bulkhead behind the front seat.

line The path through a corner that allows late braking combined with a high cornering speed and the fastest possible exit speed.

liner A replaceable, hollow tubular casting, usually of alloy iron, that fits into the cylinder bore and provides the bearing surface for the piston. Dry liners have a thin wall (on the order of 0.1 in.) and can be either a press fit or slip fit in the block. Wet liners have a thick wall, and take the place of the complete cylinder wall — the cooling water circulates around the outside of the liner. Also called a *cylinder liner* or *sleeve*.

lining See *brake lining*.

link A suspension member with a single joint at each end.

linkage Any series of rods and levers used to transmit motion from one component to another.

limited-slip differential

liquefied petroleum gas (LPG) A mixture of petroleum compounds, principally butane and propane. Comparatively low cost made LPG one of several alternate fuels to generate interest as gasoline prices rose steadily from the mid-seventies to the early eighties, though its high octane value alone makes it quite suitable for spark-ignition internal combustion engines. Also, because the pressurized liquid is converted to a dry gas before being routed to the cylinders, LPG doesn't leave carbon deposits or cause dilution of the engine oil, as gasoline does. As a result, maintenance and parts replacement costs are reduced, oil changes can be made at less frequent intervals, and exhaust emissions are low. However, LPG must be stored under pressure, and it yields fewer miles per gallon at a cost higher than gasoline.

liquid crystal display (LCD) A thin sealed sandwich of filament liquid crystal material between two glass plates; used with some digital displays. Transparent electrodes are arranged on the inner glass surfaces in the shape or shapes of the desired display. When voltage is applied to the front and back electrodes, the molecular orientation of the liquid crystal material is altered, modifying the amount of light that can pass through it.

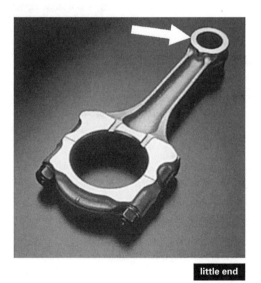

little end

liter A metric unit of capacity equal to 1000 cubic centimeters. A common measurement for engine displacement and for gasoline outside the United States. A liter is approximately equal to a quart, but the precise conversion is to divide the number of liters by 3.785 to determine the number of gallons.

little end The smaller end of a connecting rod, which connects to the piston pin. Also see *big end.*

live axle An axle that transmits power by means of a differential and axle, used in cars with front engine and rear-wheel drive. A live axle is sometimes used at the front of heavy-duty 4-wheel drive trucks. Also see *axle windup* or *Hotchkiss drive* and *monobeam suspension.*

loaded radius See *rolling radius.*

loaded section height Loaded radius minus half of the nominal wheel (rim) diameter. See illustration for *nominal wheel diameter.*

load index A number representing the load capacity (the weight a tire can safely support) of a tire when properly inflated. The most recent metric rating system gives a number and a letter with the tire size. For example, a tire marked 195/60R14 85T, has a load capacity index of 85 and a T speed rating (up to 118 mph).

The following table is not applicable at speeds above 130 mph. For higher speeds, the maximum load the tire can safely carry must be reduced. For example, at a speed of 149 mph the maximum load must be reduced by 9 percent.

Load Index	Load Capacity (lbs.)
60	551
80	992
85	1135
100	1764

L

load range An index identifying tires with their load and inflation limits (lb and psi, respectively) as well as service requirements. For example, the requirements of a passenger-car tire could be met with two- or four-ply construction; a large truck or bus might require ten plies or more. The following table shows the conversion of ply rating to load-range designation:

Load Range	Ply Rating
A	2
B	4
C	6
D	8
E	10
F	12
G	14
H	16
J	18
L	20
M	22
N	24

lobe See *cam.*

lock-to-lock See *turns lock-to-lock.*

lockup The condition that results from applying sufficient braking force to a wheel to prevent it from rotating. A common problem in panic stops and low-traction conditions such as rain or snow, and undesirable for reasons of vehicle control and safety. Locking the front wheels is especially dangerous, as a locked wheel cannot be steered. Also see *antilock braking system.*

lockup torque converter A torque converter fitted with a lockup clutch that can be engaged to eliminate the slip between the torque converter's input and output, thus improving fuel economy and performance. Also see *torque-converter lockup clutch.*

logic module An electronic control unit employing computer technology to perform control functions, as in, for example, ignition and fuel injection systems.

longitudinal link A suspension locating link positioned in a fore-and-aft direction relative to the centerline of the car.

longitudinal location (orientation) Lengthwise (north–south) placement of an engine in a vehicle; typical of front-engine, rear-drive vehicles, but also used with some front-wheel-drive vehicles.

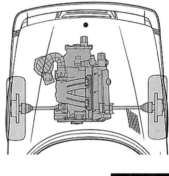

longitudinal location

loose See *oversteer.*

louver Slotted openings or vents in the hood, cowl, or other body panels, usually intended to pull air into or out of the car for ventilation or to force cooling air around a component such as the brakes.

low-back seat A car seat that lacks a head restraint, or on which the head restraint is adjustable.

low beam The primary filament in a two-headlight system or in the main (dual-filament) headlights of a four-light system. Used for most

louver

L

night driving situations when the high beams would cause severe glare to other drivers.

low gear   First gear in a manual transmission; the gear that would normally be used to start a vehicle from idle. Usually "L" (low) or "1" (first) in an automatic.

low-speed circuit   See *idle circuit*.

low-tension leads   The wiring in the ignition system carrying only 6–12 volts. Includes the battery cables, positive (plus) and negative (minus) coil connections, and wiring to the ignition switch and distributor. Compare with high-tension leads.

LPG   See *liquefied petroleum gas*.

lubricant   Any substance, but usually oil or grease, applied to moving parts to reduce friction between them. In an engine, lubricants also act as a seal to prevent leakage between parts such as piston rings and cylinder, and carry away friction heat and the abrasive metal worn from the rubbing surfaces.

lubrication system   The oil pump, oil pan (sump), oil coolers, tubing, filters, and passages in the block and head that supply, circulate, and cool oil for the moving parts and bearings of an engine.

lug bolt   A bolt used to secure a wheel to a hub; less convenient than lug nuts, because the bolts are not permanently fixed to the brake assembly.

luggage compartment   See *trunk*.

lugging   Operating an engine equipped with a manual gearbox in a gear that is too high (engine rpm too low) for a given load condition. Generally results in the driveline jerking back and forth and the engine balking (refusing to run smoothly).

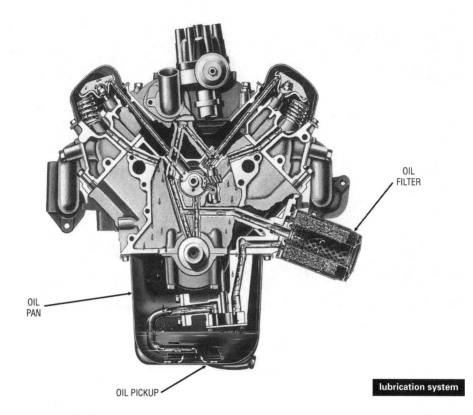

OIL
FILTER

OIL
PAN

OIL PICKUP

lubrication system

lug nut A nut used to secure a wheel to a hub; in modern cars, usually four or five per wheel.

lumbar support The degree to which a seat back conforms to the lower lumbar region of an occupant's back and provides supportive pressure to it. Good lumbar support is widely recognized by medical authorities as important in minimizing driver fatigue on long trips, thus enhancing active safety. Many car companies now offer driver's and front passenger seats with lumbar support that can be varied by a knob or lever acting on elastic bands or by inflating an air bladder to the desired firmness.

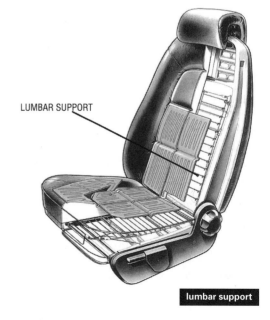

LUMBAR SUPPORT

lumbar support

MacPherson strut A type of front suspension devised by Earle MacPherson at Ford of England. A long strut incorporating the shock absorber and surrounded by a coil spring attaches to the unitized body structure; originally a simple lateral link with an anti-roll bar served as the lower arm. Most later MacPherson systems have full lower A-arms and don't rely on the anti-roll bar for wheel location. Some modifications separate the spring from the shock absorber strut — the Porsche 911 even uses a torsion bar instead of a coil spring.

mag Shortened form of magneto or mag wheel. See *magneto*. Also see *alloy wheel*.

Magnaflux Trade name for magnetic dye penetrant testing, an inspection system used to test for cracks in ferrous metals. Metal is magnetized, submerged in magnetic dye, and examined under black light. Cracks appear as red lines on the surface. Dry particles are commonly used to inspect very rough surfaces such as castings, forgings, and welds.

magnesium A light, ductile, silver-white metal that is often used to replace aluminum

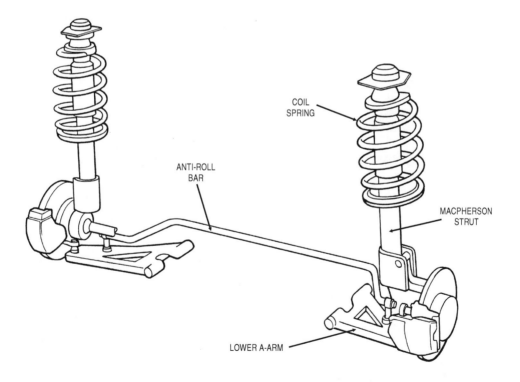

COIL
SPRING

ANTI-ROLL
BAR

MACPHERSON
STRUT

LOWER A-ARM

MacPherson strut

when ultralight weight is required. More expensive than aluminum, it is also approximately 35 percent lighter. Common uses are road wheels, engine blocks, and transmission and differential housings.

magnetic pulse generator   A device that generates pulses in an electronic ignition system to fire the spark plugs. Also see *distributor.*

magneto   A self-contained device that generates and distributes electricity to ignite the air-

fuel mixture in the combustion chamber of an internal combustion engine. The magneto not only generates the electricity but also steps up the low voltage to a high-tension voltage and distributes it to the various cylinders at the correct time. A magneto does not require any battery or other source of current and, unlike battery ignition, the intensity of the generated voltage increases rather than decreases with engine speed. Though still widely used on racing cars, magnetos were superseded by battery ignition in most automotive applications because they require higher cranking speeds than battery ignition, and a battery or some other power source is still needed for lights and other accessories.

mag wheel   See *alloy wheel.*

main bearing caps   The removable, semicircular caps that bolt to the engine block and hold the main bearings and the crankshaft in place.

main bearings   In an engine, the bearings that locate and support the crankshaft.

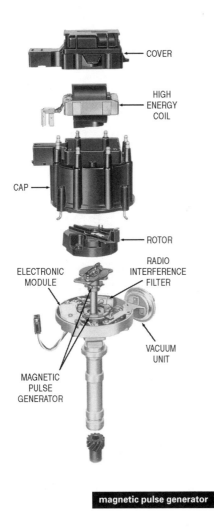

COVER

HIGH ENERGY COIL

CAP

ROTOR

RADIO INTERFERENCE FILTER

ELECTRONIC MODULE

VACUUM UNIT

MAGNETIC PULSE GENERATOR

magnetic pulse generator

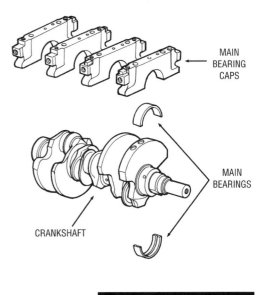

MAIN BEARING CAPS

MAIN BEARINGS

CRANKSHAFT

main bearing caps; main bearings

main shaft The primary shaft in a manual transmission. The main shaft transmits power to the differential with reductions of crankshaft rotation dictated by the size of the gears attached to the main shaft and countershaft. Also see *countershaft.*

manifold See *exhaust manifold* and *intake manifold.*

manifold heat Heat from the exhaust manifold, used to preheat the fuel mixture prior to combustion in a cold engine. Also see *heat-control valve.*

manifold pressure Positive pressure in the intake manifold, occurring in normally aspirated engines when the pistons are moving upward and the valves are closed, and also in supercharged engines. The opposite of manifold vacuum. Also see *manifold vacuum* and *supercharger.*

manifold vacuum The increment of pressure below atmospheric pressure that is created in the intake manifold by the pistons as they move downward in the cylinders on their intake strokes.

manual steering A steering system that does not use a power booster to reduce steering effort.

manual transmission A mechanism in the drivetrain with gearsets which vary the power and torque delivered to the driven wheels. It is activated by a lever on the steering column or floor in conjunction with a clutch pedal to change gears.

map In electronics, a program that determines a variable on the basis of information from two or more inputs. The most typical map in automotive use is one for ignition advance as a function of engine speed and load. In contrast to a simple two-dimensional curve (as, say, for ignition advance versus engine speed), a map is three-dimensional, with the two inputs drawn at right angles to each other and the third variable forming a "surface" whose appearance gives rise to the term "map."

M

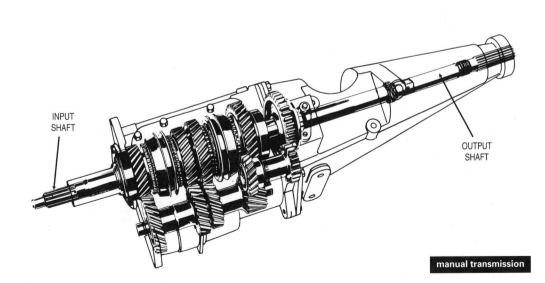

INPUT SHAFT

OUTPUT SHAFT

manual transmission

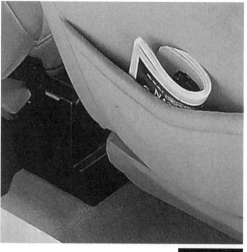

map pocket

map pocket   A small storage compartment in the doors or behind the front seats for stowing maps, newspapers and other thin items.

mass airflow sensor   See *airflow sensor*.

master cylinder   See *brake master cylinder* and *clutch master cylinder*.

maximum power, maximum torque   In every internal combustion engine, power and torque vary as a function of engine speed. Typically, an engine's maximum torque occurs at a speed somewhere around the middle of its speed range; maximum power occurs at a speed near the top of its range. See *power* and *torque*.

mean effective pressure (MEP)   The steady pressure which, if applied to each piston during each power stroke, would produce the power an engine is capable of developing. MEP is a theoretical quantity used mainly for comparing engines; in reality the pressure in an engine's cylinders varies widely during the power stroke.

mechanical brake   A brake using cables or other mechanical linkages rather than hydraulic pressure to actuate the shoes or pads. The parking or emergency brake is the only mechanical brake still found on contemporary cars.

mechanical efficiency   The ratio of the actual power available at the engine crankshaft or flywheel divided by the power produced on the pistons. The former is always less than the latter because of frictional and heat losses and the power required to drive the valve gear, oil pump, and other accessories.

mechanical valve lifter   A valve lifter that provides direct contact between the camshaft and the pushrod in overhead-valve engines or direct camshaft-to-valve contact with overhead-cam engines. Mechanical valve lifters require periodic adjustment of the valve clearance to compensate for expansion in the valve train and for wear. Also called *solid lifters*. Also see *cam follower* and *hydraulic valve lifter*.

memory   In computers, a device in which information can be stored and held available for retrieval. The memory used most often in automobiles — such as in engine computers or power-seat mechanisms — is read-only memory (ROM), which cannot be altered in normal use of the systems.

MEP   See *mean effective pressure*.

metering rod   A thin rod with several steps or tapers on its lower end, used in a carburetor to vary the size of a jet opening. As the rod is raised

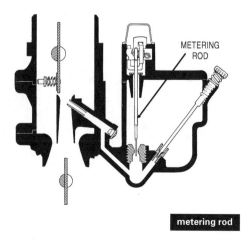

METERING ROD

metering rod

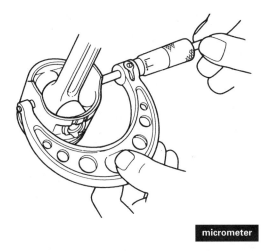

in the jet, it enlarges the effective size of the fuel orifice, permitting more fuel to flow through the circuit. The needle in an SU carburetor performs the same function.

methanol A poisonous alcohol frequently used as a fuel for racing cars because it contains more stored heat energy than gasoline and thus produces more power when burned, albeit at the expense of faster fuel consumption. However, studies have been conducted using gasoline-

methanol mixtures in passenger-car engines with the aim of decreasing the rate at which petroleum resources are depleted. Also called *methyl alcohol* or *wood alcohol*.

methyl alcohol See *methanol*.

metric rating system The European system of tire marking or sizing which is very similar to the P-metric system. Tires do not have a letter P and European regulations require the inclusion of a speed rating in the tire markings. Also see *P-metric*.

microchip A small silicon board with miniature electronic circuitry; it functions as a complete circuit board. Often shortened to chip.

micrometer An instrument for making precise measurements in thousandths and sometimes tens of thousandths of an inch or millimeter. Also called a *mike*.

microprocessor A semiconductor processing unit and a principal component of a microcomputer.

mid-engine The positioning of a car's engine wholly or partly within the wheelbase. Long

M

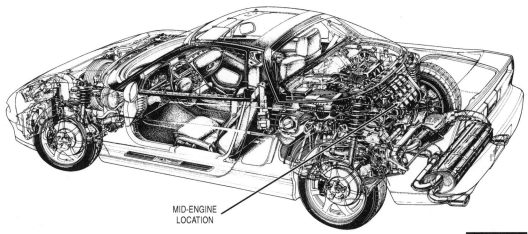

MID-ENGINE
LOCATION

mid-engine

favored for racing and high-performance cars, it results in more even front–rear weight distribution than most front- or rear-engine layouts, benefiting handling and roadholding. A mid-engine car is most commonly thought of as one in which the engine sits immediately behind the passenger compartment and ahead of or over the rear wheels' centerline; but some front-engine cars (such as the Mazda RX-7) are considered front mid-engine designs because their engines are positioned aft of the front-wheel centerline.

mike See *micrometer.*

miles per hour (mph) A measure of speed or velocity.

Miller cycle A refinement of the four-stroke Otto cycle engine in which more air is forced into the cylinders of a small engine to make it work like a larger engine; named after Ralph Miller, an American who conceived of it in 1947.

A compressor is used to force additional air into the cylinders. Miller devised a cycle in which the compression stroke is shortened, reducing the overheating that causes knocking while still allowing a full power-producing expansion stroke. The piston travels the full distance during the compression stroke, but the intake valve is left open during the first part of the expansion stroke so that no compression can occur. This lets some air escape before it can overheat and cause knocking.

The shortened compression stroke does not hamper the engine's performance because the air compressor has already pumped in about twice the supply of air when the valve does close. When compression begins there is still more mixture in the Miller-cycle cylinder than in a conventional naturally aspirated engine during compression.

minivan A small, compact van with seating for seven passengers, powered by a four- or six-cylinder engine. Popularized by Chrysler, the Dodge Caravan and Plymouth Voyager were based on the K-car four-cylinder front-drive platform. Minivans have a car-like driving position with the engine in front under the hood and the driver seated behind the front wheels. They are purchased primarily by families as an alternative to a conventional station wagon. Also see *van.*

misfire The failure of the mixture in a cylinder to fire or ignite when it should; also called a

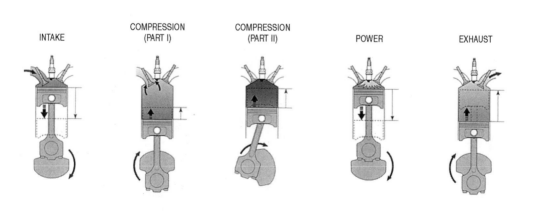

| INTAKE | COMPRESSION (PART I) | COMPRESSION (PART II) | POWER | EXHAUST |

Miller cycle

miss. A driveability problem, it detracts from smooth engine running and, in extreme cases, can lead to internal damage. Also see *autoignition* and *driveability.*

miss   See *misfire.*

mixture   See *air-fuel mixture.*

modesty panel   See *valance panel.*

modesty skirt   See *valance panel.*

modular wheel   A wheel in which the rim and center section bolt together, allowing wheels of different offsets or widths to be created. An exotic and expensive design usually found on racing cars and high-performance street machines, modular wheels often feature cast magnesium centers bolted to light alloy rim halves for strength combined with light weight.

modulation   In automobile braking, the capability of applying the brakes in a controlled manner to avoid locking the wheels and skidding. In assisted brake systems, modulation depends mainly on the amount of assistance (boost) provided, the extent to which it is proportional to an increase in pedal effort and travel, and the degree to which a driver can feel brake action through the brake pedal (often termed pedal feedback). Modulation is usually considered a component of a car's active safety. Also see *lockup* and *antilock braking system.*

modulator   In automatic transmissions, a pressure-regulating device used to vary internal oil pressure to meet engine needs. Under conditions of high engine power (high loading), the modulator increases line pressure to provide more "holding" power for the clutches; under a

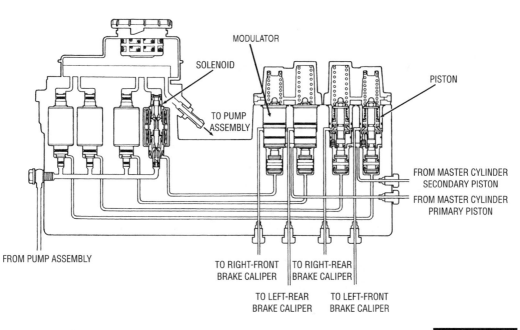

modulator (ABS)

light load, it reduces line pressure to promote smooth shifts.

In antilock braking systems, the modulator reduces hydraulic pressure in one or more brake lines according to signals of actual or incipient wheel locking received from a central processing unit, which receives signals from wheel-mounted speed sensors.

molding   A piece of trim, generally a plastic or metal strip, used either for decoration or to cover exposed seams or edges in an automobile interior. Also, the strips of plastic, metal, and rubber attached to the sides of a car to protect against dings and scrapes, and similar material surrounding the windshield and backlite. See illustration for *body-on-frame construction.*

moment   See *torque.*

moment of inertia   The rotational equivalent of inertia; the tendency of an object to resist rotational acceleration. A car's polar moment of inertia — its moment of inertia about a vertical axis through the center of rotation — has considerable influence on cornering ability, steering, and overall handling response.

When a car's mass — the driver, engine, transmission, and fuel tank — is placed within the wheelbase of the car, the polar moment of inertia about a car's center of gravity is relatively low and the tires can easily alter course. As a result, steering is usually more responsive and more sensitive. This is the principal reason the mid-engine configuration with its low polar moment of inertia has long been popular for racing cars. Also see *inertia.*

MON   Motor Octane Number. See *octane number.*

monitor   A display linked to one or more systems to report on their status and any failure or malfunction, usually by means of warning lights but increasingly by audible and/or visual means. Also see *cathode-ray tube (CRT).*

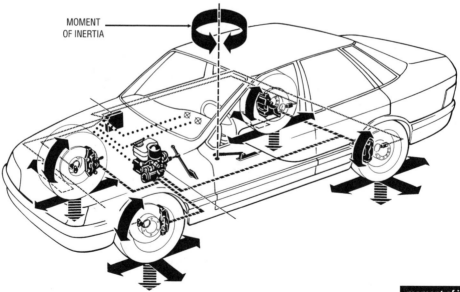

MOMENT OF INERTIA

moment of inertia

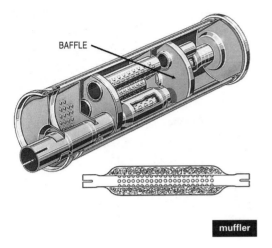

BAFFLE

muffler

monobeam suspension   A simple and rugged form of front suspension used in trucks. In a rear-drive truck, a simple beam axle supported by leaf springs is typically used. In a truck with 4-wheel drive, the single beam would consist of a live axle, one that transmits power by means of a differential and axle, again typically supported by leaf springs. Also see *beam axle* and *live axle*.

monobloc   An engine block with the cylinder and crankcase in one integral casting.

monocoque   A kind of car construction with a rigid, load-bearing skin or shell; especially efficient, though expensive, with a high strength-to-weight ratio. Monocoque race cars are as near to closed section as possible, with openings for the driver and engine. A model of a monocoque chassis is found in nature: the eggshell.

monoposto   Italian for single-seat. See *single-seater*.

moonroof   See *sunroof*.

motor   A machine that converts electrical energy to mechanical energy, as opposed to an engine, which converts heat energy derived from some fuel into mechanical energy. The two words are often used synonymously.

motor mounts   See *engine mounts*.

Motor Octane Number (MON)   See *octane number*.

mph   See *miles per hour*.

muffler   A chamber attached to an engine's exhaust pipe and fitted with baffles or porous plates that reduce or muffle the noise created by the exhaust.

multi-grade   Oil formulated to flow more easily at low temperatures and/or lubricate better at high temperatures. The modification is accomplished with additives called viscosity-index improvers. Virtually all modern synthetic motor oils are multigrade. Also called *multiviscosity*. Also see *viscosity* and *viscosity index*.

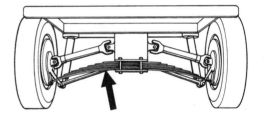

multi-leaf spring

multi-leaf spring   A leaf spring with several individual leaves mounted on top of one another and clamped together.

multi-link suspension   A front or rear suspension system in which a number of links or arms (and no struts) are used to give longitudinal, vertical, and lateral support to the wheels. Because of the multiplicity of links, such a suspension can be tuned or adjusted to give excellent steering, braking, ride, and handling characteristics.

M

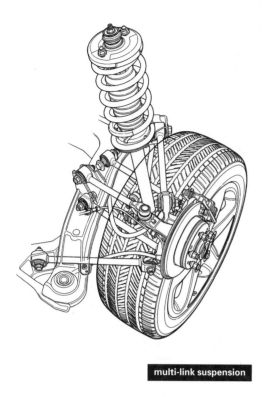

multi-link suspension

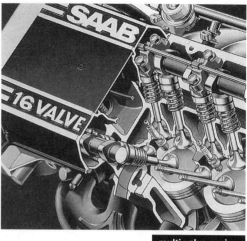

multi-valve engine

multiple disc   A clutch with two or more discs and pressure plates. Multiple-disc clutches are generally used to transmit the power of very high-output engines. Also sometimes a space-saving measure, because for a given torque capacity, a multiple-disc clutch can have a smaller diameter than a single-disc clutch.

multi-point injection   See *fuel injection*.

multi-valve engine   An engine with more than one intake and/or one exhaust valve per cylinder.

multi-valve head   See *multi-valve engine*.

multi-viscosity oil   See *multi-grade oil*.

NACA duct A low-drag inlet duct developed by the National Advisory Committee for Aeronautics after extensive research into the design of inlet ducts with minimum drag for jet engines. NACA ducts are used extensively on racing cars and some production models (such as the Lamborghini Countach) for efficiently feeding air to the engine, for cooling the engine and/or cockpit, and for channeling air to intercoolers and water and oil radiators.

National Highway Traffic Safety Administration (NHTSA) The agency within the Department of Transportation charged with establishing and enforcing automotive safety regulations.

naturally aspirated An engine relying on vacuum in the intake manifold and cylinders to induct air or the air-fuel mixture at atmospheric pressure. Also called *normally aspirated.*

navigation system A computerized system, also called a navigator, for directing a driver to a destination. Usually features an in-car screen that displays the car's position on a representation of a street or road map; some navigators operate in conjunction with a system built into the transportation infrastructure. Also see *Automatic Radio Information.*

navigator See *navigation system.*

needle See *metering rod.*

needle-and-seat The assembly that controls fuel flow into a carburetor's float bowl. Movement of the float moves the needle off its seat, allowing fuel to enter the bowl when the

NACA DUCT

NACA duct

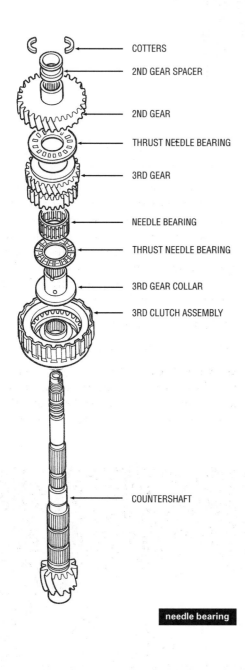

COTTERS

2ND GEAR SPACER

2ND GEAR

THRUST NEEDLE BEARING

3RD GEAR

NEEDLE BEARING

THRUST NEEDLE BEARING

3RD GEAR COLLAR

3RD CLUTCH ASSEMBLY

COUNTERSHAFT

needle bearing

fuel in the bowl drops below a predetermined level and shutting off fuel to the bowl when the level exceeds the specified height. See illustration for *carburetor*.

needle bearing   A roller bearing using rollers of small diameter in relation to their length. The small diameter is useful in components where radial space is at a premium, such as in gearboxes, clutches, and universal joints.

negative camber   See *camber*.

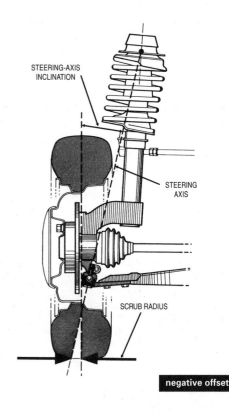

STEERING-AXIS INCLINATION

STEERING AXIS

SCRUB RADIUS

negative offset

negative offset   Steering geometry in which the axis about which the wheels are steered meets the ground outside the center of the tire's contact area with the ground. Also see *steering offset*.

net horsepower   An engine's maximum output (horsepower and/or torque) as measured on a dynamometer with standard intake and exhaust systems and all accessories such as the alternator connected.

net torque See *net horsepower.*

neutral The gear position in automatic and manual transmissions in which the engine is disengaged from the drive wheels.

neutral handling Handling characteristics in which neither understeer nor oversteer predominates; i.e., the front and rear tires are running at equal slip angles. See *oversteer* and *understeer.*

neutral steer Steering characteristics in which the slip angles generated at the front and rear are identical. When such a car exceeds the limit of adhesion, the front and rear tires break loose at the same time and the car slides sideways. While this might seem to be the ideal state of balance, in reality a car with mild understeering tendencies is more stable to drive and less "nervous" than one with neutral steer characteristics. Also see *neutral handling, oversteer, slip angle,* and *understeer.*

NHTSA See *National Highway Traffic Safety Administration.*

nibble A condition in which a car's tires tend to follow pavement irregularities such as grooved sections of freeways or the metal surfaces of bridges. Nibble is felt as a slight back-and-forth tugging on the steering wheel as the tires attempt to run in the grooves. Tire design plays a critical role in nibble; designers need to space the tread grooves such that they don't match the grooves in the pavement. Radial tires, with their more flexible sidewalls, are less prone to nibble. The British call this condition tramlining.

nitrous oxide (N₂O) Commonly known as laughing gas; often used in drag racing to boost engine performance for short periods. When burned, N₂O breaks up into nitrogen and oxy-

gen; the oxygen provides the power boost by allowing more gasoline to be burned.

nominal section height See *section height.*

nominal section width See *section width* and *tire width.*

nominal wheel diameter Diameter of the rim seat supporting the tire bead given in the nearest whole number, for example 14 in.

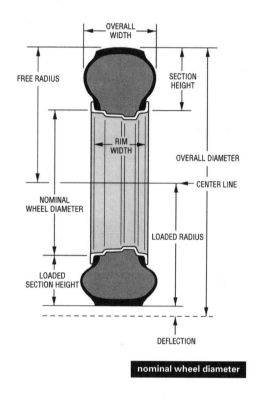

nominal wheel diameter

normally aspirated See *naturally aspirated.*

north–south See *longitudinal location.*

notchback A two- or four-door body type (not a station wagon) characterized by a discrete rear deck set at or near right angles to the rear window, thus creating a roughly L-shaped

notchback

notch in profile view. Originally referred to bodies featuring a reversed-slope rear window in the manner of the English Ford Anglia. Sometimes called a bustleback. A notchback may also be a hatchback, but should not be confused with a fastback.

notchy   Jargon; a shift linkage in a manual transmission that resists gear lever movements from one position to another. The driver feels this resistance ("notchiness") as a sticky hesitation in the lever's travel, as though the linkage were moving around an obstruction.

numeric rating system   The oldest passenger tire sizing system. When the standard was established, tires came in aspect ratios of either 92 or 82. A typical numeric tire size is 6.00-14 where the section width is 6 inches and the wheel size is 14 inches. Section widths ending in 0.00 or 0.50 represent tires with an aspect ratio of 92, while section widths ending in other decimal fractions represent an aspect ratio of 82.

observed horsepower Dynamometer horsepower of an engine before being corrected to a set of standard conditions. Also see *SAE net horsepower*.

octane number An expression of a gasoline's antiknock quality. For octane numbers below one hundred, the scale is arbitrarily based on the knocking tendencies of two hydrocarbons, isooctane and normal heptane. The latter has an assigned octane number of zero because it has much greater knocking tendency than commercially available gasoline. Isooctane has an assigned number of one hundred because it has much less tendency to knock than did the gasoline available when the scale was devised. An octane number below one hundred represents the percentage by volume of isooctane in a blend with normal heptane that will give borderline detonation under the same conditions as the fuel under test. A number above one hundred represents the milliliters of tetraethyl lead that must be added to isooctane to knock with the same intensity as the test fuel.

There are two test methods for evaluating antiknock quality, the major difference being engine operating conditions: the Research Octane Number (RON) is obtained under relatively mild conditions, the Motor Octane Number (MON) under relatively severe conditions. Generally, the octane numbers posted on gasoline pumps in the United States are an average of the two and are four numbers less than equivalent RONs. Thus, for example, if a carmaker recommends gasoline with a minimum RON of ninety-one, fuel from a pump with a rating of eighty-seven or higher can be used.

odometer An instrument for measuring and registering the miles (and often tenths of miles) a vehicle has been driven. Most cars also have an independent trip odometer that can be reset to zero for convenient measurement of the miles driven on a trip or between fuel fill-ups.

offset See *steering offset* and *wheel offset*.

OHC See *overhead cam*.

OHV See *overhead-valve engine*.

oil control ring

oil control ring The lowermost piston ring, which scrapes excess oil from the cylinder walls and returns it to the oil pan via vents in the ring and in the piston itself. The oil control ring prevents oil from getting into the combustion chamber, where it would burn and form carbon that could clog valves and piston rings, short out spark plugs, and increase exhaust emissions. Also see *expansion ring*.

oil-cooled piston A piston cooled by a jet located in the engine block that sprays oil under

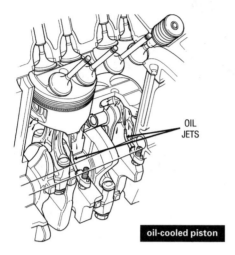

OIL
JETS

oil-cooled piston

the piston. Found in some high-performance and diesel engines.

oil cooler   A small heat exchanger similar to the radiator used in the engine cooling system. In passenger cars, usually used for cooling engine oil or automatic transmission fluid; in racing cars, also used to cool manual gearbox and differential lubricants.

oil filter   See *filter*.

oil galleries   Small passages cast into the engine block and cylinder head through which oil circulates for lubricating and cooling the engine.

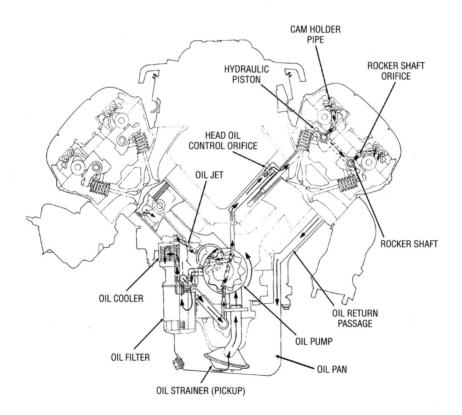

CAM HOLDER
PIPE

HYDRAULIC
PISTON

ROCKER SHAFT
ORIFICE

HEAD OIL
CONTROL ORIFICE

OIL JET

ROCKER SHAFT

OIL COOLER

OIL RETURN
PASSAGE

OIL FILTER

OIL PUMP

OIL PAN

OIL STRAINER (PICKUP)

oil cooler; oil filter; oil galleries; oil pan

oil pan A removable part of an engine, usually made of stamped steel or cast aluminum alloy, that attaches to the bottom of the cylinder block and acts as an engine's oil reservoir.

oil pressure The pressure created by the oil pump to force oil through the engine to cool and lubricate it.

oil pump A pump, usually driven from the camshaft either by gears or cams, that delivers oil to all moving parts of an engine. Most commonly a gear pump or a rotor pump. Automatic transmissions also have an oil pump, usually called a hydraulic pump, and so do many racing manual transmissions.

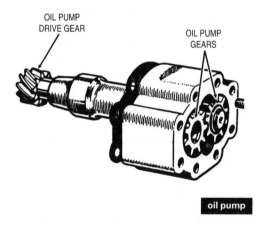

OIL PUMP DRIVE GEAR

OIL PUMP GEARS

oil pump

oil scraper ring A piston ring placed below the compression ring and above the oil control ring to remove any oil left on the cylinder wall by the oil control ring. Also see *oil control ring*.

oil slinger A cone-shaped collar fitted to a shaft that removes oil by centrifugal force.

onboard diagnostics See *diagnostics*.

on-center feel The tendency of the steering wheel to return to center when slightly deflected; the feel, responsiveness, resistance, and free play, if any, felt in a car's steering system when the steering wheel is close to its center position. Good on-center feel helps the driver instinctively keep a car on course as the car encounters influences such as crosswinds, road undulations, and varying road surfaces.

one-way clutch See *freewheel.*

one-way valve See *check valve.*

opera window See *quarter window.*

opposed engine See *flat engine.*

opposite lock A driving technique in which the wheels are steered in a direction opposite to that in which the car is turning, to counter or control a rear-wheel skid. For example, if the tail swings out to the left in a right turn, the driver would correct by steering to the left.

original equipment The parts and components with which a vehicle was fitted when it came from the factory, including standard and optional equipment and some port-installed options, but not dealer-installed accessories.

original equipment manufacturer (OEM) A generic description of any of the auto companies. Also includes supplier companies that provide components that are installed during the original assembly of a vehicle.

O-ring A type of sealing ring, usually of rubber or similar flexible material, shaped like the letter O and compressed into adjoining grooves to provide the seal.

oscilloscope An instrument using a cathode-ray tube to display changing voltage or current as sine-wave patterns. In automotive applications it can be used to tune various engine functions, such as ignition timing. Often shortened to *scope.*

Otto cycle See *four-stroke cycle.*

outboard brakes Brake discs or drums and associated components located at or near the wheel hubs. Also see *inboard brakes.*

O

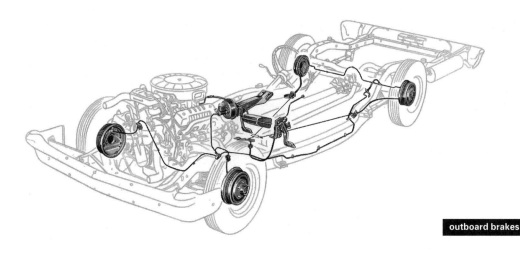

output shaft   A shaft carrying a driven gear. In a transmission, for example, the shaft that receives power from a gearset and transmits it to the driveshaft.

outward vision   The field of view available to a car's occupants, especially the driver; determined by design factors such as total glass area, placement and thickness of roof pillars, the driver's position, and the car's interior layout.

overall diameter   The outer diameter of an unloaded tire when mounted and fully inflated.

overall length   The distance from the frontmost point on a vehicle to the rearmost point.

overall width   Linear distance between the sides of a vehicle, including trim and moldings but excluding the side mirrors. See illustration for *track*. For a tire, the cross-sectional dimension of an inflated, unladen tire including protruding side ribs and decorations. See illustration for *nominal wheel diameter*.

overdrive   A gear ratio of less than 1:1. Also, a transmission that includes one or more overdrive ratios. Advantages include reduced fuel consumption, lower engine noise, and reduced engine wear.

Formerly, a small auxiliary gearbox, usually mounted behind the car's main gearbox or attached to the differential, giving another gear in addition to those of the main transmission. It caused the driveshaft to rotate faster than the engine crankshaft, thus "over-driving" it and providing a higher (numerically lower-geared) cruising ratio. It was typically engaged by a separate switch, not by the shift lever. Such auxiliary gearboxes are now almost extinct on passenger cars.

overflow tank   See *expansion tank*.

overhang   The front and rear portions of a car extending longitudinally beyond its wheelbase; more precisely, the distances from the

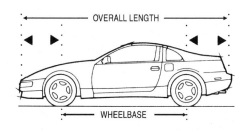

wheel centers to the vehicle's foremost and rearmost points.

overhaul Engine repair that includes a valve job plus replacement of such items as the piston, rings, rod bearings, and head and intake/exhaust manifold gaskets. A major overhaul could require replacement of the pistons, main bearings, timing chain, and gears.

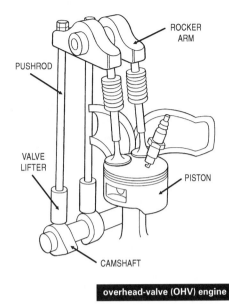

overhead-valve (OHV) engine

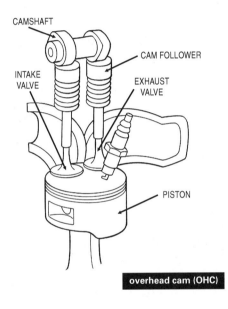

overhead cam (OHC)

overhead cam (OHC) A camshaft located above the cylinder head or heads rather than in the engine block. An OHC eliminates pushrods, and some also dispense with rocker arms. A valve train with an in-block camshaft uses pushrods and rocker arms; an OHC valve train reduces the number of moving parts and thus the inertia of the valve train, making for higher rotational speeds and, as a consequence, higher power output. Also see *single overhead cam* and *dual overhead cam*.

overhead-valve (OHV) engine An engine in which the intake and exhaust valves are directly over the piston. The term, adopted before camshafts were also generally above the cylinders, denotes a camshaft located in the block and valves actuated by pushrods and rocker arms. Also called an *I-head* or *valve-in-head engine*.

overlap The degrees of crankshaft rotation during which the intake and exhaust valves in one cylinder are open at the same time. The overlap period occurs at the end of the exhaust stroke and the start of the next intake stroke. The

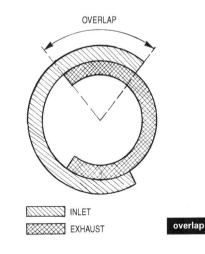

INLET
EXHAUST

overlap

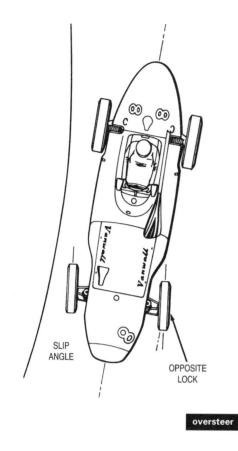

SLIP
ANGLE

OPPOSITE
LOCK

oversteer

exhaust valve closes late to give the burned gases as much time as possible to leave the combustion chamber (after they have expended most of their useful work); the intake valve opens early to give the fresh mixture time to fill the combustion chamber.

overrunning clutch See *freewheel.*

oversize Larger-than-standard tires, used to increase load-carrying capacity or to modify handling characteristics. Can also refer to modified bearings, pistons, and valve stems.

overslung A vintage automobile with the chassis frame attached to the axles from above. Also see *underslung.*

oversquare An engine whose cylinder bore is greater than its stroke.

oversteer A handling characteristic in which less steering lock is applied as car speed increases around a constant-radius turn. In the oversteering condition, the rear tires are the first to slide because the rear tires run at larger slip angles than the front. Race drivers will say an oversteering car is "loose" because the rear end tends to swing wide. Also see *neutral steer, slip angle,* and *understeer.*

oxides of nitrogen (NO$_X$) Any compound composed entirely of one part nitrogen and one or more parts of oxygen; produced when hydrocarbon fuels are burned at very high temperatures in an engine, and a constituent of photochemical smog. Emissions can be reduced by lowering peak combustion temperatures. Two common ways of accomplishing this are by lowering compression ratios and recirculating exhaust gases.

oxygen sensor An integral part of a three-way catalyst system, an oxygen sensor feeds back information on the oxygen content of the exhaust gases to a control unit which then precisely controls the air-fuel ratio to optimize combustion for the lowest possible emissions.

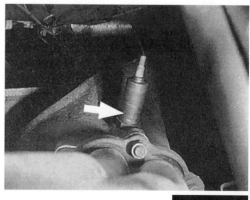

oxygen sensor

package The general concept and arrangement of a vehicle, including dimensions. Also, the group of options and accessories that are sold together at a price lower than if purchased individually.

package tray The shelf behind the rear seat and over the bulkhead, that extends to the base of the rear window.

pad See *brake pad*.

pancake engine See *flat engine*.

Panhard rod A lateral locating link, attached to the body at one end and to a live, beam, or de Dion axle at the other. Also called a *track bar*.

parallel steering See *four-wheel steering*.

parking brake See *emergency brake*.

particulates The solid constituents of an engine's exhaust, mainly carbon particles or soot. A diesel engine's exhaust contains a high percentage of particulates and in recent years the Environmental Protection Agency has come up with particulate emission standards similar to those for CO, HC, and NO_X emissions for engines fueled with gasoline.

parting line The slightly raised line on a cast part indicating the seam of the mold.

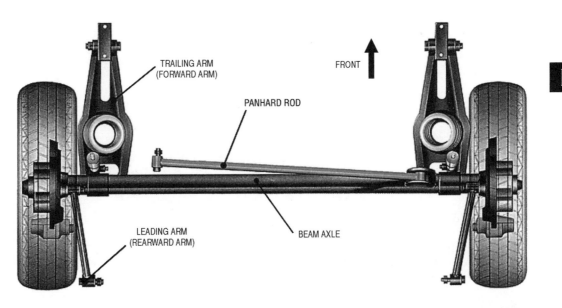

TRAILING ARM
(FORWARD ARM)

FRONT

PANHARD ROD

LEADING ARM
(REARWARD ARM)

BEAM AXLE

Panhard rod (seen from above)

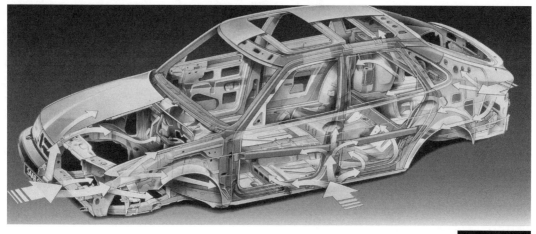

passenger cell

passenger cell   The structure enclosing a vehicle's passenger compartment. In modern cars, it is designed to resist deformation by the force of a collision, thereby reducing the likelihood of occupant injury and allowing the doors to open normally so that occupants may escape. Also see *crush zone*.

passive restraint   Any device that serves to limit or inhibit the body movements of a car's occupants in a collision, but which functions without any action on the part of the occupants. The most common passive restraints are the airbag and automatic seat belt.

passive safety   Characteristics of a motor vehicle designed to protect its occupants in a crash, including passive restraints, energy-absorbing steering components, and reinforced crush zones. Also see *active safety*.

pawl   A pivoted bar that slides over the teeth of a ratchet wheel to prevent or impart motion.

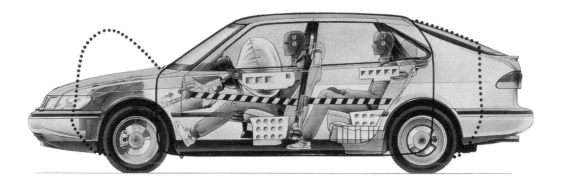

passive restraint

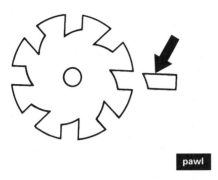

pawl

In an automatic transmission, for example, the parking pawl locks the transmission in the "Park" position.

PCV Positive crankcase ventilation. See *closed crankcase ventilation.*

pedal A floor-mounted, foot control to remotely transfer motion to a component such as the clutch, brake, throttle, or emergency brake, typically through a mechanical or hydraulic linkage. Also see *drive-by-wire.*

pedal effort The force required to depress a car's accelerator, brake, or clutch pedal.

pedal feedback See *modulation.*

pentroof combustion chamber A combustion chamber which, viewed in longitudinal section, has a wedge or "sloping-roof" form.

petcock A small valve placed in a fluid circuit for draining liquids.

petroleum A complex mixture of hydrocarbons and small amounts of various other elements, occurring widely in nature as deposits of decomposed organic matter. Gasoline, lubricating oils, propane, diesel fuel, and other products are refined from these various liquids and gaseous compounds.

photochemical smog See *smog, oxides of nitrogen,* and *hydrocarbon.*

pickup truck A lightweight truck with an enclosed cab seating two or three passengers and an open bed with low sides and a tailgate. Extended cab models include space behind the front seat for additional passengers and/or cargo. Pickup trucks now feature carlike passenger compartments as well as the ability to haul heavy bulky supplies and equipment and tow heavy loads. Compact pickups may be powered by either four- or six-cylinder engines; full-size pickups generally have six- or eight-cylinder engines. Rear- and four-wheel-drive models are available.

pillarless A four-door body design without a central B-pillar to obstruct ingress and egress. The front door is hinged at the front and opens in a conventional manner; the rear door is hinged at the rear and swings open toward the trunk of the car. Pillarless designs result in a greenhouse uninterrupted by metalwork, resulting in a clean uncluttered look appreciated by owners and stylists alike. The 1965 Lincoln Continental is one well-known example.

The term can also be applied to any closed four-door body style in which the door glass is

P

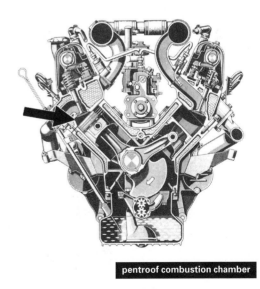

pentroof combustion chamber

freestanding and unsupported. Also, a two-door sedan or coupe in which the door glass is unframed and the corresponding rear quarter window is set without a vertical frame member at its leading edge.

pilot bearing   The bearing at the output end of the crankshaft supporting the transmission input shaft.

pilot production   A new or modified assembly or manufacturing line constructed to evaluate the machines, tooling, production processes, and organization, needed for a new car or component. Vehicles or their components are made at a rate far slower than that for which the line was designed, and pilot units are typically retained by an automaker to evaluate the manufacturing plant's quality control rather than being offered for public sale.

ping   See *detonation.*

pinion gear   A gear with a small number of teeth, designed to mesh with a larger geared wheel or rack. Used in rack-and-pinion steering, the starter motor and the differential ring-and-pinion. Also see *planetary gears* and *rack-and-pinion steering.*

piston   A partly hollow cylinder, closed at one end and moving in a cylinder. Pistons are used to convert the motion of a brake pedal into

PISTON-PIN
BUSHING   RING GROOVES   PISTON
SKIRT

piston

hydraulic pressure and to convert hydraulic pressure into the motion of a disc brake's friction pads. In an internal combustion engine, a piston is fitted to each of the engine's cylinders and attached to the crankshaft by a connecting rod. Each piston moves up and down in its cylinder, transmitting the force of the combustion-chamber explosion to the crankshaft through the connecting rod. Pistons are fitted with rings used to seal the piston in the cylinder.

piston displacement   See *displacement.*

piston pin   The cylindrical or tubular metal shaft, with its axis at right angles to that of the

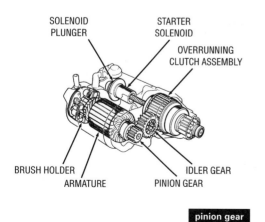

SOLENOID
PLUNGER   STARTER
SOLENOID

OVERRUNNING
CLUTCH ASSEMBLY

BRUSH HOLDER
ARMATURE   IDLER GEAR
PINION GEAR

pinion gear

piston pin

piston, that attaches the piston to the connecting rod. Also called *wrist pin*.

piston-pin bushing   The removable bushing inserted on the small end of the connecting rod, serving as a bearing surface for the piston pin. Also see *bushing, connecting rod,* and *piston pin*.

piston rings   Thin metal rings installed at the top of a piston to form a seal with the cylinder walls and prevent oil from entering the combustion chamber. There are typically two compression rings and an oil control ring, but in some low-friction, high-fuel-economy engines the second compression ring may be eliminated. Also see *oil control ring* and *compression ring*.

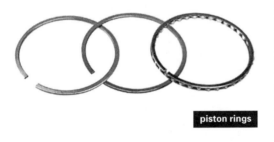

piston rings

piston skirt   See *skirt*.

piston slap   A hollow, muffled, rattling sound made by a loose or worn piston as it contacts the cylinder wall while moving up and down.

pitch   A ride motion in automobiles; a fore-and-aft rocking motion, alternately compressing a car's front springs while extending the rear springs and vice versa. Also see *ride*.

Also, the distance between two threads on a bolt or screw.

pitman arm   The lever, extending from the steering gear, to which the steering linkage is attached. A pitman shaft extends downward from the steering box and is splined to the pitman arm, which converts the shaft's rotary motion to lateral movement of the arm. Also see *idler arm*. See illustration for *steering box*.

planetary gears   A gear system consisting of a central sun gear surrounded by two or more planet gears that are, in turn, meshed with a ring gear (internal gear). The planet gears (pinions) turn on their own axes while rotating around the sun gear in a manner similar to planets rotating around the sun; hence the name. By holding any one of the three gear elements motionless, different ratios can be produced between the other two. Frequently used in overdrives and automatic transmissions.

plan view   The overhead view of an object.

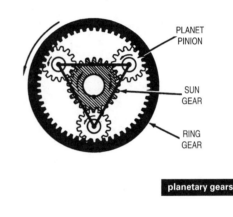

PLANET
PINION

SUN
GEAR

RING
GEAR

planetary gears

platform   A car's basic structural foundation, i.e., its body-and-frame design or unit body/chassis assemblage. The concept is helpful in identifying common components of nominally different models. Chrysler Corporation's front-wheel-drive K-car is a well-known example; more recently, Saab, Lancia, and Alfa Romeo developed a platform which was the basis for the Saab 9000, the Lancia Theta, and the Alfa 164.

Also, a synonym for the automobile frame, especially early ladder types with straight chassis side rails. Also see *ladder frame*.

plenum   A container or chamber filled with air or some other gas under greater than atmospheric pressure. The plenum chamber in an intake manifold contains air or the air-fuel mixture.

Plexiglas   Trade name for a transparent plastic, often used as a substitute for glass.

plies   The layers of cord, fiberglass, steel, or structural fabric making up a tire's carcass and reinforcing belts. Also see *bias tire*.

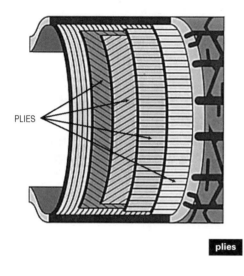

PLIES

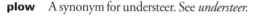

plies

plow   A synonym for understeer. See *understeer*.

plug   See *spark plug*.

Plus fitments   A tire/wheel system designed to permit cars to accommodate high-performance tires that are lower and wider than those originally fitted. A car equipped with 185/70R13 tires can easily be fitted with the wider 195/70R13 (Plus 0). However, the latter is also taller, making it a tighter fit in the wheel wells and altering the car's gear ratios and speedometer readings.

A better solution would be to choose a tire with a lower aspect ratio. A 205/60R13 would work, if the rim is wide enough and if there is adequate clearance, but it has a lower load-carrying capacity than the 185/70R13. The best

solution is to move up to a wheel one inch larger in diameter, or Plus 1. A 195/60R14 tire mounted on a fourteen-inch wheel is almost identical in height, circumference, and load-carrying capacity to the 185/70R13, but it's wider and the sidewalls are shorter so its performance is enhanced.

A performance enthusiast might go a step further with Plus 2, fitting a wheel with a diameter of fifteen inches and mounting a 205/50R15 tire.

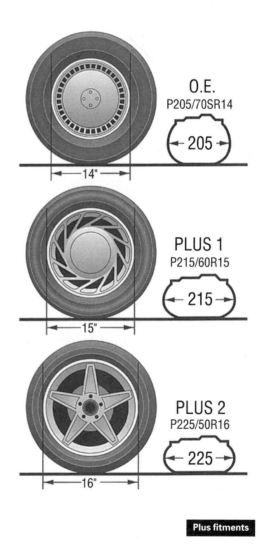

Plus fitments

ply rating An index of a tire's strength, although no longer representing the actual number of plies in the tire. Tires can now have equivalent strengths using different materials or by arranging the materials in different ways. To compare various casings, manufacturers have agreed to refer to a standard type of ply. Until recently, this indication was stamped on the tire (i.e., 4 p.R.) giving the actual strength of the plies, regardless of the number and type of plies used in the tire's construction.

P-metric A new generation of tires introduced in 1976 by U.S. tire manufacturers and designed to run at higher inflation pressures in order to lower rolling resistance and achieve better fuel economy. P-metric tire sizes begin with the letter P (for passenger), followed by the section width in millimeters, a slash, and the aspect ratio. The next letter is either D (diagonal, or bias, construction) or R (radial construction). The last number indicates the wheel diameter.

An example would be P215/75R15. A letter preceding the construction type indicates the speed rating of the tire. If the aspect ratio is not indicated (as in 175R14), then, by definition, the aspect ratio is 80. Also see *speed rating* and *tire ratings*.

pneumatic tire A tire made of natural or synthetic rubber materials and containing compressed air to support the weight of the car and cushion road impacts.

pneumatic trail A phenomenon in which dynamic forces acting on a tire move its contact patch to the rear of its geometric center. Also see *self-aligning torque*.

points See *breaker points*.

polar moment of inertia See *moment of inertia*.

pollutant See *exhaust emissions*.

polyellipsoid See *ellipsoid*.

pop-off valve A simple valve that limits pressure in an enclosure or system to a predetermined level. Seldom used in passenger cars today, but found on turbocharged racing engines as a boost-limiting device.

poppet valve A mushroom-shaped valve found in the cylinder heads of virtually all modern car engines. It is designed to open and close a circular opening or port, and is so named because it "pops" up and down. See *intake valve* and *exhaust valve*.

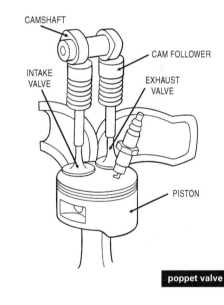

poppet valve

pop rivet A small metal fastener that can be applied with access from only one side. A breakaway mandrel crushes the rivet from the inside, securing it.

porpoising A ride motion in automobiles; the front end's alternating rhythmic rise and fall on undulations. Also see *ride*.

port See *exhaust port* and *intake port*.

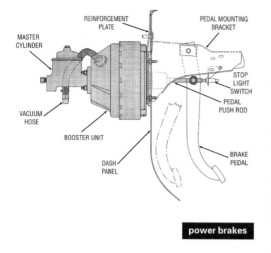

REINFORCEMENT PLATE

MASTER CYLINDER

PEDAL MOUNTING BRACKET

STOP LIGHT SWITCH

PEDAL PUSH ROD

VACUUM HOSE

BOOSTER UNIT

DASH PANEL

BRAKE PEDAL

power brakes

port fuel injection   A fuel injection system that injects fuel directly into the intake ports of an internal combustion engine. See *fuel injection.*

positive camber   See *camber.*

positive crankcase ventilation (PCV)   See *closed crankcase ventilation.*

positive offset   Steering geometry in which the axis about which the wheels are steered meets the ground inboard of the center of the tire's contact area with the ground. Also see *steering offset.*

pound-feet   A measurement of torque, the product of the magnitude of a force (measured in pounds) and the force arm, the perpendicular distance from the axis of rotation of the body to the line of action of the force (measured in feet). Also see *torque* and *foot-pound.*

pounds per square inch (psi)   A unit of measure of pressure. Also see *pressure.*

pour point   The lowest temperature at which oil will flow; an indicator of an oil's ability to lubricate in cold weather.

power   The rate at which work is done. If work is expressed in ft-lb and time in seconds, the basic English unit of power is one ft-lb/sec.

Since this unit is inconveniently small, a larger unit called the horsepower is commonly used instead. See *horsepower.*

power-assisted brakes   See *power brakes.*

power-assisted steering   See *power steering.*

power band   The range, expressed in rpm, over which an engine delivers a major portion of its peak power. This subjective power band generally starts slightly below the engine's torque peak and extends to slightly above its power peak. Also see *power curve, power peak, torque curve,* and *torque peak.*

power brakes   A brake system using vacuum or hydraulic assist to reduce the driver's effort in slowing and stopping a car. When the assist is from the engine's intake vacuum or a vacuum pump, the preferred term is vacuum-assisted brakes. When the assist is from an engine-driven pump, they are called hydraulically assisted brakes. Also see *hydraulic assist, vacuum assist,* and *brake booster.*

power curve   An engine's power output relative to its crankshaft speed; also a graphic representation of the same. Power output is determined by dynamometer measurements at various points in the engine's crankshaft-speed range; these figures are then plotted as points on a graph, usually with the horizontal scale representing crankshaft speed (in rpm) and the vertical scale representing power (usually in horsepower, though in Europe kilowatts are also used). When connected, the points form a curve that permits easy visual comparison of an engine's power delivery characteristics to those of other engines.

power peak   An engine's maximum power; appears as the highest point on the power curve.

power plant   A synonym for an automobile engine.

power steering   A steering system generally using hydraulic pressure to reduce the driver's

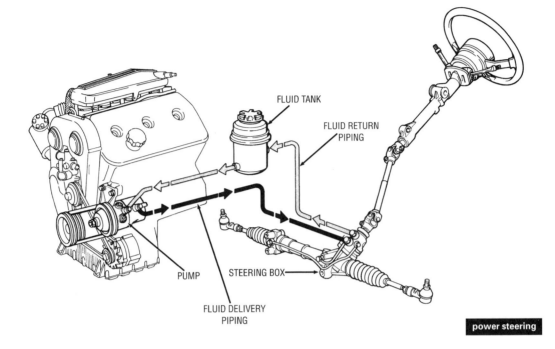

FLUID TANK

FLUID RETURN
PIPING

PUMP

STEERING BOX

FLUID DELIVERY
PIPING

power steering

effort in steering a car. Also called *power-assisted* or *assisted steering*.

power stroke   The third stroke of the four-stroke cycle, in which the piston moves downward from top dead center to bottom dead center as a result of the force of combustion acting on the top of the piston. Also called *expansion, working,* or *combustion stroke.*

power train   All the power-producing and transmitting components of an automobile: the engine, transmission, differential, and driveshafts.

power valve   A vacuum- or mechanically-operated carburetor valve that provides additional fuel at wide-open throttle.

prechamber injection   See *fuel injection.*

preignition   Ignition of the air-fuel mixture in an engine cylinder before the ignition spark occurs at the spark plug; causes can include a random spark, high pressure, a flame, or a hot surface.

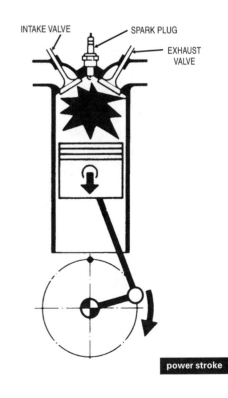

INTAKE VALVE   SPARK PLUG

EXHAUST
VALVE

power stroke

P

preload To install a part by applying pressure to it. An antifriction bearing, ball joint, or spring may be preloaded to eliminate looseness or to give it a specific operating characteristic.

press-fit To fit two parts — a piston pin in a pin bushing, for example — by applying pressure, often from a hydraulic press.

pressure Force per unit area. Measured in such units as pounds per square inch and kilograms per square centimeter.

pressure cap A radiator cap with a valve that maintains pressure in the cooling system. Placing the coolant under pressure raises its boiling point, allowing the engine to operate at a higher and thus more efficient temperature without loss of coolant. The cap's vacuum valve lets air into the cooling system when the pressure falls, to prevent external air pressure from collapsing the radiator.

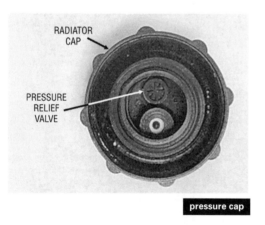

RADIATOR
CAP

PRESSURE
RELIEF
VALVE

pressure cap

pressure plate See *clutch pressure plate.*

pressure-relief valve A one-way valve that opens above a set pressure to relieve excessive internal pressure. In an engine's lubrication system, a pressure-relief valve opens to relieve excess

pressure that the oil pump might develop. Also see *blowoff valve.*

pressure-wave supercharger A type of supercharger in which energy is transferred from the exhaust gas to the engine's intake air by means of pressure waves in the cells of an engine-driven rotor.

primary brake shoe In drum brakes, the shoe that initiates a self-energizing action. Self-energizing is obtained by locating the brake anchor pin so that the rotating drum tends to drag the lining along with it. When the drum is rotating in one direction, frictional force between the brake drum and the primary shoe tries to turn the shoe around the anchor pin. Because the drum itself prevents this, the shoe is forced against the drum with greater force than the force pushing it. There is no self-energizing if the drum is revolved in the opposite direction. However, as there are two shoes, one or the other is effective either way the drum turns. When self-energizing is amplified to include both shoes by letting the primary shoe push the secondary shoe, the amplification of forces is known as servo action.

primary circuit The path of low-voltage current in an ignition system from the battery to the primary winding of the coil through the breaker points and back to the battery.

Also, the main fuel passage in a carburetor containing the primary jet(s).

profile See *aspect ratio.*

programmable read-only memory (PROM) The electronic memory that cannot be altered by the user. Automotive electronic control units make extensive use of PROM.

progressive-rate springs See *rising-rate suspension* and *spring rate.*

progressive transmission An early type of transmission in which it was necessary to engage all the intermediate gears in sequence when

pulley

shifting from the lowest to highest gears, and vice versa.

PROM See *programmable read-only memory.*

propane A type of liquefied petroleum gas used in some piston engines. Propane can be used in very cold conditions because its freezing point is −44 degrees Fahrenheit. See *liquefied petroleum gas.*

propeller shaft See *driveshaft.*

proportioning valve See *brake proportioning valve.*

propshaft See *driveshaft.*

proving ground Facility in which motor vehicles are tested and developed extensively, generally by manufacturers before the vehicles are put into production. A proving ground is a more extensive facility than a test track; it attempts to duplicate the terrain and surfaces encountered on public roads, and includes a skid pad, water splash, banked oval, high-speed loop, engineering shops, and other areas for spe-

cialized testing and building of prototypes and components. Also see *test track.*

pull A condition in which a vehicle swerves to one side without being steered in that direction, as a result of irregular tire wear, improper front and/or rear wheel alignment, or worn or improperly adjusted brakes.

pulley A wheel with a V-shaped groove around its circumference in which a fan belt or V-belt is fitted to drive engine accessories such as the fan and the alternator.

pull-rod suspension See *push-pull suspension.*

pulsed air injection See *air injection system.*

pulsed injection A fuel injection system that meters fuel to the engine by electronically controlling the amount of time that the fuel injectors are open. In contrast to a continuous injection system, in which the injectors are open and fuel flows from the moment the engine starts, pulsed injectors open and close in time with the engine to deliver the fuel. Also called *timed injection.*

pump octane See *octane number.*

push A handling characteristic in which additional steering lock is required as speed increases around a constant-radius turn. Also called *understeer.* Also see *oversteer.*

push-pull suspension A racing suspension in which inboard spring/shock units are actuated by complicated linkages. A tension rod connects the outer upper ball joint to the lower inner shock attachment, which is located by a roller guide or its own control arm. This arrangement effectively triangulates the linkage and reduces stress on the system. The purpose of such suspensions is to remove the spring/shock unit from the sidepod airflow, where it would reduce downforce, and to create rising-rate geometry. Pushrods are sometimes used in a similar way to get a slightly different variable

P

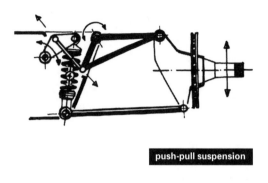

push-pull suspension

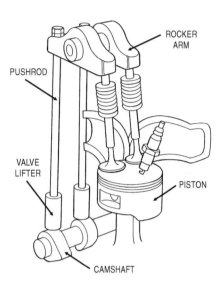

pushrod

spring rate. Also called *pull- or push-rod suspension.* Also see *rising-rate suspension.*

pushrod   In general, a connecting link in an operating mechanism. In overhead valve engines, the rod interposed between the valve lifter and the rocker arm.

push-rod suspension   See *push-pull suspension.*

pyrometer   An instrument used to measure high temperatures, usually through contact with the object whose temperature is being measured. In racing and tire testing, pyrometers are used to check tire temperatures.

quality   A synonym for workmanship, specifically the thoroughness with which a vehicle is assembled, the fit and finish of its various components, the nature of the materials used in its overall construction, its level of durability and reliability, and the degree to which obvious flaws are absent.

quarter-elliptic leaf spring   A type of leaf spring no longer in use, that takes its name from being shaped like roughly one-fourth of an ellipse. Also see *leaf springs*.

quarter panel   Another name for a car's fender. The front quarter panel extends from the headlights to the front door openings and from the wheel wells to the hood. The rear quarter panel extends from the rear door openings to the taillights and from the wheel wells to the trunk or hatch opening.

Also refers to an internal trim panel that "finishes" an area in one corner or quadrant of the passenger compartment or cargo area.

quarter window   Small windows incorporated in the front and/or rear door frames and separate from the main windows. Originally designed to pivot open for interior ventilation (and thus once called vent windows, vent wings, or wind wings) but fixed glass on many modern cars. Rear quarter windows sometimes appear in the C-pillar area aft of the doors, such as the

small, usually vertical opera windows popular on many seventies American coupes.

quartz halogen bulb   A bulb made of quartz glass, a tungsten filament, and filled with an inert gas containing iodine or another of the five halogen gases. The gas allows the filament to carry a high current and serves to remove the tungsten deposits from the bulb wall, redepositing them on the filament and thus preventing the bulb surface from blackening. The high filament and operating temperatures necessitate the use of quartz glass, but produce an efficient and brilliant white light.

quench area   A zone in the combustion chamber of some engines in which the cylinder

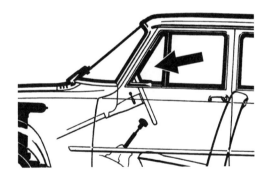

quarter window

head is very close to the piston at top dead center. The piston and combustion chamber surfaces forming the quench area are cooler than the end gas and conduct heat away from the end gas. Such cooling reduces (quenches) detonation, though the cooler metal surfaces also promote the formation of unburned hydrocarbons.

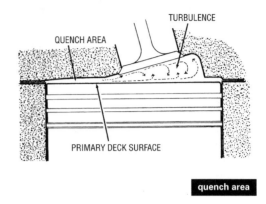

quench area

race   In bearings, the finished inner and outer surfaces in which balls or rollers move.

rack-and-pinion steering   A steering system in which a pinion gear on the end of the steering column mates with a rack, which is basically an open flat gear. The pinion turns with the steering wheel, moving the rack to the left or right, and the motion is carried through tie rods to the steering arms at the wheels.

radar (radio detection and ranging)   A system or device using reflected radio waves to determine the speed and location of an object.

radial engine   An engine, often used in aircraft, in which the cylinders are mounted in a circle around the crankshaft.

radial ply   A tire in which the main carcass plies or cords run radially, usually at right angles

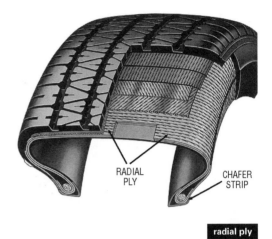

radial ply

to the bead. By itself, this construction is very weak — the smaller the bias angle, the stiffer the structure and this is the largest possible angle. A circumferential belt of plies at a low angle (usu-

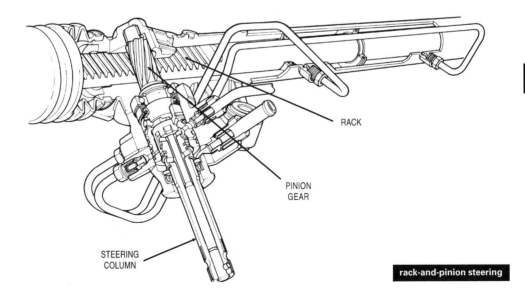

rack-and-pinion steering

177

ally around 15 degrees) is added to make the tread area stiff and the relatively independent sidewalls flexible.

radial runout   See *runout.*

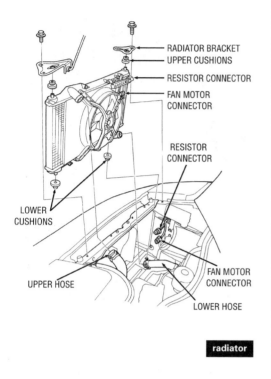

radiator

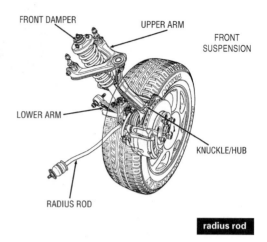

radius rod

radiator   A heat exchanger connected to a car's engine, through which a mixture of water and antifreeze circulates. Air passing through the radiator transfers heat from the coolant to the atmosphere before the coolant is returned to the engine. A thermostat regulates the volume of coolant in order to maintain the engine at an optimum operating temperature. See *heat exchanger.*

radius rod   A rod or arm used to locate a front or rear suspension component. When used to locate a live rear axle, the rods attach to the frame and to the axle to prevent fore–aft movement while allowing vertical motion. Attached to the frame in front of the axle, a radius rod is equivalent to a trailing arm; attached at the rear, it is equivalent to a leading arm.

ragtop   A convertible.

rails   See *fuel rail.*

rain gutter   See *drip molding.*

rake adjustment   See *seat-back angle.*

ram air   A form of natural supercharging in which an intake duct, typically a hood scoop, pulls in air flowing over a moving car and forces it into the carburetor or fuel injection system.

ram effect   See *resonance induction.*

ramp angle   In profile, the angle created with a horizontal road surface by a line drawn from a car's tires to the lowest point of its front or rear overhangs; defines the steepness of transitions the car may traverse without scraping. A deep front spoiler, for instance, reduces the ramp angle.

read-only memory (ROM)   See *memory.*

rear air dam   See *air dam.*

rear deck   The flat or mostly flat upper surface of a notchback body's trunk area, including the trunk lid and flanking rear fender surfaces.

rear engine

rear drive See *rear-wheel drive.*

rear end The differential and final drive assembly on a rear-drive vehicle.

rear engine Placement of a car's engine so that its mass is concentrated mainly behind the rear-wheel centerline. Once widely favored for racing cars and some production models, but now seldom used because its extreme rearward weight bias makes a car more prone to oversteer than mid- or front-engine layouts. Well-known rear-engine cars include the Volkswagen Beetle, Chevrolet Corvair, and Porsche 911.

rear-wheel drive (RWD) A drive system in which the transmission is connected by the driving axle(s) to the rear wheels. Also called *rear drive.*

R

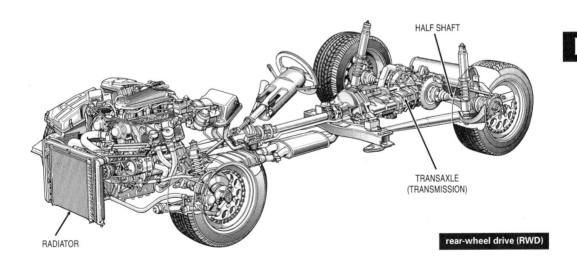

HALF SHAFT

TRANSAXLE
(TRANSMISSION)

RADIATOR

rear-wheel drive (RWD)

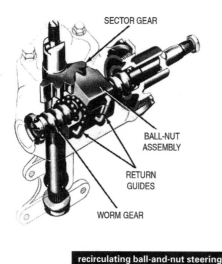

recirculating ball-and-nut steering

rebound   Downward movement of a car wheel and its suspension in reaction to jounce.

rebuild   Engine repair that could include replacing the crankshaft, camshaft(s), and cylinder head(s) if excessively worn and replacing or rebuilding the carburetor or fuel injection system, starter motor, or oil pump, in addition to overhauling the engine. Also see *overhaul*.

reciprocating   Motion of an object in two directions between two limiting positions; a term sometimes applied to piston engines (as opposed to rotary engines) because of the up-and-down or reciprocating motion of its pistons.

recirculating ball-and-nut steering   A steering system in which turning forces are transmitted through ball bearings from a worm gear on the steering shaft to a sector gear on the pitman arm shaft. A ball-nut assembly is filled with ball bearings which roll along grooves between the worm teeth and grooves inside the ball nut. Thus, as the steering wheel is turned, the worm gear on the end of the steering shaft rotates and the movement of the recirculating balls causes the ball nut to move up and down along the

worm. Movement of the ball nut is carried by teeth to the sector gear, which in turn moves with the ball nut to rotate the pitman arm shaft and activate the steering linkage. The balls recirculate from one end of the ball nut to the other through a pair of ball-return guides. Also called *ball-and-nut steering*, *recirculating-ball steering*, and *worm-and-sector steering*.

recirculating ball steering   See *recirculating ball-and-nut steering*.

rectifier   Electrical component in the alternator that converts alternating current to direct current.

redline

redline   A red mark or zone on most tachometers indicating the maximum rotational speed at which the engine may be safely operated. Exceeding this limit can result in internal engine damage. Many car tachometers also have a yellow or orange sector covering a rotational-speed band immediately below redline as an additional driver warning.

reed valve A type of one-way valve used in some two-cycle engines, consisting of a flat metal strip that covers a hole in the crankcase connected to the carburetor. As the piston moves up, the crankcase vacuum lifts the reed valve off the hole, causing the air-fuel mixture to flow from the carburetor into the crankcase. Then, as the piston starts to move down, pressure increases in the crankcase, pushing the reed valve down to close the hole and seal the crankcase.

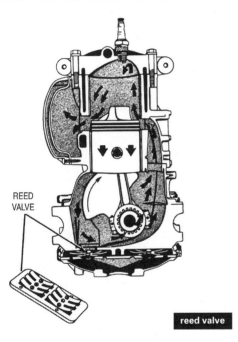

REED
VALVE

reed valve

refrigerant Substance used in an air-conditioning system that absorbs and gives up heat as it changes from a liquid to a gas to a liquid. Until recently, Freon-12 was used, but most new cars use R134a, a refrigerant that contains no chemicals harmful to the ozone layer.

regulator See *voltage regulator.*

relay See *cutout.*

reliability The extent to which a vehicle and its various components perform without failure throughout the vehicle's service life, i.e., resist normal wear-and-tear given only the routine maintenance specified by the manufacturer. Widely regarded as a component of quality. Also see *durability.*

relief valve See *pressure-relief valve.*

Research Octane Number (RON) See *octane number.*

reservoir A container in which a fluid is held. Automotive applications include reservoirs for coolant recovery, for brake and clutch fluids, and for windshield washer fluid.

MAX
MIN

reservoir

resistance In physics, a force opposing any motion. Resistance forces an engine must overcome to propel a car include the air through which it must be pushed, friction in tires and mechanical components, and (in uphill motion) gravity.

In electricity, resistance to the flow of current exists in all conductors. In an electric circuit, the current is equal to the voltage divided by the resistance.

resistor spark plug See *suppressor spark plug.*

resonance induction A supercharging effect resulting from harmonic resonance of

R

vibrating columns of air in an engine's intake pipes; boosts engine torque and power in a specific speed range determined by the pipes' length and diameter. Also called *ram effect*.

resonator   A small auxiliary muffler that assists the main muffler in reducing exhaust noise. Generally, the main muffler reduces noise in one frequency range and the resonator reduces noise in another.

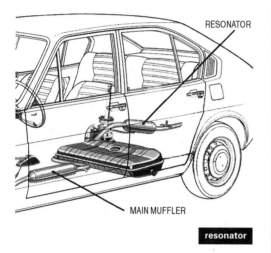

RESONATOR

MAIN MUFFLER

resonator

retard   To adjust the timing of a camshaft, distributor spark, or valve operation so that a valve opens or a spark plug fires later in the engine's cycle; also, the mechanism for doing this. The opposite of *advance*.

returnability   A characteristic of the steering and suspension geometries which causes the steering wheel to positively return to the on-center position after completing a turn. Also see *kingpin inclination*.

rev counter   See *tachometer*.

rev limit   The maximum crankshaft rotational speed at which an engine may be operated for sustained periods without incurring damage. Also see *redline*.

rev limiter   A device that prevents an engine from exceeding a specified rotational speed. Used to reduce undue wear and tear on an engine and thus prolong its life, especially on high-performance production models. Also sometimes necessary because one or more internal components, such as the valve train, are not designed for sustained operation above a certain rotational speed. The most common type of rev limiter is the ignition cutout, which interrupts electrical current from the distributor to the spark plugs above a given rotational speed.

revolutions per mile   Measured number of revolutions for a tire traveling one mile. This can vary with speed, load, and inflation pressure.

revolutions per minute (rpm)   Standard measure for rotational speed; used to express the speed at which an engine's crankshaft and other rotating components turn.

ribbed belt   A fan belt or accessory drive belt with a ribbed cross section.

rich   An air-fuel mixture that has more fuel than is needed for normal operation of the engine. Caused by maladjustment and/or malfunction of one or more fuel system components. May inhibit starting and smooth running. An excessively rich mixture can foul spark plugs and may result in black smoke emitted from the exhaust pipe. The opposite of lean. Also see *driveability* and *lean*.

ride   The dynamic behavior of a car's suspension, wheels, and tires over various road surfaces, as experienced by passengers. The ride motions of a given car are largely determined by its suspension geometry, spring and shock-absorber rates, sprung and unsprung weight, and the design and inflation pressure of its tires. The word ride is used primarily to describe a car's riding comfort or lack of it; handling and roadholding are used to describe its response to steering forces. Also see *porpoising, pitch, wheel patter* or *bump-thump, float,* and *bottoming* or *crashing through*.

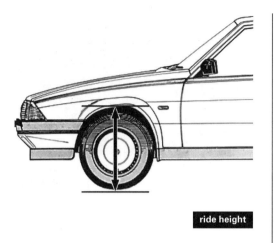

ride height

ride height The distance from the ground to a fixed reference point (which varies with different automakers) on a car's body. This dimension can be used to measure the amount of suspension travel or the height of the body from the ground. With many current race cars, maintaining a constant ride height is critical to achieving consistent downforce from air being tunneled under the car.

ride steer See *bump steer.*

rigid axle See *axle.*

rim That portion of a wheel to which a tire is mounted. Its primary functions include ensuring, together with the tire bead, an airtight seal for the tire, transmission of all forces and torques required for traction (acceleration, braking, and cornering) to the ground through the tire, and easy mounting and demounting of the tire.

rim diameter Diameter of the rim bead seats supporting the tire.

rim width Linear distance between rim flanges.

ring-and-pinion A gearset consisting of a small pinion gear which turns a large-diameter annular (ring) gear. An example is a differential's

driving (pinion) and driven (ring) gears. Also see *final drive ratio* and *hypoid gear.*

ring gear A ring-shaped bevel gear that bolts to a flange on the differential case and meshes with the drive pinion on the end of the driveshaft. Also used at the circumference of the flywheel to engage the starter motor. Also see *planetary gears* and *starter.*

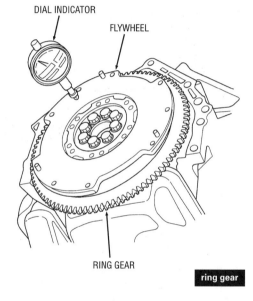

DIAL INDICATOR

FLYWHEEL

RING GEAR

ring gear

ring groove A slot in a piston into which a piston ring is fitted.

rings See *piston rings, oil control ring,* and *compression ring.*

rising-rate suspension A suspension system in which the spring rates increase as the wheels move farther into jounce. This can be achieved with rising-rate geometry, progressive-rate springs with varying wire diameter or varying distances between coils, two or more springs, or progressive compression of rubber springs or rubber jounce stops. The aim is to maintain consistent ride and handling characteristics under maxi-

R

mum and minimum passenger, fuel, and luggage loads; to provide a soft ride over minor road irregularities and firm control over major ones; or to achieve a soft ride in straight-line driving without sacrificing roll stiffness in cornering. On race cars, another purpose is to keep the car on an even keel on bumpy surfaces so that the wings can generate consistent downforce.

roadster

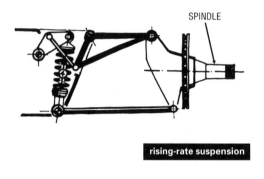

rising-rate suspension

road feel See *self-aligning torque.*

roadholding The degree to which a car maintains contact with the road surface in various types of directional changes and in a straight line. Lateral acceleration on a skid pad and time and speed through a slalom course are the measurements most frequently used to assess roadholding objectively.

roadster A two-door open body type often confused with a convertible coupe. Traditionally, a roadster had side curtains rather than roll-down windows and often a soft top that was not permanently attached to the body nor folded into a stowage well. Traditional British roadsters often employ a tonneau for full or partial cockpit protection in wet weather. Today, the term is more widely applied and includes two-seat convertibles with roll-down windows. Also see *tonneau cover.*

rocker arm A lever located on a fulcrum or shaft, one end contacting the valve stem, the other contacting either a pushrod (in overhead-valve engines) or a camshaft lobe (in some overhead-cam engines). As the camshaft rotates, the arms rock on their fulcrums, causing the valves to open and close.

rocker-arm suspension A suspension system developed primarily for open-wheel race cars and initially designed to remove the spring/shock hardware from the sidepod airflow to improve the aerodynamics of the car. The complex arms/linkages developed to actuate the

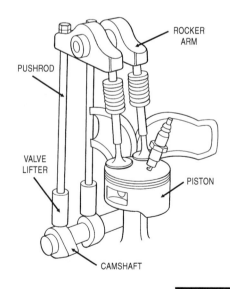

rocker arm

spring/shock mechanisms operate in a manner similar to the rocker arms that open and close the valves in a pushrod engine. Also see *rising-rate suspension* and *push-pull suspension*.

rocker panel   The area on a car body immediately below the door sills and extending longitudinally between the front and rear wheel arches.

rocker panel

rod   See *connecting rod.*

rod bearing   The bearing that fits between the connecting rod and the crankshaft in a piston engine. Also called *big-end bearing.*

roll   The rotating motion about a car's longitudinal centerline that causes the springs on one side to compress and those on the other side to extend. Also known as *body lean.*

ROLL ANGLE   GROUND LINE
roll

roll axis   A longitudinal line drawn through the front and rear roll centers, about which the entire body rotates or rolls. The slope of the roll axis affects handling; one sloping downward toward the front tends to increase understeer and one sloping downward toward the rear tends to increase oversteer. Also see *roll center.*

roll bar   A tubular steel structural bar, installed above and behind the driver and extending across the car, to protect the driver from injury if the car overturns.

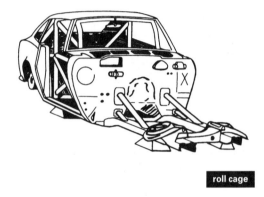
roll cage

roll cage   A tubular steel structure incorporating a roll bar plus additional bars along doors, windshield header, and roof rails; built into some racing cars to protect the driver from injury in case of accident. Adding a roll cage also usually increases chassis strength and stiffness, thus providing more predictable and consistent handling characteristics.

roll center   That point about which a car body rolls when cornering. On any suspension system whose movement is controlled entirely by linkages, the roll center can be determined by suspension geometry.

   To find the roll center, first find the point at which the linkages on one side intersect with an imaginary line drawn to the center of the tire's contact patch on the same side of the car. The

R

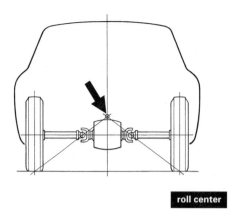

roll center

point at which this line intersects with the car's vertical centerline is the roll center.

The front roll center is generally at a different height than the rear roll center. All other things being equal, the lower the roll axis, the greater the amount of roll, so the height of the roll centers have an important influence on handling. Also see *roll axis*.

roll couple   A couple is defined as two equal forces acting in opposite directions in the same plane. In the illustration, force A produces a torque about X. This torque can also be described as being produced by forces B and C,

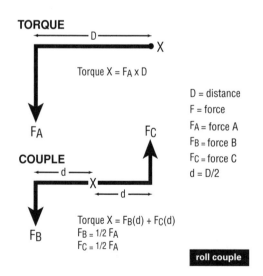

TORQUE

Torque X = F_A x D

COUPLE

Torque X = F_B(d) + F_C(d)
F_B = 1/2 F_A
F_C = 1/2 F_A

D = distance
F = force
F_A = force A
F_B = force B
F_C = force C
d = D/2

roll couple

which are equal and act in opposite directions at equal radii from X. B and C are the roll couple. In automotive engineering the concept is used to describe cornering forces. Also see *torque*.

roller bearing   A mechanical bearing using cylindrical rollers to reduce friction.

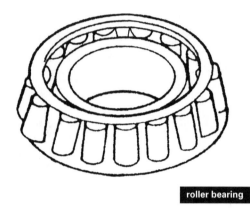

roller bearing

rolling circumference   The distance covered in one complete revolution of a tire on an asphalt road at the speed of 62 mph or 100 kph, under the load and pressure conditions shown in standard tables. In radial-ply tires, rolling circumference remains constant; in cross-ply tires, however, it varies according to speed, load, and air pressure.

rolling radius   The distance from the center of a tire's contact patch to the center of the wheel rim, i.e., a tire's effective radius when rolling. The distance will vary based on air pressure and the weight supported by the tire. To measure this distance, one applies the formula:

$$r = \frac{D}{6.28n}$$

where D = distance traveled, n = number of revolutions the tire rolled in distance D, and r = rolling radius. Also see *static loaded radius*.

rolling resistance   The friction in bearings and in the flexing of tires that must be overcome for a car's wheels to turn or to maintain speed. Rolling resistance does not include air resistance, and is affected by tire construction and tread design. Most of the power expended in a rolling wheel is converted into heat within the tire. The consequent rise in temperature reduces both the abrasive resistance and flex fatigue of the tire material and becomes the limiting factor of a tire's performance and longevity. On normal road surfaces, rolling resistance decreases with increasing tire pressure and increases with vehicle weight.

roll resistance   See *roll stiffness*.

roll steer   A handling characteristic that results in a slight over- or understeer as the suspension moves in body roll. Roll steer is often purposely designed into the suspension to achieve some desired handling characteristic, but can also result from improper suspension location.

roll stiffness   When a car's body rolls, the turning moment or torque exerted by the suspension to try to pull the body back to its normal upright position. Roll stiffness is expressed in lb-ft/degree of roll and is basically a function of the spring rates and the perpendicular distance from the springs to the roll center. The stiffer the springs or the greater this distance, the larger the roll stiffness and the flatter the car will corner. Also called *roll resistance*.

ROM   Read-only memory. See *memory*.

RON   Research Octane Number. See *octane number*.

roof rail   See *drip molding*.

Roots supercharger   A type of supercharger with two hourglass-shaped rotors, named for its inventors, Francis and Philander Roots. Also see *supercharger*.

rotary engine   The general term for an engine in which the burning of the air-fuel mixture is used to spin a rotor or wheel, thus producing rotary motion directly instead of using the rec-

iprocating motion of pistons to turn a crankshaft. Because of this, rotary engines are inherently more balanced than conventional piston engines. The most common rotary internal combustion engine is the Wankel. See *Wankel engine*.

rotary valve   A semicircular rotating disc in the cylinder wall of a two-stroke engine which opens and closes the intake port.

rotational speed   The speed at which an object or machine rotates, normally expressed in revolutions per minute.

rotor   In a mechanical ignition distributor, the small rotating device mounted on the breaker cam inside the cap. It connects the center electrode and the various outer spark plug terminals as it turns, distributing high voltage

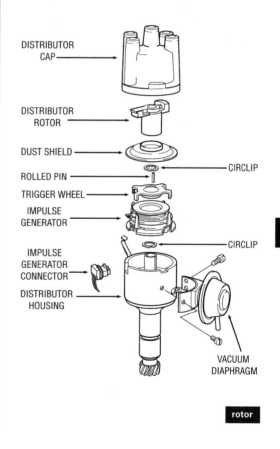

DISTRIBUTOR CAP

DISTRIBUTOR ROTOR

DUST SHIELD

ROLLED PIN

TRIGGER WHEEL

IMPULSE GENERATOR

IMPULSE GENERATOR CONNECTOR

DISTRIBUTOR HOUSING

CIRCLIP

CIRCLIP

VACUUM DIAPHRAGM

rotor

R

from the coil's secondary winding to the proper spark plug.

In a rotary engine, the element or elements driven by the force of the air-fuel explosion.

In a disc brake, the circular component that rotates with the wheel.

rotor seal   See *apex seal.*

rpm   See *revolutions per minute.*

rubbing compound   See *glaze.*

rumble   A noise found particularly in high-compression engines and associated with the bending vibration of the crankshaft. It is caused by an abnormally high degree of pressure rise as the pistons near top dead center.

Also, a type of low-frequency road noise resulting from a tire rolling over a surface — the more aggressive the tread pattern and the rougher the road surface, the louder the rumble.

rumble seat   An auxiliary seat in early roadsters for one or two passengers, situated outside the main passenger compartment and some-times furnished with a separate, shallow windshield but otherwise open to the elements. Popular in the twenties and early thirties, it has since been revived for the occasional show car but has yet to reappear on a production model.

run-in   See *break-in.*

running gear   The components attached to the underbody of a vehicle, including the wheels, tires, steering, suspension, brakes, and drivetrain.

run-on   A form of auto-ignition in which a gasoline engine continues to fire after the ignition has been shut off. In late-model emission-controlled engines, run-on or dieseling is caused by the heat and unusually high manifold pressure that result from retarding the spark at idle.

runout   The amount a gear or wheel moves in and out from its true center as it is rotated. If runout is excessive, the gear or wheel can be seen to wobble as it rotates.

RWD   See *rear-wheel-drive.*

SAE   See *Society of Automotive Engineers*.

SAE net horsepower   The dynamometer brake horsepower of an engine corrected to SAE standards, which include an ambient temperature of 60 degrees Fahrenheit and a barometric pressure of 29.0 inches of mercury.

safety belt   See *seat belt*.

safety glass   A heat-treated or tempered glass with a very thin but tough surface layer. When seriously damaged, tempered glass shatters into a flimsy "mosaic" of blunt crystals that seriously impairs visibility and will cause lacerations upon impact. Tempered glass is used for the side and back windows of an automobile. Also see *laminated glass*.

safety rim   Wheel rim with a channel to secure the tire bead on the rim in case of a blowout.

sail panel   See *C-pillar*.

saloon   British term for sedan; see *sedan*.

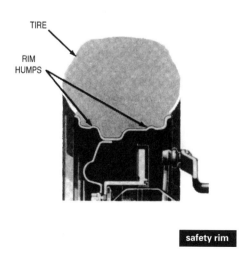

TIRE

RIM
HUMPS

safety rim

same-steer   See *four-wheel steering*.

sandblast   To clean or polish a surface or part using compressed air or steam to force an abrasive material such as sand against it.

scavenge pump   In a dry sump lubrication system, the pump that returns oil to the sump.

scavenging   Removal of exhaust gases from an engine cylinder using the momentum of the exhaust gases in a long exhaust pipe or by taking advantage of the pressure waves set up in the exhaust pipe by the discharge of the gases.

scoop   See *air scoop*.

scope   See *oscilloscope*.

score   A scratch, ridge, or groove marring a finished surface.

SCR   See *silicon-controlled rectifier*.

scrub   See *tire scrub*.

scrub radius   See *steering offset*.

SCS   See *Stop Control System*.

scuffing   Unwanted friction. Roughening of the cylinder bore surface due to lack of lubrication between the piston and the cylinder wall is called cylinder scuffing. Roughening of the piston is called piston scuffing. A worn or unbalanced crankshaft can cause excessive thrust on the piston leading to cylinder wall and piston scuffing. Also see *skirt*.

scuttle   See *cowl*.

sealed beam   A hermetically sealed headlight unit in which the filament is an integral part of the unit and the lens itself is the bulb. Relatively

S

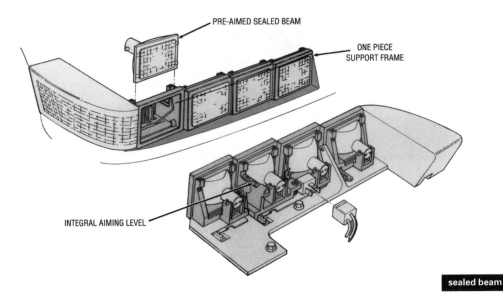

PRE-AIMED SEALED BEAM

ONE PIECE
SUPPORT FRAME

INTEGRAL AIMING LEVEL

sealed beam

inexpensive, the entire unit is replaced when it burns out or if the lens cracks.

seat   A surface, usually machined, upon which another part such as a valve face rests or seats. Also see illustration for *valve*.

seat back   Vertical portion of a car seat supporting the occupant's back and shoulders. Also called *backrest*. Also see *lumbar support*.

seat-back angle   The number of degrees from vertical that the seat back is raked rearward. On most seats the angle can be individually adjusted

via a rotating knob, a lever, or electrically. Also called *rake adjustment*.

seat belt   The primary device in a vehicle to restrain the driver or passenger in the event of an accident, typically consisting of a lap belt attached across the hips and a shoulder belt running diagonally across the chest and connecting to the seat belt assembly. Also called *safety belt*.

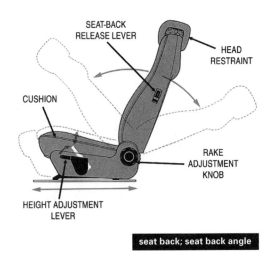

SEAT-BACK
RELEASE LEVER

HEAD
RESTRAINT

CUSHION

RAKE
ADJUSTMENT
KNOB

HEIGHT ADJUSTMENT
LEVER

seat back; seat back angle

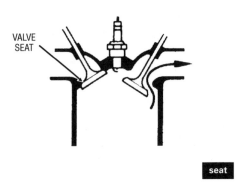

VALVE
SEAT

seat

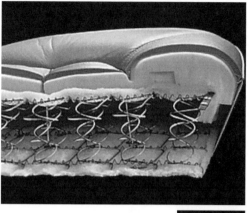

seat cushion

seat cushion   The horizontal portion of a car seat supporting the occupant's posterior and thighs.

secondary brake shoe   The rear or trailing shoe on a drum brake. Also see *primary brake shoe.*

secondary circuit   The path of high-voltage current in the ignition system from the coil secondary winding to the distributor cap and rotor to the spark plug cables to the spark plugs.

Also, the secondary fuel passages, containing the secondary jet(s), in a carburetor.

section height   The distance from the rim seat to the outer tread surface of an unloaded inflated tire. Section height can be approximated by multiplying the section width by the aspect ratio.

section width   The measurement, sidewall-to-sidewall, in millimeters, of an inflated and unloaded tire, not including protective side ribs, lettering, or embellishments.

sector gear   A gear used in recirculating ball-and-nut steering; so-named because it is a portion of a circle. Also see *recirculating ball-and-nut steering.*

sedan   Typically a closed car with four doors (but sometimes two and possibly three or five in a hatchback), four or six side windows, fixed B-pillars, and seating for four or more occupants. Sedans are intended for family transport and are generally driven by the owner. The term is derived from a kind of handcart used in the township of Sedan in France to transport fish; it was later applied to the sedan chair, a single-seat conveyance carried by two bearers. Also see *saloon* and *Berlina.*

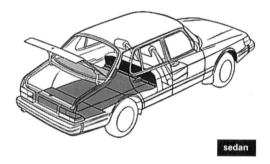

sedan

seize   To bind or weld together two materials, typically metal, generally as a result of excessive heat caused by improper lubrication. Common examples are a piston seizing to a cylinder wall and a bearing seizing to the crankshaft.

self-aligning torque   Torque created at the dynamic road contact patch because the force generated by the tire when the car is cornering actually acts at a point somewhat to the rear of the actual wheel center due to a phenomenon known as pneumatic trail. Self-aligning torque has the same effect as — and can be magnified by — increasing positive caster. The trail distance (from the point at which the cornering force acts to the center of the wheel or steering axis) is a moment arm that results in a torque that tends to force the wheel back to the straight-ahead position. This self-aligning torque is transmitted through the steering mechanism to the steering wheel and can be felt as steering effort or road feel.

S

self-energizing brakes See *primary brake shoe.*

self-leveling suspension See *automatic leveling.*

semiconductor An electrical conductor whose conductivity is similar to a metal at high temperatures and to an insulator at low temperatures. Semiconductors are frequently used in integrated circuits.

semi-elliptic spring A leaf spring that takes its name from being shaped like roughly half an ellipse. Also see *leaf spring.*

semi-floating axle A drive-axle construction in which the axle shaft supports the weight of the car in addition to being the means of propulsion. Unlike a full-floating axle, in which each wheel hub is fully supported by bearings on both sides of the hub, a semi-floating axle uses a single bearing. The drawbacks of this design are that to remove the axle, the wheel must first be removed, and if an axle shaft breaks, the wheel also comes off.

semi-monocoque A tubular chassis with stressed body panels. Also see *monocoque.*

semi-trailing arm A popular, relatively simple type of independent rear suspension in which a single control arm per side pivots along an axis other than the car's transverse or longitudinal axis. This gives rear-wheel camber between that of a swing axle (negative camber on the outside rear wheel under roll) and a pure trailing arm (positive camber on the outer wheel under roll). By combining the two, it is possible to design a system to give minimal camber change under roll.

sending unit A mechanical, electromechanical, electric, or electronic sensing device which measures a physical property such as temperature or pressure and transmits a signal to a gauge or warning light. Also called a *sensor unit.*

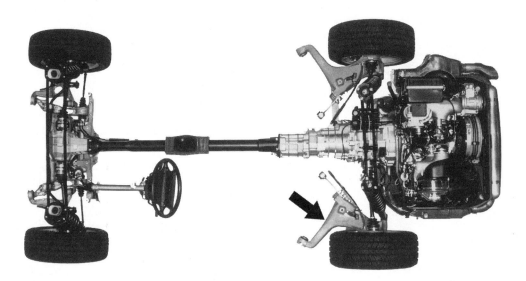

semi-trailing arm

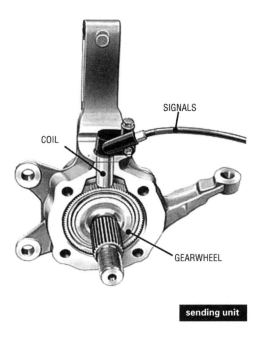

COIL

SIGNALS

GEARWHEEL

sending unit

serpentine belt

sensor plate In a continuous-flow fuel injection system, the plate in the intake airstream which measures the airflow.

sensor unit See *sending unit*.

sequential fuel injection See *fuel injection*.

series See *aspect ratio*.

serpentine belt A flat, grooved fan or drive belt which follows a path over, under, and around a number of pulleys to drive several engine accessories such as the alternator and water pump. This single belt takes the place of various individual fan belts.

servo action See *primary brake shoe*.

setscrew A type of screw, typically with a point that fits into a matching recess in a shaft, used to secure a small gear, cam, or pulley to a shaft.

shackle A swinging support by which one end of a leaf spring is attached to the car frame

to accommodate the change in a spring's length as it deforms in response to wheel deflection.

shaved tire A tire whose tread has been planed to extremely low depths (typically 3/32 in.) for racing.

shell See *body-in-white*.

shift fork Rod with a U-shaped end which slides the gears or synchronizers inside a manual transmission. See illustration for *bell housing*.

shift lever See *gearshift*.

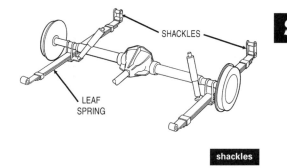

SHACKLES

LEAF SPRING

shackles

S

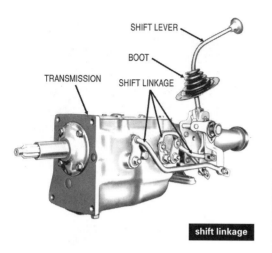

SHIFT LEVER

BOOT

TRANSMISSION

SHIFT LINKAGE

shift linkage

shift linkage   Rods, levers, and cables used to convert motion of the shift lever into movement of the gears in a gearbox.

shim   A thin metal strip used as a spacer between parts.

shimmy   Rapid lateral movement of a car's front wheels, typically experienced as vibration in the steering wheel. Often caused by unbalanced wheels/tires, improper alignment of the suspension and/or steering linkage, or poor front-suspension geometry.

shock   See *shock absorber.*

shock absorber   A friction device, often shortened to shock, that controls and damps spring oscillations. Thus "shock absorber" is a misnomer; springs actually absorb road shocks. Shock absorbers convert the energy imparted to them into heat (by friction) that is then dissipated to the atmosphere or the car's chassis. They are distinguishable by the type of friction involved, mechanical or hydraulic, but contemporary cars all use tubular-shaped hydraulic units. Because shocks affect up-and-down wheel motion, they are an important element in tuning a car's ride and handling. In Britain, called a *damper.* Also see *friction shock absorber.*

shoe   See *brake shoe.*

shooting brake   See *station wagon.*

short   See *short circuit.*

short block   An engine block with all internal components such as pistons, rods, and crankshaft, but minus all bolt-on components such as the heads, manifolds, carburetor/fuel injection, and other accessories.

short circuit   Defect in an electrical circuit that permits current to take an alternate, usually shorter path to ground instead of the prescribed path, often resulting in a burned out circuit and/or failure of an electrical device. Abbreviated as *short.*

short-long arms   See *unequal-length A-arms.*

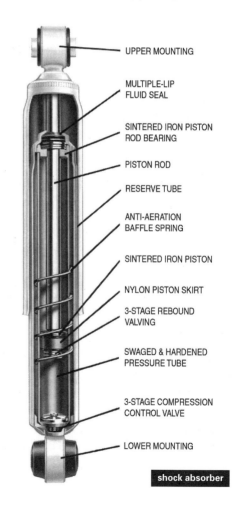

UPPER MOUNTING

MULTIPLE-LIP FLUID SEAL

SINTERED IRON PISTON ROD BEARING

PISTON ROD

RESERVE TUBE

ANTI-AERATION BAFFLE SPRING

SINTERED IRON PISTON

NYLON PISTON SKIRT

3-STAGE REBOUND VALVING

SWAGED & HARDENED PRESSURE TUBE

3-STAGE COMPRESSION CONTROL VALVE

LOWER MOUNTING

shock absorber

shot peen A surface treatment for metals. In a process similar to sandblasting, a part is blasted with steel shot to strengthen it and reduce the chance of stress cracks.

shrink fit An extremely tight fit achieved by heating a part above its normal temperature and/or chilling its mating part before assembly, then allowing them to return to normal temperature.

shroud See *fan shroud*.

siamesed Joined or paired parts. Engine ports arranged with their intake or exhaust valves in pairs, allowing two-into-one passages to be cast into the cylinder head. Also applies to two cylinders connected solidly together instead of each being surrounded by water jackets, and to two exhaust pipes joined together.

side curtain A detachable window typically consisting of a metal frame surrounding a panel of fabric and a transparent material, used to provide a degree of side protection for open cars in inclement weather.

side-draft carburetor A carburetor with a horizontal barrel through which the air-fuel mixture flows horizontally to the intake manifold and cylinders.

side force The lateral force acting on a turning vehicle that attempts to push it out of the turn. When the side force exceeds the tires' cornering force, the vehicle reaches its cornering limit and begins to slide. Also see *centrifugal force, oversteer, understeer,* and *neutral steer*.

sidepod That portion of the body work on a single-seater race car that extends on either side of the cockpit and bridges the opening between front and rear wheels. Often contains openings and ducts for internal radiators and intercoolers. See illustration for *blown* and *single-seater*.

sidepod airflow Air flowing over the sidepods of a single-seater race car to create downforce. See illustration for *blown* and *single-seater*.

side rail In an automotive frame, the parallel longitudinal members connected by cross members.

side valve See *flathead*.

sidewall The part of the tire lying between the bead and the tread. It consists of the set of casing plies covered with a thin layer of rubber that protects it from accidental friction (such as against curbs). Because it undergoes distortion from the load bearing down on the tire, it's most significant property is its flexibility.

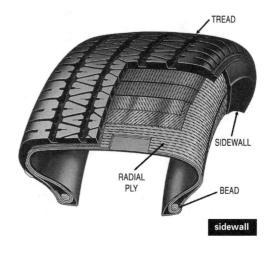

sidewall

sidewall height See *section height*.

sidewinder A vehicle with its engine mounted transversely. Also called *east-west location*. Also see *transverse engine*.

silencer An exhaust muffler. Also see *muffler*.

silicon-controlled rectifier (SCR) An electrical device that converts alternating current to direct current.

silicon-impregnated aluminum Material used in cylinder blocks, in which silicon is mixed with the aluminum before casting. After casting, a chemical process etches away a thin layer of aluminum, leaving the silicon crystals as the cylinder walls' actual working surface. Saves

weight by eliminating the need for separate iron cylinder liners.

sill   The horizontal frame member underneath the doors of a car body.

single overhead cam (SOHC)   An engine in which one overhead camshaft operates all the valves of a given cylinder head. Also see *overhead cam.*

single-point injection   See *fuel injection.*

single-seater   A term generally applied to Grand Prix, Indy, and other Formula and racing cars of single-seat design.

SIDEPOD

sintered metal   Metal heated below its melting point, then forced into molds or dies.

skid pad   A flat, smooth expanse of pavement marked with a circle of known radius and used for various handling tests. Also see *lateral acceleration*.

skirt   The main section of a piston that forms a bearing surface in contact with the cylinder wall and takes the lateral thrust transmitted from the crankshaft through the connecting rod. Also see *airdam*. See illustration for *piston*.

slalom

slalom   A maneuverability test used by automakers and car magazines in which several cones or markers are placed in a straight line at equal intervals. The object for the driver and car is to negotiate the slalom course by steering to the left and right of successive markers as quickly as possible.

Also, a competition-driving event consisting of a series of turns and straightaways defined by cones. Generally set up in a parking lot, the object is to drive around the course as quickly as possible without knocking down cones. Touching or knocking down a cone usually results in a time penalty being added to the competitor's lap time. In a slalom, competitors race against the clock, not against other competitors who are on the course at the same time. Also called *autocross*.

slap   See *piston slap*.

slave cylinder   A cylinder and piston directly controlled by hydraulic pressure from a master cylinder to operate a mechanical component on a clutch or brake. A typical example would be a hydraulically actuated clutch.

sleeve   See *liner*.

sleeve valve   A reciprocating or oscillating cylinder sleeve that functions as a valve as it covers or uncovers the intake and exhaust ports. Primarily found in older engines.

slick

slick   A wide treadless tire of soft rubber used for racing on dry surfaces.

sliding caliper   See *floating caliper*.

sliding-gear transmission   See *constant-mesh gearbox*.

slip angle   The angular difference between the direction a wheel is traveling and the direction of the tread, resulting from the tire carcass's flexibility. If, when cornering, the slip angles of the rear tires are greater than those of the front tires, a car is said to oversteer. Greater slip angles

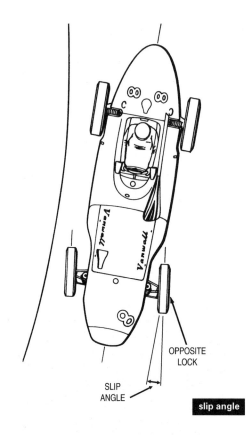

OPPOSITE
LOCK

SLIP
ANGLE

slip angle

SKIRT

slipper skirt piston

at the front result in understeer, and equal slip angles at the front and rear result in neutral steering. Also see *neutral steer, oversteer,* and *understeer.*

slip joint Variable-length connection that permits the driveshaft or axle shaft to change length as it moves up and down.

slipper skirt piston A piston with its lower edge cut away so that the piston skirt is short. Such a design lightens the piston, making it easier to accelerate and decelerate, thus reducing power loss and bearing wear. Cutting away the skirt also allows for a shorter connecting rod, but leaves enough room between counterweights and pistons so that the engine's overall height can be reduced.

slipstream The low-pressure area created behind a vehicle at high speeds. Also see *drafting.*

sludge Composite of oxidized petroleum products, oil, and water forming a pasty substance that can clog oil lines and passages and interfere with engine lubrication.

slush box Jargon for an automatic transmission.

smog A combination of the words smoke and fog. Smog is composed of smoke, moisture, and chemicals produced by combustion from power plants, burning garbage, automotive engines, and natural and industrial processes. Formation is aided by the presence of sunlight, which reacts with chemicals and combustion products to form other, more noxious compounds, often seen as a fog-like layer hanging over metropolitan areas.

snap ring Ring-shaped clip used to prevent lengthwise movement of cylindrical parts and shafts or to retain a cylindrical part within a housing. An internal snap ring is used in a groove in a housing; an external snap ring fits in

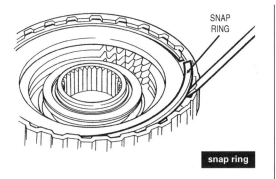

SNAP
RING

snap ring

a groove cut on the outside of a cylindrical piece such as a shaft.

snubber   A rubber bump stop used to limit suspension travel. Also see *bump stop*.

Society of Automotive Engineers (SAE) A professional engineering organization that publishes research papers and defines various standards of measurement for the American automobile industry. Their field of influence and expertise has expanded to other engineering fields, and today the organization prefers the title "SAE International, The Engineering Society for Advanced Mobility Land Sea Air and Space." Also see *SAE net horsepower*.

sodium-cooled valve   An exhaust valve having a hollow stem filled with sodium. When

the valve heats to 280 degrees Fahrenheit, the sodium melts and splashes up and down in the stem, absorbing heat from the valve head and carrying it away to the cooler stem and thus into the valve guide in the cylinder head. This circulation cools the valve head, resulting in lower valve temperatures.

soft top   The fold-down top on a convertible, or the vehicle itself.

SOHC   See *single overhead cam*.

solenoid   An iron core, surrounded by a coil of wire, which is activated by magnetic attraction when electric current is fed to the coil, thus converting electrical energy to mechanical energy. This movement can be used to open and close a valve or as a switch.

solid axle   See *axle*.

solid-state ignition   An ignition system using electronic components such as diodes and transistors instead of mechanical parts such as points and a rotor to control spark timing.

space frame   Frame construction consisting of numerous lengths of tubing welded into a weblike structure to which the engine, suspen-

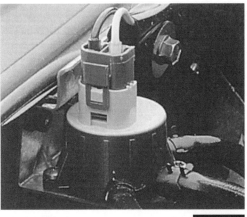

solenoid

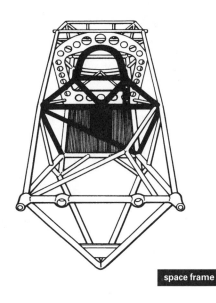

space frame

S

space-saver spare tire

wheel so as to occupy minimum space in a car. Typically designed only for speeds below 50 mph and distances of one hundred miles or less, and thus sometimes called a "get you home" spare.

spark advance   See *advance.*

spark gap   See *gap.*

spark ignition   An internal combustion engine in which the air-fuel mixture is ignited in a combustion chamber by an electrical spark.

spark knock   See *preignition.*

spark plug   Electrical device inserted into the combustion chamber of an internal combustion engine to ignite the air-fuel mixture. High-tension voltage jumps across a gap formed by two electrodes to create a spark. The plug's center electrode is connected to the ignition coil's secondary winding through the distributor, and is insulated from the spark plug shell. The other electrode protrudes from the shell's bottom edge

sion, and other components are attached; offers high rigidity for minimum weight. Used in some racing and low-volume production cars.

space-saver spare tire   A temporary tire with a very narrow tread, mounted on a similarly slim

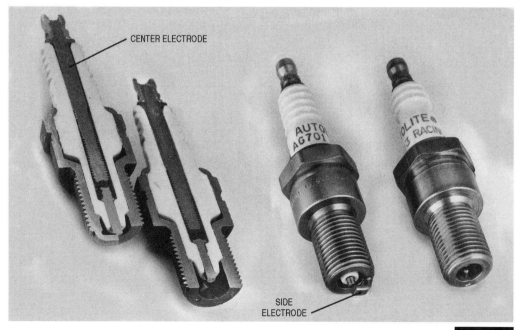

CENTER ELECTRODE

SIDE
ELECTRODE

spark plug

and is positioned to form a small gap with the center electrode.

specific fuel consumption See *brake specific fuel consumption.*

speed The rate of motion at which an object travels, usually measured in ft/sec, km/h, or mph. Also see *velocity.*

speed control See *cruise control.*

speedometer An instrument for measuring and indicating the speed at which a car is traveling.

speedometer

speed rating A letter imprinted on a tire's sidewall to indicate its maximum speed for short periods of time when properly inflated and not overloaded. The speed rating appears in one of two forms: as a letter preceding the construction type (as in P175/70**H**R13 or 225/50**V**R15) or following the load index (as in 195/60R14 85**T**).

All European tires carry a speed rating, ranging from A5 (a maximum of 15 mph for forklift tires) to Z (speeds above 149 mph).

Only some tires produced in the United States carry speed ratings, but all new tires must be capable of 85 mph. The most common speed ratings are: S (112 mph), T (118 mph), H (130 mph), V (149 mph), W (168 mph), and Z (over 149 mph).

The ability to withstand higher sustained speeds is only one characteristic of speed-rated tires. Speed ratings are not so much a measure of speed as they are a measure of performance and quality. Generally, the higher a tire's speed rating, the better its resistance to heat build-up. High-speed tires provide better wet and dry traction and stability and thus will have enhanced ability to corner, brake, and accelerate.

speed-sensitive power steering

speed-sensitive power steering A steering system in which engine or vehicle speed is measured, typically by an electronic sensor, and the power steering assist pressure is increased or decreased through a series of valves. These adjustments make the steering wheel easier to turn at lower speeds or while parallel parking. At higher speeds the system increases the steering effort to provide better road feel, and more turning effort is required to alter the car's course. Also see *variable-assist power steering.*

S

speed shift   A drag racing technique in which the driver keeps the accelerator flat to the floor while upshifting a manual transmission. Executed correctly, this technique reduces the time needed to complete each upshift, resulting in a quicker elapsed time, but is also extremely abusive to the entire drivetrain.

spherical rod end   See *Heim joint.*

spider

spider   Originally a light, spindly horse-drawn conveyance. The term was applied to early lightweight two-seat motorcars and was revived by the Italians after World War II to designate an open two-seat sporting car. Also called *spyder.*

spider gear   One of two to four small gears in the differential that mesh with bevel gears on the

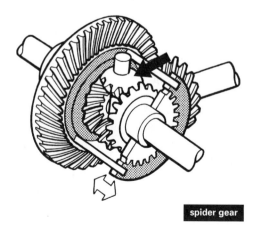

spider gear

ends of the axles. Spider gears allow each wheel to rotate at its own speed as the vehicle goes around a corner. Also see *pinion gear.*

spindle   The short shaft on which a wheel rotates. Generally refers to the front wheels but can also be applied to certain types of independent rear suspension. Also called *stub axle.* See illustration for *rising-rate suspension.*

spline   One of several lengthwise grooves cut internally or externally into a shaft or gear. Meshing splines enforce mutual rotation of parts and, at the same time, permit freedom of lengthwise motion.

spoiler   Aerodynamic device attached to a car, usually under the front bumper or on the deck lid, to either reduce drag or induce downforce.

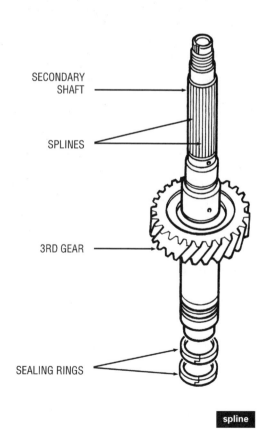

SECONDARY SHAFT

SPLINES

3RD GEAR

SEALING RINGS

spline

spoiler

So called because it "spoils" normal airflow over or under the car.

sports car   Once used to describe any open car with sporting pretensions, current use embraces two-seat and two-plus-two open designs with low sleek bodies as well as their closed coupe equivalents, which should be more precisely called Grand Touring, Gran Turismo, or simply GT cars. In truth, these days a sports car can include almost any performance car that is exhilarating to drive and puts a smile on the driver's face.

sport utility vehicle (SUV)   Basically a hybrid of a pickup truck and a station wagon. Typically uses a trucklike frame and suspension and a wagonlike extended body to combine comfort and good off-road performance with heavy-duty carrying and towing capabilities. All but the smallest offer seating for five or more,

rear- or four-wheel-drive, and six- and eight-cylinder engines.

spring   An elastic metal or fiberglass device that yields under stress or pressure to absorb energy, then returns to its original state when the energy is released. Springs are used to support a car's frame, engine, and body, and to absorb shocks that result from the wheels hitting holes or bumps in the road. The most common types of springs are leaf springs, coil springs, and torsion bars, although air springs — deformable units inflated with air — are occasionally used. Also see *air suspension.*

spring rate   A constant that determines a spring's resistance to compression or extension. Spring rate is measured in pounds per inch (lb/in.). For example, if 100 lb. of force is required to compress a coil spring 1.0 in., and each addition of 100 lb. compresses the spring

S

an additional inch, its spring rate would be 100 lb./in.

The spring rate may not be a constant. For instance, using the previous example, if 100 lb. is required to compress the spring 1.0 in. but an additional 200 lb. is required to compress it an additional 1.0 in., then the spring is said to have a variable or progressive rate.

spring shackle   See *shackle*.

sprocket   A set of teeth or projections on a wheel's periphery, shaped to engage with a chain or drive belt.

sprocket

sprung weight   The parts of a car that are supported by its springs, including the frame, engine, and body. Also see *unsprung weight*.

spur gear   A gear whose teeth are parallel to its centerline. Not often used in modern gearboxes because they are noisier than helical gears. Also called *straight-cut gears*.

spyder   See *spider*.

squareback   A synonym for station wagon, but most often associated with rear-engine Type 3 and 411/412 Volkswagens. Also see *station wagon*.

squat   Settling of a car's rear end under hard acceleration.

squish area   Area in the combustion chamber of some engines in which the piston squeezes or "squishes" part of the air-fuel mixture at the end of the compression stroke. As the piston approaches top dead center, the mixture is pushed out of the squish area, which promotes turbulence and thus further mixing of the air-fuel charge for more efficient (complete) combustion.

SRS   See *supplemental restraint system*.

stability   The ability of a vehicle to remain under the driver's control during cornering or other dynamic maneuvers such as lane changes or when affected by wind or changing road surfaces. Stability implies that the vehicle's handling characteristics are predictable and linear, not twitchy or nervous, as the limit of adhesion is approached. Tires, suspension geometry, and aerodynamics all contribute to a car's stability.

Stability should not be confused with a vehicle's cornering limit. It is possible for a car with a lower cornering limit to be driven around a given corner faster than a car with higher limits if the latter exhibits dynamic behavior that makes it difficult for anyone except the most skilled driver to maintain control.

stabilizer bar   See *anti-roll bar*.

stagger   In racing, the practice of using different-sized tires on a car's two sides or adjusting the chassis for uneven ride height side-to-side to improve cornering in one direction.

stall   Unintended stopping of an engine. Stalling can occur due to electrical or fuel system problems or, in a vehicle with a manual transmission, if the driver releases the clutch pedal too abruptly when moving away from rest.

stall speed   In a torque converter, the speed at which the stator begins to rotate in the same direction as the impeller and the turbine. This

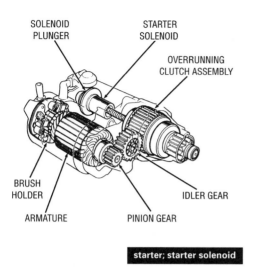

SOLENOID PLUNGER
STARTER SOLENOID
OVERRUNNING CLUTCH ASSEMBLY
BRUSH HOLDER
ARMATURE
PINION GEAR
IDLER GEAR

starter; starter solenoid

is the speed at which maximum torque multiplication occurs. Also see *torque converter*.

stamping   Cutting and forming a piece of sheet metal into a desired shape by a pair of hardened metal blocks called dies.

starter   Small electric motor that engages teeth on the engine flywheel and causes the engine to crank or turn over until it begins to run under its own power. Also called the *starter motor*.

starter motor   See *starter*.

starter solenoid   An electrical switch that transfers electricity from the battery to the starter when the ignition key is turned.

static balance   See *wheel balancing*.

static loaded radius   The distance from the center of the wheel rim to the contact surface when the tire is fitted on the measuring rim, inflated to the recommended air pressure, and the prescribed load is applied. Also see *rolling radius*.

station wagon   A two- or four-door closed body type resembling a sedan but whose roof extends to the very rear of the car to form a canopy (with side windows) over a cargo hold behind the passenger compartment; also referred to as a wagon. The roof terminates in a flat panel (the tailgate) angled at or near vertical in profile and containing the rear window. Almost all wagons have a folding back seat and/or fold-down rear seat back(s) to enlarge the cargo bay; some larger models also have a folding third seat.

Station wagon stems from the wagon-like wood-bodied utility vehicles of the early twenties used to ferry passengers and baggage between hotels and railroad stations. All-steel bodies replaced structural wood beginning in 1949, but simulated wood trim continues to echo the past on many wagons built since.

S

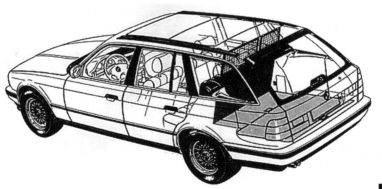

station wagon

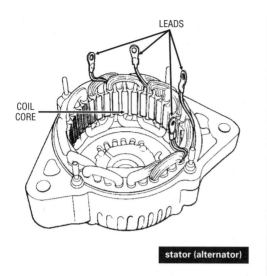

LEADS

COIL
CORE

stator (alternator)

Most station wagons now employ one-piece tailgates hinged at the top or side, and are thus termed three- and five-door models. Some older designs split the tailgate horizontally into a top-hinged liftgate and a bottom-hinged tailgate that lowers to form a platform for carrying long objects.

In England station wagons are referred to as shooting brakes, a vehicle which originally featured seats arranged in rows along each side of the body, the occupants sitting sideways to the motion of the vehicle and facing each other. A shooting brake catered to hunting parties and their equipment.

The French refer to a station wagon as a break.

stator In a torque converter, the vaned wheel interposed between the impeller and turbine that redirects oil flow from the turbine to boost impeller action and thus multiply engine torque.

In an alternator, the three stationary windings that give overlapping pulses of alternating current.

steam engine External combustion engine in which water is converted to steam in a boiler outside the cylinder. Steam is admitted to the cylinder, where it expands against a piston. As it expands, the steam cools and begins to condense. This mixture of water droplets and steam is forced out of the cylinder on the return stroke and into a condenser, where the remaining steam is condensed into water. This water is forced into the boiler by a pump, and the cycle is repeated.

Steam engines have some notable drawbacks: slow warm-up, water-system freezing in cold weather, and easy water contamination by scale, oil, and sludge that can wreak havoc on the boiler, pumps, and condenser. But they also offer certain advantages: potential high fuel economy with low emissions, the ability to start from rest against a load so that a clutch is not needed, and maximum torque at low rpm, so that in some applications a multiple-ratio gearbox is not necessary.

steel In its simplest form, essentially an alloy of pure iron with less than 2 percent carbon. Small amounts of other elements such as nickel, manganese, and chromium are frequently added to steel to vary its properties. Various types of steel are used throughout a vehicle, most notably for the frame/unit body and for the sheet metal body panels.

steering See *steering system.*

steering arm A linkage attached to the steering knuckle that turns the knuckle and wheel for steering.

steering axis The line through the center of the ball joints in a front suspension system. See illustration for *negative offset.*

steering-axis inclination The steering axis angle formed by a line drawn through the ball joint centers and the vertical tire centerline. The choice of steering axis inclination is a compromise between steering effort, returnability, and possible wheel pull while braking. Also called *kingpin inclination.* See illustration for *negative offset.*

steering box A gearbox located near the lower end of the steering shaft that converts the rotary motion of the steering wheel into the straight-line motion of the steering arms and steering knuckles.

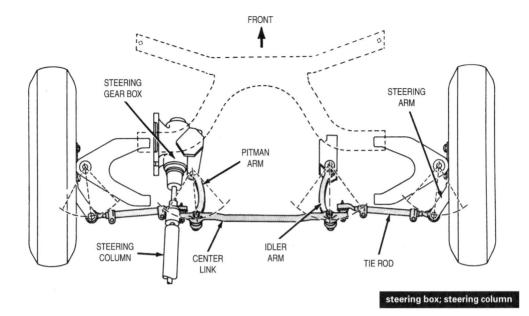

steering column A shaft connecting the steering wheel with the steering box. Also called *steering shaft*.

steering effort The general relationship between handling and the forces at the steering wheel; also called steering feel. Steering effort should build up smoothly as the wheel is moved off center. Also, steering effort should increase in a linear fashion as the cornering forces at the steered wheels increase, and friction built into the steering system should be small relative to the handling-related steering forces. Also see *self-aligning torque*.

steering feel See *steering effort*.

steering fight See *kickback*.

steering gain The relationship between steering wheel position and effort and yaw. Responsive steering demands that all three of these factors build up smoothly and be proportional.

steering geometry The relationship of the front wheels to the frame and the attachment points, including camber, caster, steering-axis inclination, and toe-in and toe-out.

steering knuckle That part of the steering system attached to the ends of the steering

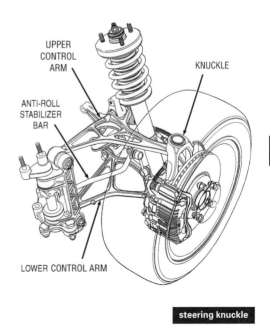

S

arms and supported by upper and lower ball joints or the kingpin, and about which the front wheels pivot.

steering linkage Rods, arms, and other links that carry movement of the pitman arm to the steering knuckles. Also see *pitman arm.*

steering lock The number of degrees that the front wheels can turn from straight ahead to extreme left or right. Generally, the more lock designed into the front geometry, the smaller the turning circle, but the more the tires scrub as the wheels approach the extreme lock positions. Also see *turns lock-to-lock.*

Also, the locking mechanism usually contained in the steering column that locks the steering wheel when the ignition switch is turned off or the key is removed from the switch.

steering offset The distance between the point where the steering axis intersects the pavement and the center of the tire's contact patch.

Also called scrub radius, it acts as a lever arm that converts road-to-tire forces into torque on the steering mechanism that must be counteracted by the driver if the forces do not act equally on each steered wheel. If offset is positive, any asymmetrical force on a steered wheel (such as increased drag caused by a tire losing air) tends to turn the steering in the direction of the side with increased friction. If offset is negative, the effect is opposite and increased drag self-cancels to some extent. Scrub radius can be affected by installing different size tires and by wheels with nonstock offsets. Also see *negative offset* and *positive offset.*

steering overall ratio Ratio of the degrees the steering wheel must turn in order to turn the road wheels one degree from their straight-ahead position.

steering ratio Ratio of the steering gears — the rack to the pinion or the worm gear to the

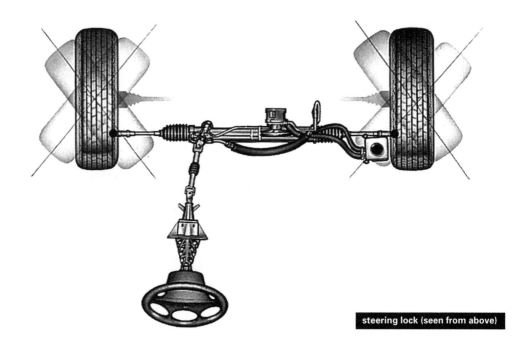

steering lock (seen from above)

recirculating nut. The higher the numerical ratio, the slower the steering.

steering response   A combination of steering effort and steering gain. See *steering effort* and *steering gain.*

steering shaft   See *steering column.*

steering spindle   Shaft-like projection from the steering knuckle to which the wheel is mounted. Also see *spindle.*

steering system   The entire mechanism that allows the driver to guide and direct a car. Includes the steering wheel, steering column, steering gear, linkages, and wheel supports.

steering wheel   The wheel by which the driver directs a vehicle. Steering linkage converts the motion of the driver's hands into movement of the road wheels.

stick shift

stick shift   A manual transmission, usually with a floor-mounted gearshift. Also see *floor shift.*

stiction   Starting friction. See *friction shock absorber.*

Stirling engine   External combustion engine in which heat is applied through the wall of a chamber within which a gas is successively heated and cooled, alternately expanding and contracting to power a piston inside the chamber. Its advantages include exceptional quietness, lack of vibration, long life, high efficiency, extremely low emissions, and adaptability to many different kinds of fuel. Drawbacks are the need for extremely effective seals, inflexible control systems, and high cost.

stoichiometric ratio   An air-fuel ratio of 14.7:1. It is the best compromise between a rich air-fuel ratio for best power and a lean air-fuel ratio for best economy. Also called the *ideal air-fuel ratio.*

Stop Control System (SCS)   A low-cost mechanical antilock braking system compatible with front-wheel drive devised by Lucas-Girlin. It employs a hydromechanical modulator for each front wheel driven by belts from the constant velocity joints and containing a flywheel that acts as a wheel-speed sensor. When one wheel begins to lock, a ball-and-ramp drive in the modulator actuates a relief valve that reduces pressure in the appropriate line. Also see *antilock braking system.*

stopping distance   See *braking distance.*

storage battery   An electrochemical device for converting chemical energy to electrical

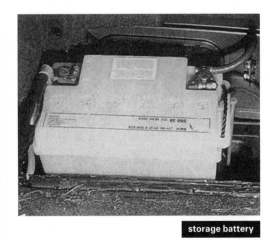

storage battery

S

energy. The typical lead-acid automotive battery supplies power for cranking the engine and the necessary electrical energy for the ignition system. In addition, it can, for a limited time, furnish current for operating electrical accessories when the ignition is switched off, or when the car's electrical demands exceed alternator or generator output. Also called the *battery.*

straight-cut gear   See *spur gear.*

straight eight   In-line eight-cylinder engine.

straight-line stability   See *directional stability.*

straight-line tracking   The ability of a car to resist road irregularities and run in a straight line without steering corrections. Straight-line tracking can be influenced by such factors as caster, pneumatic trail, and tire tread design. The width of the wheels and tires also plays a role in proper tracking. Also see *self-aligning torque.*

stratified charge   A combustion system that provides a rich mixture near the spark plug, surrounded by progressively leaner mixtures as the distance from the spark plug increases. The small amount of rich mixture ignites relatively easily and spreads combustion to the lean mixtures which would otherwise be prone to misfire. This can result in lower peak combustion temperatures, reduced exhaust emissions, and improved fuel economy. Honda's early CVCC engine, which initiated combustion in a small auxiliary chamber, is one type of stratified-charge engine (more precisely, a dual-combustion engine). Another was a mid-seventies design sponsored by Texaco in which turbulence in the incoming mixture was used to induce stratification.

stressed body   Car body whose outer panels share a proportion of the total load or stresses fed to the entire structure, rather than the frame taking all the loads. The Jaguar E-Type is an example.

stroke   The distance the piston in an engine moves from bottom dead center to top dead center, or vice versa.

stroking   To increase the piston stroke by lengthening an engine's crankshaft throws, thus increasing displacement.

strut   See *MacPherson strut* and *Chapman strut.*

stub axle   See *spindle.*

stud   A headless bolt threaded at both ends. Also, metal spikes installed in snow tires to increase traction on ice and hard-packed snow. Studded tires have been banned in many areas because of the damage they inflict on road surfaces.

stumble   A driveability problem similar to, but more severe than, hesitation. See *hesitation.*

subframe

subframe   A partial frame sometimes used in unitized construction to support the engine, transmission, and suspension. Such an arrangement, though expensive, improves road isolation and reduces harshness.

sump   See *oil pan.*

sun gear   See *planetary gears.*

sunroof In closed body styles, a partial or full-length covered roof opening that can be exposed as weather permits to admit extra air and/or light or to assist interior ventilation. Full-length sunroofs, like that of the Citroen 2CV, typically have cloth covers that fold accordion-style as they slide on longitudinal tracks built into the surrounding roof structure. A partial sunroof is generally a metal panel over the front seats that retracts into the rear roof structure — and often tilts up at its rear edge — either manually or by electric motor. Sometimes the panel is called a moonroof when it is a clear or tinted panel. A variation is a panel that can be tilted (sometimes electrically) but must be removed to be open.

sun visor See *visor*.

supercharger A pump that compresses air delivered to an engine into a denser charge, which can thus combine with extra fuel to produce a more explosive air-fuel mixture in order to increase engine power; often called a blower. A supercharger may be driven mechanically by the engine (usually via a pulley off the camshaft) or by using the energy in a portion of the exhaust gases, in which case it is technically a turbocharger.

Mechanical superchargers are traditionally either centrifugal, in which air compression or boost is accomplished via a turbine, or the Roots type, in which two small rotors take in air from one side of a housing and discharge compressed air from the opposite side. The main advantage

of the Roots type is relatively high boost at low rpm. Unlike a turbocharger, a supercharger does not require any lag time before it starts to operate because it is, in effect, constantly operating. However, being mechanically driven, it does consume a certain amount of engine power when not providing positive boost (i.e., an air charge above normal atmospheric pressure). Also see *pressure-wave supercharger*.

supplemental restraint system (SRS) A combination of passive restraint devices and/or systems, such as an airbag and knee bolster. Also see *passive restraint*.

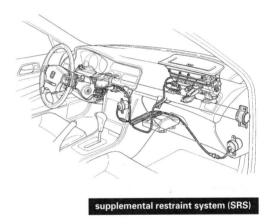

suppressor spark plug A spark plug incorporating radio frequency interference (RFI) suppression so that the ignition does not create static in radio reception. RFI suppression is achieved by giving the spark plug a certain amount of electrical resistance. Also called *resistor spark plug*.

surge Driveability problem in which an engine is unable to run smoothly at steady speeds; generally the result of a very lean air-fuel mixture and/or retarded timing. The almost universal use of modern electronic engine controls has rendered surge far less prevalent now than with the carbureted cars of the early to mid-seventies.

surge tank   See *expansion tank*.

suspension   The various springs, shock absorbers, and linkages used to suspend a car's frame, body, engine, and drivetrain above its wheels.

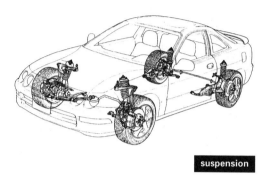

suspension

suspension geometry   The arrangement of a car's front or rear suspension components relative to each other (the system's geometry).

suspension travel   Maximum vertical distance through which a car wheel may move on its suspension; its combined travel in jounce and rebound. All other things being equal, the greater a car's suspension travel, the better its ride over large road irregularities. Also called *wheel travel*.

SUV   See *sport utility vehicle*.

sway bar   See *anti-roll bar*.

swept volume   The volume displaced by the piston of an engine as it moves downward in its cylinder; in a multi-cylinder engine, the sum of these volumes for all the cylinders. Displacement is the primary measure of engine size, representing the theoretical volume of air-fuel mixture that can be inducted by a cylinder on its intake stroke. Also called *displacement*.

swing axle   A type of independent rear suspension using half shafts with universal joints at the inboard end only, on either side of the differential. The small swing radius results in large camber changes as the wheels move up and down. When cornering hard, swing-axle cars are prone to large positive camber at the outside rear wheel, which can induce sudden oversteer or jacking.

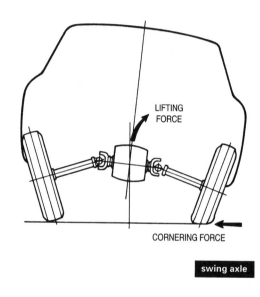

LIFTING FORCE

CORNERING FORCE

swing axle

swirl intake ports   Ports positioned and shaped to create a swirl of air in the combustion chamber for more even fuel distribution and ignition.

switch   A device that opens and closes an electrical circuit.

synchro   See *synchronizer*.

synchromesh transmission   A manual gearbox employing synchronizers, usually for the forward ratios only but not necessarily for all of them.

synchronizer   A cone or sleeve that slides back and forth on the transmission main shaft

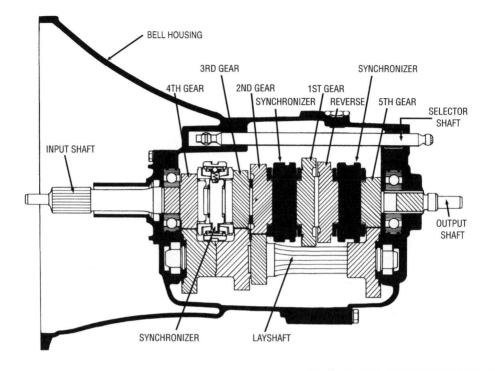

BELL HOUSING

3RD GEAR

SYNCHRONIZER

4TH GEAR   2ND GEAR   1ST GEAR

SYNCHRONIZER   REVERSE   5TH GEAR

SELECTOR SHAFT

INPUT SHAFT

OUTPUT SHAFT

SYNCHRONIZER   LAYSHAFT

synchromesh transmission; synchromesh

to make a gear rotate at the speed of the main shaft, thus preventing clash when the gears mesh. The transmission main shaft turns and the clutch gear spins whenever a car moves. Although the clutch is disengaged, the clutch gear continues to spin until friction slows or stops it. Thus, during a shift the gears may be moving at different speeds. Synchronizers reduce the possibility of broken or damaged gear teeth, ease shift effort, and eliminate the need to double-clutch. Abbreviated as *synchro*.

synthetic oil A lubricant that is artificially produced in a laboratory instead of being refined from naturally occurring organic petroleum. Typically refers to newer motor oils engineered to resist breakdown and consequent loss of lubricity under extreme heat and friction.

S

tach   See *tachometer.*

tachometer   An instrument for measuring and indicating the speed at which the engine crankshaft is turning, universally calibrated in revolutions per minute (rpm). Often shortened to *tach*; also known as a *rev counter.* Also see *redline.*

tachometer

tailgate   A hinged rear door on a station wagon or minivan.

Also, to follow another car at a dangerously close distance.

taillamp   See *taillight.*

taillight   One of two typically red lights at the rear of a vehicle that light when the parking lights or headlights are turned on, to enable following traffic to see the vehicle at night and in

tailpipe

low-visibility conditions. Taillights usually incorporate at least two bulbs, one of which is for the brake lights. Also called *taillamp.*

tailpipe   The steel tube through which engine exhaust gases are routed from the muffler to the atmosphere.

tapered roller bearing   A roller bearing, often used in wheel bearings, rear axle shafts, and transmissions, in which the cylindrical rollers are larger in circumference at one end than at the other. Also see *roller bearing.*

tappet   See *cam follower.*

Targa   A semiconvertible coupe design, introduced in the mid-sixties by Porsche, in which the forward portion of the roof may be opened by removing a single full-width panel that attaches to the windshield header at the front and to a roll bar at the rear. The original 911 Targa also had a removable rear window behind the roll bar; later models had a fixed rear window. The name stems from Sicily's famed Targa Florio road race; Targa has since become a generic description for this hybrid body style and thus is sometimes written lowercase. Also called *Targa top.*

A variation on the theme is seen in the Jaguar XJ-S Cabriolet, whose metal front and rear win-

T

T-bar roof

dow frames are retained. Like a Targa, the Jaguar has a solid, removable one-piece forward section, but the rear area is a cloth quarter-top that folds like a convertible roof and may be covered with a boot.

Targa top   See *Targa.*

T-bar roof   A semiconvertible coupe design, pioneered in production by the 1968 Chevrolet Corvette, in which the forward portion of the roof may be opened. It consists of two removable panels attached to a central longitudinal member extending from the windshield header to the rear roof structure; the windshield and longitudinal member are T-shaped. The panels are generally of steel, fiberglass finished to match the rest of the roof, glass, or transparent acrylic plastic. Also called a *T-top.*

TBI   See *throttle-body injection.*

TDC   See *top dead center.*

temper   In lay terms, the hardness of a metal. In metallurgical terms, the degree of hardness obtained by either heat-treating or cold-working a metal.

tempered glass   See *safety glass.*

tensile strength   A material's resistance to stretching; measured in lb/in.^{2}.

terminal post   The post to which a cable is attached on a battery. The positive terminal is called the plus (+) terminal or anode; the negative terminal is called the negative (-) terminal or cathode.

test track   A facility designed for automobile racing and/or testing, with a road or series of roads not directly accessible from public thoroughfares. Compare with *proving ground.*

tetraethyl lead   A lead compound used as a gasoline additive to increase octane rating and to reduce knock. The addition of tetraethyl lead to gasoline is being phased out because of the emission of lead, a toxin, into the atmosphere when the fuel is burned.

T-head engine   An engine with the intake valves on one side of the cylinder and the exhaust valves on the other. Widely used on cars built until about 1915, after which it disappeared entirely.

thermal efficiency   The ratio of the work accomplished by an engine to the total quantity of heat contained in its fuel. When fuel burns in

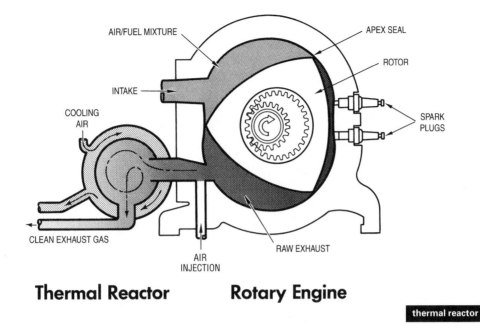

AIR/FUEL MIXTURE

APEX SEAL

ROTOR

INTAKE

COOLING
AIR

SPARK
PLUGS

CLEAN EXHAUST GAS

AIR
INJECTION

RAW EXHAUST

Thermal Reactor   Rotary Engine

thermal reactor

an engine, all of its energy is not converted to power — some is lost in overcoming friction and some escapes in the exhaust gases — so this ratio is always less than one.

thermal reactor   A high-volume thermally isolated chamber replacing the exhaust manifold and providing a place for high-temperature afterburning of exhaust pollutants.

thermistor   A resistor whose resistance changes according to temperature. Often used in sending units for gauges or as thermally sensitive switches.

thermostat   A heat-controlled valve used in an engine's cooling system to regulate the flow of coolant between the cylinder block and the radiator. Because automotive internal combustion engines operate more efficiently within

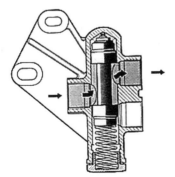

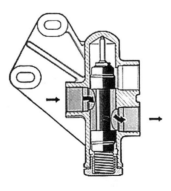

thermostat

T

a narrow temperature range, the thermostat closes off the coolant flow from the engine to the radiator until the engine has reached its operating temperature.

Other thermostats are used in the electrical circuit of a car's heating system to control the amount of heat supplied to the passengers; in the manifold heat-control system that preheats the air-fuel mixture going to the cylinders; and in the automatic choke.

three-way catalyst   A catalytic converter that changes an engine's emissions of oxides of nitrogen, hydrocarbons, and carbon monoxide into less harmful products.

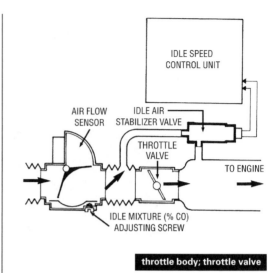

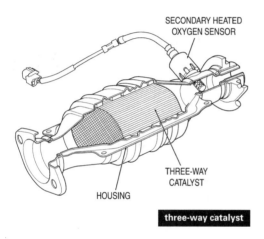

three-way catalyst

throttle   The accelerator pedal. In the early days of the automobile the throttle was a hand control that governed the speed of an engine. Also see *accelerator*.

throttle body   The section of an engine's intake system in which the throttle valve (butterfly) is located.

throttle-body injection (TBI)   A system that injects fuel at the throttle body. See *fuel injection*.

throttle plate   See *throttle valve*.

throttle valve   A valve that varies the amount of air entering the intake manifold. Usually

consists of a flat round disc mounted on a shaft that can be tilted at various angles by means of a linkage from the accelerator pedal. Also called *throttle plate*.

throw   Distance from the center of the crankshaft main bearing to the center of the connecting-rod journal. The piston stroke is twice the throw distance.

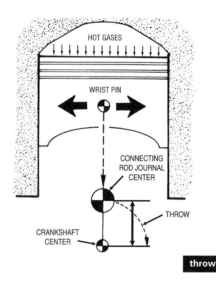

throw

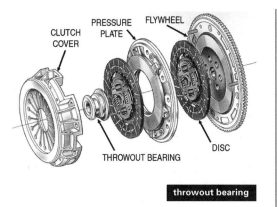

CLUTCH COVER

PRESSURE PLATE

FLYWHEEL

THROWOUT BEARING

DISC

throwout bearing

throwout bearing   The clutch bearing that moves into the release levers by activating the clutch pedal, disengaging the clutch and disconnecting the engine from the drivetrain. Also called *clutch release bearing*.

thrust bearing   A bearing with flanges on its sides that prevent a shaft, such as the crankshaft, from moving forward or backward. In the engine crankshaft assembly, the flanges fit close to the two sides of the crankpin. If the crankshaft tends to shift one way or the other, the crankpin sides come up against the flanges, preventing excessive end-to-end movement. See illustration for *needle bearing*.

tie rod   In a steering system, rods that link the pitman arm and the idler arm to transmit lateral

motion to the steering knuckle arms. Also see *idler arm* and *pitman arm*. See illustration for *steering box*.

timed injection   See *pulsed injection*.

timing   Refers to the crankshaft angles at which the valves and ignition points open and close.

timing belt   A cogged or toothed belt by which the crankshaft drives the camshaft(s). See illustration for *flat engine*.

timing chain   A chain by which the crankshaft drives the camshaft(s).

timing gears   A set of gears by which the crankshaft drives the camshaft(s). Used only where long life and extra-hard service are expected, as in commercial vehicles and racing cars. Generally noisier in operation than a timing chain or belt.

tip plate   A plate on a wing's outboard end, also known as an end plate, used to control turbulence around the wing and thus reduce aerodynamic drag.

tip seal   See *apex seal*.

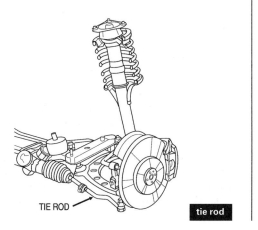

TIE ROD

tie rod

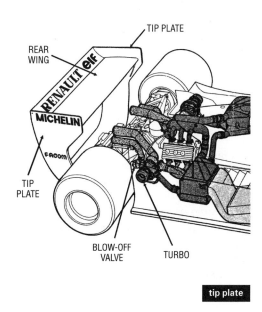

TIP PLATE

REAR WING

TIP PLATE

BLOW-OFF VALVE

TURBO

tip plate

T

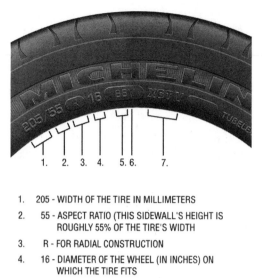

1. 205 - WIDTH OF THE TIRE IN MILLIMETERS
2. 55 - ASPECT RATIO (THIS SIDEWALL'S HEIGHT IS ROUGHLY 55% OF THE TIRE'S WIDTH
3. R - FOR RADIAL CONSTRUCTION
4. 16 - DIAMETER OF THE WHEEL (IN INCHES) ON WHICH THE TIRE FITS
5. 88 - NUMERICAL CODE ASSOCIATED WITH THE MAXIMUM LOAD A TIRE CAN CARRY
6. V - SPEED RATING (THIS TIRE COULD SUSTAIN SPEEDS UP TO 149 MPH)
7. XGT V - MANUFACTURER'S NAME FOR TREAD DESIGN AND ARCHITECTURE

tire ratings

tire   A rubber covering fitted to a wheel and usually containing compressed air to support a vehicle's load. The acceleration, braking, and cornering forces acting on a vehicle are resisted by the tires.

tire grading   See *Uniform Tire Quality Grading.*

tire patch   See *contact patch.*

tire plug   A plug used to repair a tire puncture.

tire ratings   The numbers and letters imprinted on the sidewall of a tire which list such things as load capacity, size, speed capability, and tire type. For example, a P215/60VR15 tire is a metric tire with a cross-section width of 215 millimeters, an aspect ratio of 60, a V speed rating (maximum speed

149 mph), of radial construction, and with a wheel diameter of 15 inches.

tire rotation   Moving the tires from front to rear and possibly from one side of the car to the other to equalize tire wear. Bias ply tires are rotated in a cross-over pattern: typically, LF to RR, RR to LF, RF to LR, LR to RF when the spare tire is not included. When radials first became popular, tire manufacturers recommended keeping them on the same side of the car so they would always run in the same direction. Today, many tire makers say this is no longer necessary.

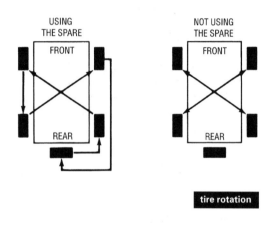

tire rotation

tire scrub   A scuffing or scrubbing of the outside tire which results when a car is turning a corner and its steering system is not designed to compensate for the larger circle tracked by the outside wheel versus the inside wheel. Ackermann steering minimizes scrub in the typical conditions encountered by production cars. For a rear-wheel-drive car, the differential performs a similar function, allowing the outer driving wheel to turn faster than the inner when the car goes around a corner. Tire scrub will be especially noticeable in a vehicle equipped with 4-wheel drive and the ability to lock the differentials. The binding in the steering and the jud-

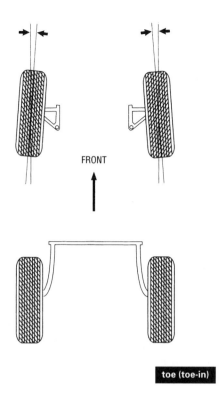

toe (toe-in)

in front; toe-out is when they are closer together at the rear.

A slight amount of toe-in is usually specified to offset other forces that tend to spread the front wheels apart; the major force is the backward thrust of the road against the tire treads while the car is moving forward. Other factors include play in the tie-rod assembly and allowance for angular changes caused by wheel bounce or variations in road conditions. With most independent rear suspension systems, rear wheels assume toe-in or -out as they experience acceleration, braking, and cornering forces.

toe board See *floorboard*.

toe control Rear-suspension geometry that actively influences the amount of toe change at a wheel to enhance cornering or braking ability. Well-known examples of cars whose rear suspension incorporates toe control are the

dering of the rear end during tight, low-speed maneuvers on pavement are indicators of severe tire scrub. This is the reason manufacturers recommend the use of 4-wheel drive with locked differentials only on slippery surfaces that will compensate for scrub by small amounts of tire slip. Scrub can also result from misaligned suspension geometry and from the tire running at a slip angle, the angular difference between the direction the wheel is traveling and the direction of the tread. Also see *Ackermann steering, differential,* and *slip angle.*

tire stagger See *stagger.*

tire valve See *valve.*

tire width See *section width.*

toe A condition in which a car's wheels are closer together at the front or rear in plan view. Toe-in refers to the wheels being closer together

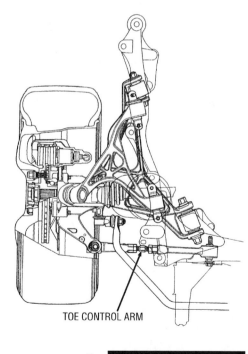

TOE CONTROL ARM

toe control (seen from above)

T

Mercedes 190 and 200/300 series, second-generation Mazda RX-7, and Porsche 928.

toe steer Changes in the direction of a wheel that occur without driver steering input. Several factors can induce toe steer, including body roll and deflections in the suspension linkages caused by acceleration, braking, and cornering forces. For example, a condition in which the outside rear wheel toes-in during cornering results in increased understeer. Conversely, an outside rear wheel that toes-out when cornering induces more oversteer. Also see *roll steer*.

tolerance The allowable deviation of a part from a nominal standard. Also see *blueprinting*.

tonneau cover

tonneau cover A cover of leather, vinyl, canvas, or other soft, pliable material used to protect the interior of a convertible or roadster when its soft top is down. It typically fastens around the dash, sides, and rear of the car, and often has a longitudinal zipper so the car can be driven with the passenger side covered.

top dead center (TDC) The highest point of piston and connecting-rod travel in a cylinder in a four-cycle engine, at the ends of the compression and exhaust strokes.

top gear See *high gear*.

torch ignition A combustion system utilizing two combustion chambers: a large, conventional chamber connected to a smaller chamber where the spark plug is located. The larger chamber contains a very lean air-fuel mixture, the smaller one a relatively rich mixture. The smaller chamber ignites first; flame spreads from it (in the form of a "torch") to the larger one. The system uses leaner air-fuel mixtures than does a conventional single combustion chamber. Torch ignition is a kind of stratified-charge system. Also see *stratified charge*.

torque Turning or twisting effort, usually measured in lb-ft or Newton-meters. It differs from work or power in that torque does not necessarily produce motion. The torque acting on a body is the product of the magnitude of a force and its force arm (the perpendicular distance from the body's axis of rotation to the line of action of the force). This product is called the moment about this axis, or the torque.

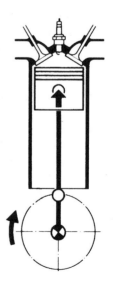

top dead center (TDC)

torque converter   In an automatic transmission, three vaned elements — the impeller, turbine, and stator — rotating in a fluid-filled housing that serve as a hydraulic clutch to transmit and multiply engine torque and to cushion the flow of power.

The engine drives the impeller, which in turn impels fluid against the vanes of a turbine connected through the transmission gears to the driveshaft. The stator is the middle element. At low speeds, the stator is held stationary (hence its name) against the oil flow by a one-way clutch, redirecting the flow from the turbine to boost impeller action and thus multiply engine torque. As speed increases, the oil flow shifts and rotates the stator in the same direction the other elements are turning; torque multiplication

ceases and the torque converter then functions as a simple fluid coupling.

torque-converter lockup clutch   An automatic mechanism that effects mechanical connection of a torque converter's impeller and turbine. Thus engaged, the lockup clutch eliminates part or all of the slippage associated with a converter's transmission of torque through oil, increasing efficiency and fuel economy.

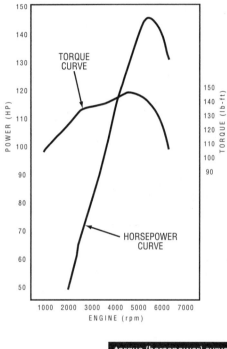

torque (horsepower) curve

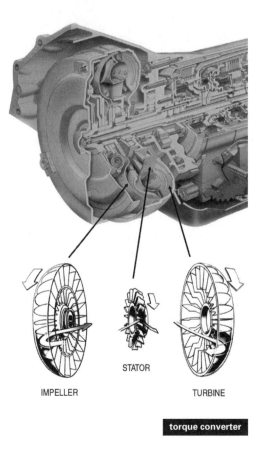

IMPELLER   STATOR   TURBINE

torque converter

torque (horsepower) curve   The degree to which an engine's torque (horsepower) output varies with crankshaft speed; also, the graphic representation of same. To measure a torque (horsepower) curve, dynamometer measurements are made of the torque (horsepower) produced at various points in the engine's speed (rpm) range; these measurements are plotted as points on a graph, usually with the horizontal scale repre-

T

senting engine speed and the vertical scale representing torque horsepower. When connected, the points form a curve that permits visual comparison of the engine's torque (horsepower) delivery with that of other engines.

torque peak Maximum torque developed by an engine, appearing as the highest point on a torque curve.

torque steer The tendency of some front-wheel-drive cars, especially those with unequal-length driveshafts, to pull to one side or the other during hard acceleration. Typically experienced by the driver as a tugging through the steering wheel, and most pronounced in high-powered cars. It results from an application of engine torque sufficient to unevenly twist different-length driveshafts, and may be reduced, if not always eliminated, through the use of equal-length driveshafts. Not to be confused with tuck-in, the tendency of front-drive cars to straighten out energetically when power is applied while cornering. Also see *tuck-in.*

torque tube A rear drivetrain in which the driveshaft is inside a stout tube anchored to the rear axle housing. Only one universal joint is used, at the driveshaft's front end. The torque tube prevents the axle housing from twisting when engine power or braking torque is applied. When this type of drive was widely used, before the advent of sophisticated link-

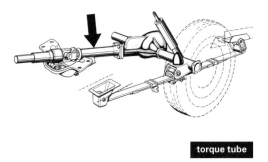

torque tube

ages for live rear axles, torque tubes generally resulted in a relatively smooth ride because the springs didn't have to be firm enough to absorb any driving or braking torque; they only had to cushion the ride.

torsen differential A type of limited-slip differential whose name derives from torque sensing. Noted for its smooth engagement and disengagement characteristics. Also called *Torsen-Gleason differential.*

torsen differential

Torsen-Gleason differential See *torsen differential.*

torsion The twisting of a body by two equal and opposite torques; the twisting moment around a car's longitudinal axis.

torsional rigidity Resistance of a car body or frame to twisting forces. Usually measured in lb/degree of twist.

torsion bar A long straight bar fastened to the frame at one end and to a suspension part at the other. In effect, an unwound coil spring that absorbs energy by twisting. Its main advantage over the coil spring in a front suspension is the relative ease of adjusting suspension height. Also, because of its slender configuration, it is more adaptable than a coil or leaf

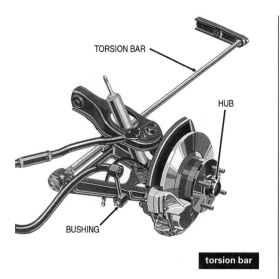

torsion bar

spring to some car layouts and in off-road truck applications.

tossable Term used by road testers to describe car handling characterized by quick responses to, and controlled behavior in, sudden directional changes, such as rounding sharp corners, negotiating a slalom course, and making U-turns.

touring car A coachbuilding term for a vintage open car with two or four doors and seating for at least four occupants. Weatherproofing varied from literally none to a folding top complete with side curtains.

track The distance from the longitudinal center plane of one wheel or tire to the center of the wheel or tire on the opposite side. Also called *tread*.

track bar See *Panhard rod*.

Track Link A BMW-patented design for rear semi-trailing-arm suspension in which an additional locating link is used with a smaller angle for the arm's pivot axis to reduce camber and toe changes as the wheels move up and down. The Track Link adds a helical motion to the semi-trailing arm's normal swinging motion.

track rod See *Panhard rod*.

traction The adhesive friction of a tire and a road surface.

traction control Computer-controlled system that increases control and stability on slippery surfaces by automatically reducing the throttle opening, pumping the brakes, or both, to control wheelspin. Traction control can be thought of as the opposite of antilock braking: ABS prevents wheels from locking during deceleration; traction control prevents wheelspin during acceleration. The wheel sensors used for ABS may also be used for traction control.

trail braking A driving technique in which the brakes are applied before entering a corner and braking is continued as the driver enters the turn. As cornering forces build, the driver gradually and smoothly releases brake pressure, trading braking power for cornering grip. By increasing the vertical loading on the front tires as the car enters a turn, traction at the front tires is increased, improving a car's turn-in.

trailing arm A suspension arm that pivots in a plane parallel to the longitudinal axis of the car. The wheel is fixed to and trails behind the fixed

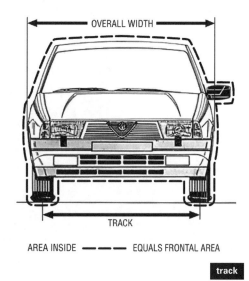

track

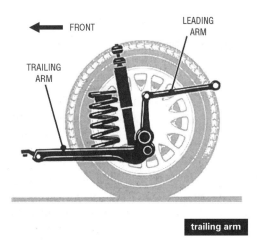

FRONT

LEADING ARM

TRAILING ARM

TRAILING ARM

pivot point on the chassis. With this type of independent rear suspension, the wheels are always upright relative to the body, and hence leaning with the body in a corner. Widely used at the rear of front-wheel-drive cars.

trailing shoe   In drum brakes, a shoe pivoted at its forward end relative to rotation of the drum.

trailing-throttle oversteer   A handling condition generally associated with rear-wheel-drive cars in which the rear tires lose cornering grip when the throttle is suddenly released during hard cornering. When power is applied to a rear-drive car, weight is transferred from the front to the rear tires. This additional weight increases straight-line and cornering grip. If this weight is suddenly removed as the result of lifting off the throttle in a corner, loss of grip at the rear can result in an oversteering condition which can be exacerbated if the driver also applies the brakes, thus transferring even more weight to the front tires. Also called *lift-throttle oversteer*.

tramlining   See *nibble*.

trammel bar   A bar used to measure between the wheels for adjusting toe-in or toe-out.

tramp   A condition is which the drive wheels move up and down, generally as a result of torque being transmitted by the axle shafts to the wheels, producing a reaction that rotates the live rear axle about its own centerline. Tramping

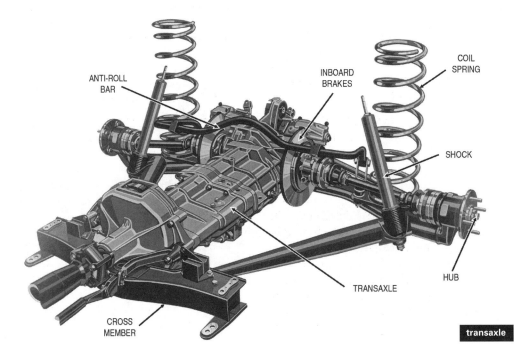

ANTI-ROLL BAR

INBOARD BRAKES

COIL SPRING

SHOCK

HUB

TRANSAXLE

CROSS MEMBER

transaxle

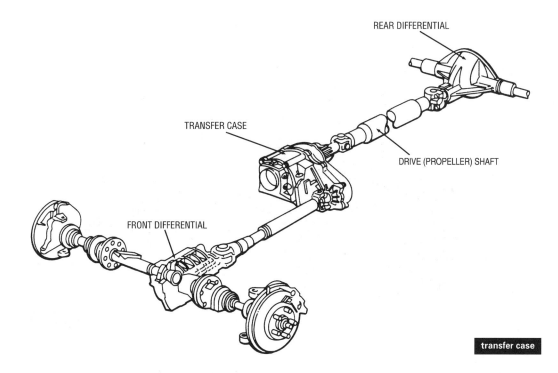

REAR DIFFERENTIAL

TRANSFER CASE

DRIVE (PROPELLER) SHAFT

FRONT DIFFERENTIAL

transfer case

is a less severe version of wheel hop, a condition in which the wheels actually leave the ground. Also see *axle windup* and *wheel hop.*

transaxle Combined transmission and axle in which the clutch, gearbox, final drive, and differential are housed in one unit. All front-wheel-drive, rear-engine, and mid-engine cars use a transaxle, as do some front-engine/rear-drive models such as the Porsche 924, 944, and 928 series and the Alfa Romeo GTV and Milano.

transfer case In a four-wheel-drive vehicle, an auxiliary gearbox through which power may be delivered to both axles simultaneously. In vehicles with offroad capability it typically incorporates a "normal" (high-ratio) gear for two- or four-wheel operation, and a much lower (numerically higher) gear that effectively lowers each of the transmission ratios for maximum four-wheel-drive pulling power. In part-time systems, the transfer case permits disconnecting

the front or rear drive for running on dry pavement. In some permanent or full-time systems, the transfer case may employ a viscous coupling in addition to or in place of mechanical gears.

transient yaw response A car's response with respect to yaw in transition, that is, while moving from one state (of cornering, braking, or acceleration) to another. Also see *yaw.*

transistorized ignition Ignition system in which the points serve to trigger a transistor that switches the heavy primary current. Transistors are much more efficient switches at high engine speeds, and don't burn, pit, or change gap spacing. The advantages of such systems include greatly increased point life, generally better starting due to improved contact condition, and voltage output not greatly affected by breaker-point dwell time, which results in better performance at high engine speeds.

T

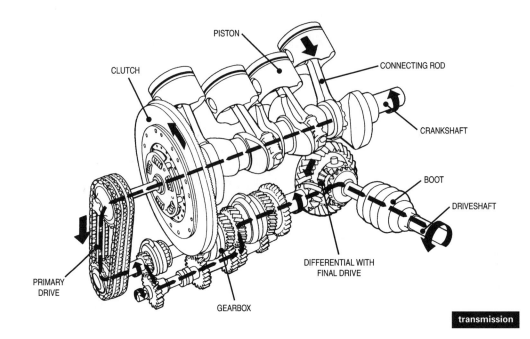

PISTON

CLUTCH

CONNECTING ROD

CRANKSHAFT

BOOT

DRIVESHAFT

PRIMARY
DRIVE

DIFFERENTIAL WITH
FINAL DRIVE

GEARBOX

transmission

transmission   The speed- and power-changing device in the power train that provides different gear ratios between the engine and the drive wheels, plus a reverse gear for backing up the car. The transmission multiplies engine torque when the car is accelerating from rest or climbing hills; when cruising on a relatively level road surface, it trades torque for higher wheel speeds and a reduction in engine speed. In manual transmissions, the transmission includes the clutch and gearbox. In a conventional automatic transmission, it includes the torque converter and gearbox.

transmission mounts   See *engine mounts.*

transverse arm or transverse link   See *lateral arm.*

transverse engine   Engine placement perpendicular to a vehicle's centerline. Positioning the engine in an east–west manner results in a shorter, more compact engine compartment and is the typical design for front-wheel-drive vehicles. Also called *sidewinder.*

transverse leaf spring   A leaf spring mounted perpendicular to the centerline of the vehicle. This simple, vintage suspension made a sophisticated comeback in the form of fiberglass transverse leaf springs at the front and rear of the 1984 Chevrolet Corvette. Also see *leaf spring.* See illustration for *multi-leaf spring.*

trap oxidizer   The diesel engine's equivalent of a gasoline engine's catalytic converter. The trap oxidizer captures particulates emitted in a diesel's exhaust and also oxidizes exhaust emissions that would otherwise wind up as soot.

tread   A circumferential band of rubber bonded to a tire's carcass, which contacts the road and protects the tire from abrasion. An engraved tread pattern assures even tire wear, directional stability, dry traction, wet traction, controlled acceleration and braking, and low noise. The wider the tread surface, the better the dispersion of the heat generated in the tire. Also see *track.*

tread

tread depth The distance from the bottom of the tread grooves to the tread surface, measured in thirty-seconds of an inch.

tread grooves Grooves in a tire's tread to make the tire lighter and more flexible, to provide edges to grip the road in straight-line driving and when cornering, and to channel water away from the tread to prevent aquaplaning when driving in the rain.

tread squirm The flexibility of a tire's tread between the tread surface and the tire carcass. A tire with deep tread and small, unsupported tread blocks (snow tires) has a large amount of tread squirm. Racing slicks have little squirm.

trip computer An electronic calculator found on many newer cars for computing time, speed, distance, and fuel use. Designs vary, but most employ a microprocessor linked to a clock, the car's odometer and speedometer drives, and the engine's fuel system. With data from these sources, the microprocessor calculates and displays precise values for variables such as average speed, instantaneous and average mpg, time and/or distance to a destination, elapsed journey time, and miles that can be traveled on remaining fuel at the existing fuel consumption rate. Operated via a set of buttons (a keypad), typically mounted on the dashboard, or by a steering column lever.

trunk The compartment at the rear of a front- or mid-engine car or at the front of a rear-engine car in which luggage and other items are stowed. Also called the luggage compartment.

trunk

T

trunk lid   The lift-up panel at the rear of a notchback car that covers and provides access to the trunk. Because the luggage compartment of a rear-engine car (if any) is at the front, the trunk lid could also be called the hood of a rear-engine car. Some mid-engine models such as the Lotus Esprit have an engine access cover extended to double as the trunk lid. Also called the *deck lid.*

T-top   See *T-bar roof.*

tube   A tire's inner tube, which holds the air. Most current passenger car tires are a tubeless design, but many truck tires still use tubes. Also see *tubeless.*

tubeless   A tire without an inner tube. Instead, an air seal is provided by a layer of special air-tight rubber which is applied on the inside of the tire casing and substitutes for the tube. The inflation valve, with rubber gaskets to assure airtightness, is fitted to a tubeless rim. The wheel flange must be in perfect condition because imperfections will cause air leaks between the tire and rim.

tuck-in   A handling condition similar to trailing-throttle oversteer, but associated with front-wheel-drive cars. A tire can generate longitudinal (acceleration and braking) and lateral (cornering) forces or a combination of both. The front tires on a front-drive car, unlike those on a rear-drive vehicle, not only steer the car, but also provide the tractive effort that pulls the car. During hard cornering, applying power can cause the front tires to exceed their total traction limits. When this happens, the car will have a tendency to understeer or "run wide" through the corner. However, if the driver lifts off the throttle in the turn, the component of force driving the tires straight ahead will be redirected into cornering force, allowing the car to corner harder with less understeer. The driver will notice this increase in cornering force by the nose of the car "tucking in" toward the inside of the corner or by a reduction in understeer, which

some drivers wrongly describe as front-wheel-drive oversteer.

tuck-under   See *turn-under.*

tumblehome   A styling term for the outward curvature from perpendicular of a car's upper body as viewed from the front or rear. Typically begins at the body's belt line. The opposite of *turn-under.*

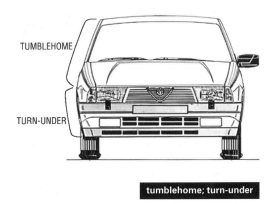

tumblehome; turn-under

tuned intake and exhaust systems   Intake and exhaust systems that harness the pressure pulses and resonances inside the various chambers and passageways of the intake and exhaust manifolds to increase the flow of mixture into and the flow of burned gases out of the combustion chambers.

tune-up   To perform careful and accurate adjustments to an engine (such as setting the timing, gapping the spark plugs, and adjusting the carburetor) for the purpose of obtaining optimum performance and lowest possible exhaust emissions.

turbine   A wheel or disc with a series of radial vanes on one or both sides that, when acted on by the force of a gas or liquid, serve to rotate the wheel and thus impart motion to a shaft attached to it. Also, an engine using one or more turbines to produce power. Also see *torque converter.*

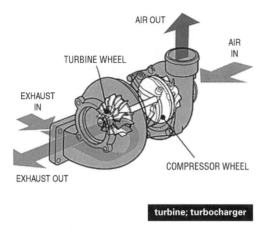

AIR OUT

AIR IN

TURBINE WHEEL

EXHAUST IN

COMPRESSOR WHEEL

EXHAUST OUT

turbine; turbocharger

turbo See *turbocharger.*

turbocharger A centrifugal supercharger driven by exhaust gases. It consists of an exhaust-driven turbine, a housing into which air is drawn for compression by another turbine (driven by the exhaust turbine), and a control system that limits boost pressure to avoid the risk of internal damage.

Unlike a supercharger, a turbocharger does not consume engine power; instead, it makes use of otherwise wasted energy in the exhaust stream to increase an engine's power output. Because of the higher internal pressures involved in "force-feeding," compression ratios of turbocharged (and supercharged) engines are generally lower than those of their normally aspirated counterparts in the interest of prolonging engine life. Often shortened to *turbo*; also called a *blower.*

turbodiesel A turbocharged diesel engine. A diesel is inherently more suitable than a spark-ignition engine for turbocharging because it does not have a throttle valve. See *turbo lag.*

turbo lag Delayed response time in a turbocharged engine after the accelerator is pressed. In a gasoline engine operating at low speeds and under minimal load, the throttle is restricting gas flow, and relatively little exhaust gas flows through the turbocharger. Once the driver demands power by opening the throttle, it takes time for the increased exhaust-gas flow to bring the turbocharger to a speed where it can produce significant boost. Typically, the slower the engine is running when the driver steps on the throttle, the longer the turbo lag.

turbulent flow See *drafting* and *laminar flow.*

turn-in The transition between driving straight ahead and cornering. How quickly and smoothly turn-in occurs is a function of suspension stiffness, wheel and tire width, steering system design, and the car's moment of inertia.

turn indicator See *direction indicator.*

turning circle See *turning radius.*

turning diameter See *turning radius.*

turning radius The diameter (twice the radius) of the circle needed by a car to make a 360-degree turn. Turning radius is measured either curb-to-curb or wall-to-wall; the latter is always larger because it takes front-end overhang into account. Also called *turning circle* or *turning diameter.*

turn signal See *direction indicator.*

turns lock-to-lock The number of steering wheel rotations required to go from one extreme lock position to the other, i.e., full left to full right or vice-versa; an indicator of a car's maneuverability and handling response. See illustration for *steering lock.*

turn-under A styling term for the marked inward curvature from perpendicular of a car's lower body as viewed from the front or rear. Typically begins at the body's widest point. Also called tuck-under. The opposite of tumblehome.

twincam An engine with double overhead camshafts. Also see *overhead cam.*

two-plus-two (2+2) A coupe with two front seats (typically buckets) and nominal four-passenger carrying capacity but whose rear seating area is so limited as to be suitable only for small

T

two-plus-two (2 + 2)

children. Some designs tacitly acknowledge this with a rear seat or seat backs that folds down to form a luggage platform.

two-seater   A roadster. See *roadster*.

two-stroke cycle   The reciprocating engine cycle in which the piston takes over some valve functions in order to obtain a power stroke on each crankshaft revolution. Ports in the cylinders are alternately covered and uncovered by piston movement; the ports are opened by the piston's downstroke so that exhaust gases can exit at the same time a fresh mixture charge enters.

Typically, the air-fuel mixture enters the crankcase through a reed valve. When the pis-

ton is at bottom dead center, a port is uncovered, allowing the already compressed mixture to flow from the crankcase into the cylinder. Further compression in the cylinder starts as soon as the piston rises and covers the ports.

As compression is occurring in the cylinder, piston movement has created a vacuum in the crankcase that draws in a fresh charge from the carburetor. The compressed charge is fired as the piston reaches top dead center. Expansion of the burning charge forces the piston down, the crankcase reed valve closes, and the mixture in the crankcase is compressed.

As the piston uncovers the ports at the bottom of its stroke, a compressed mixture again enters the cylinder and is deflected by a baffle on the piston head into the outer end of the cylinder. This incoming fresh mixture then helps to push the burned gases out of the cylinder, and the cycle is repeated. Also see *reed valve*.

two-wheel drive (2WD)   A vehicle with power transmitted to the front or rear wheels but not to both.

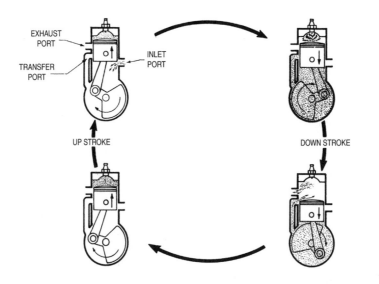

two-stroke cycle

U-joint See *universal joint*.

ultimate cornering force Maximum steady-state cornering or side force generated by the tires when a car is driven around a skid pad as fast as possible without sliding off the course.

undercoating Petroleum-based compound applied to the underside of a car and in selected areas such as rocker panels to deter rust formation and insulate the passenger compartment from noise.

underslung A vintage automobile with the chassis frame attached to the axles from below. The design allowed the car to be lower to the ground than an overslung design.

undersquare An engine whose cylinder bore is less than its stroke. Also see *oversquare*.

understeer A handling characteristic in which additional steering lock is required as speed increases around a constant radius turn. An understeering car breaks away at the front end first because the front tires run at larger slip angles than the rear tires; also called "push". A characterization usually attributed to race drivers is that cars that understeer go through the fence nose first, and cars that oversteer go through tail first. Also see *neutral steer* and *oversteer*.

unequal-length A-arm A common front suspension layout consisting of two unequal-length non-parallel A-arms for each front wheel. In

SLIP ANGLE

understeer

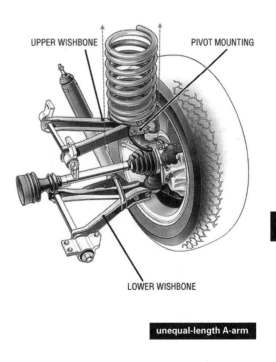

UPPER WISHBONE PIVOT MOUNTING

LOWER WISHBONE

unequal-length A-arm

some suspensions, the lateral arms may be straight or curved links. Also called short-long arms, double A-arms, or double wishbones. Also see *A-arm*.

unibody See *unitized construction*.

unidirectional tires Tires whose tread patterns are designed for optimum grip and handling response in the forward direction only. Also see *directional tire*.

unidirectional wheels Wheels designed with radial cooling slots or vanes effective in the forward direction only. Unidirectional wheels are designed for either left- or right-side installation and should not be transposed.

Uniform Tire Quality Grading (UTQG) All tires sold in the United States are subjected to mandatory tests which are defined by the U.S. government and carried out by the manufacturer. The tests were established to allow consumers to more easily compare tires produced by different manufacturers in terms of tread wear, traction, and resistance to heat generation (temperature).

The traction grades are A (the highest), B, and C, and represent the tire's ability to stop on wet pavement as measured under controlled conditions on specified test surfaces; braking traction is tested, but cornering traction is not.

The tread wear grade is a comparative rating based on the wear rate of the tire when tested under controlled conditions on a specified test course. For example, a tire graded 150 would wear one and a half times as well on the test course as a tire graded 100.

The temperature grades of A (the highest), B, and C represent a tire's resistance to the generation of heat and its ability to dissipate heat when tested under controlled conditions on a specified indoor laboratory test wheel.

unit body See *unitized construction*.

unitized construction A car engineered so that the body, floorpan, and chassis form a single structure. Generally lighter and more rigid than traditional body-on-frame construction, but more vulnerable to rust damage, particularly in the rocker panels. Less accurately termed unit body or unibody construction.

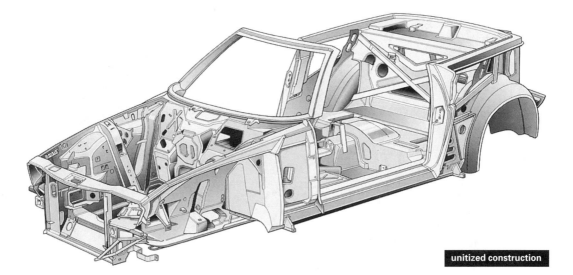

unitized construction

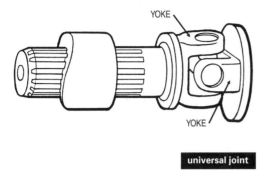

YOKE

YOKE

universal joint

universal joint (U-joint) A double-pivoted joint that allows driving power to be carried through two shafts at an angle to each other. Typically used to connect the driveshaft to the transmission and the differential in a front-engine rear-drive vehicle.

It consists of two U-shaped yokes and a cross-shaped member called the spider. The four arms of the spider are assembled into bearings in the ends of the two yokes. With this construction there is some change in speed when the drive shaft and driven shaft are angled to each other, because the driven yoke and driven shaft speed up and then slow down twice with every revolution of the drivetrain. The greater the angle between the shafts, the greater the speed variation. Constant velocity joints are used on many cars to eliminate this speed variation, which results in increased wear of the affected parts. Also known as a *Cardan* or *Hooke joint*. Also see illustration for *yoke*.

unleaded gasoline Gasoline devoid or nearly devoid of tetraethyl lead. Also see *lead-free gasoline*.

unsprung weight The weight of the parts of a car not supported by its springs, including wheels and tires, outboard brake assemblies, the rear axle assembly, suspension members, springs, shock absorbers, and anti-roll bars.

Unsprung weight can be reduced with independent rear suspension because the differential can be attached to the body. Engineers, especially race car designers, strive for low unsprung weight because it allows them to fit softer shocks and springs while still achieving the handling and ride characteristics they seek. The lower the unsprung weight, the less likely the car will be upset when encountering road irregularities. Other means of reducing unsprung weight include inboard brakes and the use of light alloys for suspension members, brakes, and wheels. Also see *sprung weight*.

updraft carburetor A carburetor in which the air-fuel mixture flows upward to the intake manifold and cylinders.

upshift In a transmission, to change from a lower gear (numerically higher ratio) to a higher gear (numerically lower ratio).

urethane Firm yet pliable plastic commonly used for suspension bushings in high-performance applications because of its rigidity. Other types of urethane are used in a car's body to reduce transmission of noise and vibration and to increase body stiffness. For example, during manufacturing of the body, urethane in the form of liquid foam can be injected into the tubelike structural members forming a car's A-, B-, and C-pillars. When the body is baked during the painting process, the urethane expands and hardens.

UTQG See *Uniform Tire Quality Grading*.

U

vacuum advance A mechanism that automatically varies the instant at which the spark occurs as a function of intake manifold vacuum. Vacuum advance provides the additional advance needed when the engine is operating at part throttle, when less air-fuel mixture gets into the cylinders and takes longer to burn after it is ignited. Without additional ignition advance, the piston would be past top dead center and moving down before the mixture had a chance to burn and produce full power.

The typical vacuum advance mechanism consists of a flexible, spring-loaded diaphragm connected by a linkage to the breaker plate on which the points are mounted. The diaphragm's sealed side is connected by a tube to the carburetor. The throttle valve is below the vacuum passage in the carburetor air horn, so there is no vacuum advance when the engine is idling because the throttle is closed. However, when the throttle is partly open, intake manifold vacuum pulls the diaphragm in, causing the breaker plate to rotate a few degrees and advance the timing. At wide-open throttle there is very little vacuum in the intake manifold, so there will be little or no vacuum advance. The vacuum advance operation with a fuel injection system is similar to a carburetor.

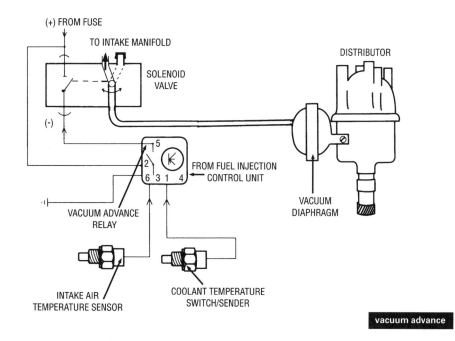

vacuum advance

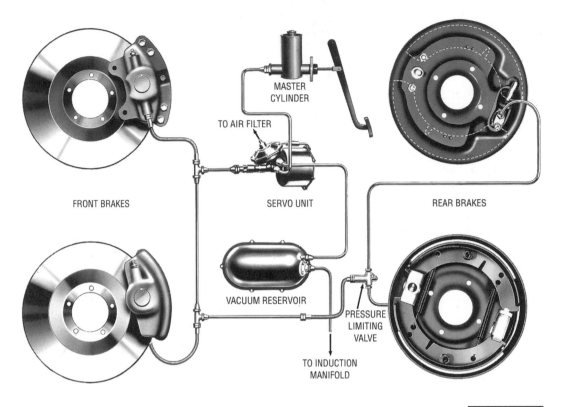

MASTER CYLINDER

TO AIR FILTER

FRONT BRAKES

SERVO UNIT

REAR BRAKES

VACUUM RESERVOIR

PRESSURE LIMITING VALVE

TO INDUCTION MANIFOLD

vacuum assist

vacuum assist   Engine vacuum used to reduce the driver's effort in performing a function such as braking.

valance   Front and rear areas under the bumpers designed to hide a car's suspension and other chassis components from view. Also called *modesty panel* or *modesty skirt.*

valve   A device that controls or restricts the flow of a liquid or gas. Also see *poppet valve.*

Also, the mechanical device used to admit, retain, and exhaust air in a tire. The tire valve typically consists of the base, the stem, an inner core, and a protective cap which also serves to retain air in the tire. Also see *exhaust valve* and *intake valve.*

valve bounce   See *bounce.*

valve clearance   The gap between the end of the valve stem and rocker arm or valve lifter; necessary to compensate for expansion due to heat. Also called *valve lash.*

valve float   A condition in an engine at high rotational speeds in which the valves no longer follow the cam contours, but "float" in a semi-open state. When valve float occurs, it effectively puts an upper limit on engine speed.

valve guide   The cylindrical hole in the cylinder head or block, usually containing a bushing to serve as a bearing surface, that keeps the valve moving up and down in a straight line.

valve-in-head engine   See *overhead valve engine.*

valve job   Engine repair that entails removing the cylinder head(s) and disassembling and machining all the valve components installed in the head: grinding the valves, grinding or replacing the valve seats in the head, repairing or replacing the valve guides, possibly replacing the valve springs and valve keepers, resurfacing (truing) the cylinder head, and reassembling the components to manufacturer specifications.

valve keeper   See *keepers.*

valve lash   See *valve clearance.*

valve lifter   See *cam follower.*

valve seat   The ring of hardened metal at the end of the valve guide nearest the combustion chamber, against which the back of an intake or exhaust valve rests (seats) when it is closed. See *seat.*

valve seat insert   See *insert.*

valves per cylinder   The number of valves in a cylinder head. The more valves per cylinder, the better the engine breathes. The smallest number is two, one intake and one exhaust. A three-valve head would generally have two intake and one exhaust valves per cylinder; a four-valve head would have two intake and two exhaust valves per cylinder.

valve spring   A small spring, generally of coil wire, that closes the valve after it has been opened by the cam, and prevents the valve from bouncing on its seat. The spring's action keeps the lifter in contact with the cam. If the spring is weak, the valve will be noisy and the valve, spring, lifter, and cam will be subjected to hammer-like blows that cause metal fatigue.

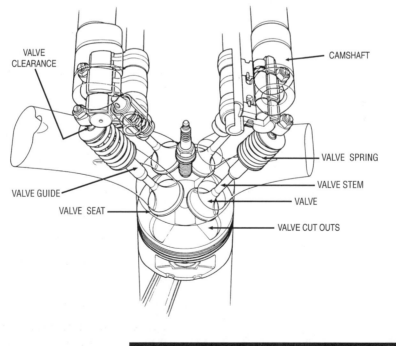

valve; valve clearance; valve guide; valve seat; valve spring; valve stem

valve stem   Long cylindrical portion of a valve that moves up and down in the valve guide.

valve train   The assembly of parts that open and close the valves. Includes the camshaft(s), the various parts that convert the camshaft's rotary motion into reciprocating motion at the valves, and the valves and their associated parts.

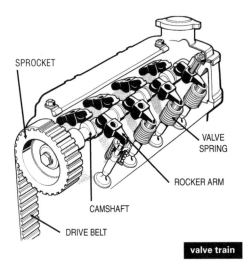

SPROCKET

VALVE SPRING

ROCKER ARM

CAMSHAFT

DRIVE BELT

valve train

van   A one-box design in which the passenger compartment and luggage compartment are integral, providing a flexible interior space with seating for up to fifteen passengers in a full-size van or, with the rear seats removed, space for cargo. A van is usually powered by a six- or eight-cylinder engine with rear drive; the driver sits well forward, often over the front wheels, and the engine is often located under a cover between the two front seats. Vans are frequently used as commercial vehicles. Also see *box*.

vanity mirror   A mirror, sometimes lighted, incorporated into the driver's and/or passenger's visor or inside the glove compartment.

vapor injection   See *water injection*.

vapor lock   A condition in which fuel boils in the fuel system, forming bubbles that retard or stop the flow of fuel to the carburetor or cause the float chamber to overflow. The overflow can flood the carburetor and result in an over-rich mixture that can stall the engine.

vapor recovery system   See *evaporative emission control*.

variable-assist power steering   A power-assisted steering system in which the degree of assistance provided at the wheel increases or decreases directly with engine speed or road speed. It provides a relatively high degree of assistance when it's needed most, namely in parking and other low-speed maneuvers, and little or none at higher road speeds when steering effort naturally decreases and a greater degree of road feel is desirable. Also called *variable power-assisted steering*. Also see *speed-sensitive power steering*.

variable power-assisted steering   See *variable-assist power steering*.

variable-ratio steering   Steering in which the steering ratio does not remain constant as the steering wheel is turned from lock-to-lock. Typically, such steering will be slower (a higher numerical ratio) when the car is being driven straight, so that the steering is not overly sensitive on-center. The ratio will quicken (a lower numerical ratio) near the extremes of steering lock to reduce the amount of steering effort required during low-speed maneuvering such as parallel parking.

variable spring rate   See *spring rate*.

variable-venturi carburetor   See *air-valve carburetor*.

V-belt   See *fan belt*.

vehicle identification number (VIN)   A number plate, typically affixed to the top of the dashboard (by law it must be visible from outside the vehicle), with the serial number identifying the vehicle by model, year of manufacture, and basic equipment.

velocity The speed of an object plus the direction in which it is moving. Not to be used interchangeably with speed. Velocity is a vector quantity, meaning it has magnitude and direction; speed is a scalar quantity, meaning it has magnitude only.

V-engine An engine configuration in which two banks of cylinders are set at an angle to each other, forming a V in end view.

vented disc brake See *ventilated disc brake.*

ventilated disc brake A disc brake whose rotors have ducts for admitting air to cool the rotor surfaces; the brakes resist heat buildup and are less prone to fade. The rotors may be vented internally by air passing between the discs or externally via holes drilled perpendicu-

lar to the rotor face. The latter are called cross-drilled. Also called *vented disc brake.*

venturi In a carburetor, the streamlined constriction or throat in the air horn that produces the vacuum which draws fuel out of a small tube or jet and into the passing air.

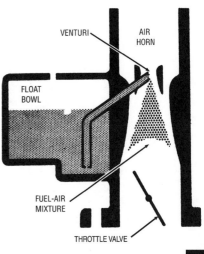

venturi

vent window See *quarter window.*

vent wing See *quarter window.*

vibration damper See *harmonic balancer.*

VIN See *vehicle identification number.*

vintage An old or historic vehicle, officially one built before 1925.

viscosity A fluid's resistance to flow. An oil with high viscosity is thick and flows slowly; an oil with low viscosity flows easily.

viscosity index The pattern of a fluid's change of viscosity relative to temperature.

V

viscous coupling A type of clutch in which a fluid, typically silicone, effects engagement. Most frequently used to limit slip in a differen-

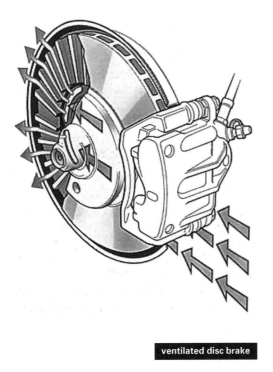

ventilated disc brake

tial and/or provide drive to a second set of wheels in a four-wheel-drive vehicle, it typically consists of two alternating sets of discs, each connected to a separate shaft. As long as no relative motion exists between the two shafts, the fluid remains relatively cool and there is no locking action. When relative motion develops, as when one wheel or one set of wheels begins to spin, the silicone fluid heats up and its viscosity increases; this locks the two sets of discs together and limits relative motion between them.

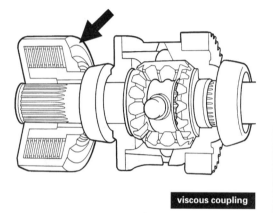

viscous coupling

viscous limited-slip differential　A differential in which a viscous coupling limits slip. Also see *viscous coupling*.

visor　A thin, flip-down panel stowed above the windshield for shading the driver's and the front passenger's eyes from glare. Generally, visors pivot to the side windows where they provide a similar function. The underside of the visor often incorporates a lighted vanity mirror.

volatility　Measure of the ease with which a fluid vaporizes. For example, gasoline is more volatile (has higher volatility) than kerosene because it evaporates at a lower temperature.

volt　A measure of electrical force. One volt produces an electric current of one amp through a resistance of one ohm.

voltage regulator　An electrical device that prevents the voltage of an electrical circuit from exceeding a safe level; also maintains a constant voltage in a car's electrical system. When the battery needs charging, the regulator cuts resistance out of the alternator field current to increase current in that circuit, with the result that output is increased. When the battery becomes fully charged, resistance is cut back into the field circuit so that the charging rate is decreased.

voltage regulator

volumetric efficiency　See *breathing capacity*.

vulcanization　A stage in the manufacture of rubber during which the chain molecules of the rubber are welded by means of the vulcanizing agent, sulphur. This restores and preserves the resilience and elasticity possessed by rubber in its natural state, but which it loses during the mechanical processing and under heat. Vulcanization is carried out in molds at about 284 degrees Fahrenheit with hot water and steam. During this process, the tire's tread pattern is formed in a metal mold by means of high pressure from within the mold.

wagon   See *station wagon.*

wall-to-wall   See *turning circle.*

wander   A vehicle's tendency to stray or wander from its intended direction of travel as a result of steering abnormalities, worn tires, suspension misalignment, crosswinds, or pavement irregularities. Also see *directional stability.*

Wankel engine   Rotary internal combustion engine developed in Germany by Felix Wankel. It consists of an equilateral triangular member with curved sides orbiting about an eccentric on a shaft inside a stationary housing. The rotor is in sliding contact with the eccentric and imparts power to the eccentric shaft in a manner similar to a connecting rod and a crankshaft. With one-third of a rotor revolution per shaft revolution and a power impulse for each of the rotor's three sides, the Wankel generates one power impulse per revolution per rotor, twice that which a four-cycle piston engine produces. Thus it has become accepted practice to multiply a Wankel's geometry displacement by a factor of two for comparison with Otto-cycle piston engines.

The Wankel's advantages include compact size, light weight, and, because there are no reciprocating parts, smooth operation. Early drawbacks included relatively high fuel consumption and exhaust emissions, and possible sealing problems at the rotor tips. Mazda, the only automaker currently using the Wankel engine, has made significant improvements in all three of these areas. Widely known as a rotary engine.

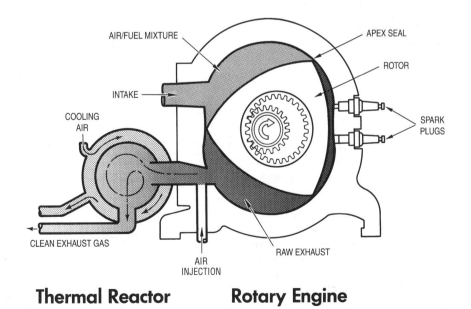

Thermal Reactor   Rotary Engine

Wankel engine

warning light   An indicator light that alerts the driver to specific or unsafe conditions such as low fuel level, low oil pressure, the need for engine servicing, brake failure, or that the headlights are on. Drivers who prefer gauges for certain of these functions, such as oil pressure, sometimes refer to these as idiot lights.

washboard   A road whose surface is rippled. Named for a device with a rippled surface on which one rubs clothes with soap and water to clean them. Also see *wheel patter*.

wastegate   A valve that diverts exhaust gas around the exhaust turbine or to the atmosphere to limit the boost produced by a turbocharger.

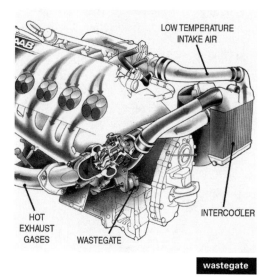

LOW TEMPERATURE INTAKE AIR

HOT EXHAUST GASES

WASTEGATE

INTERCOOLER

wastegate

water injection   A system that injects a small amount of water or alcohol-water mixture into the air-fuel mixture as it passes through the carburetor. Theoretically, as the water evaporates it should cool the incoming charge, which then becomes denser, leading to higher volumetric efficiency. In turn, this should lead to improved performance and economy, and allow the use of lower-octane fuel because the cooler charge suppresses detonation. Also called *vapor injection*.

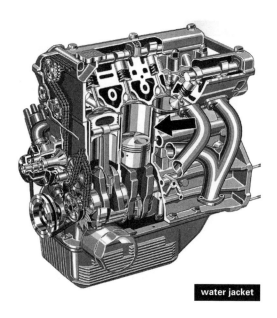

water jacket

water jacket   Space between the inner and outer shells of the cylinder block, head, or intake manifold in which coolant circulates.

water pump   A pump driven by a pulley and belt from the crankshaft that forces coolant through the cooling system.

Watt linkage   Three-bar linkage used for transverse location of a de Dion or live axle. Two methods are used to arrange a Watts link-

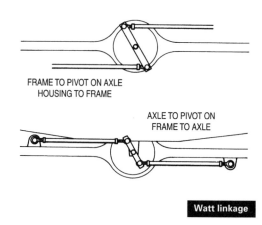

FRAME TO PIVOT ON AXLE HOUSING TO FRAME

AXLE TO PIVOT ON FRAME TO AXLE

Watt linkage

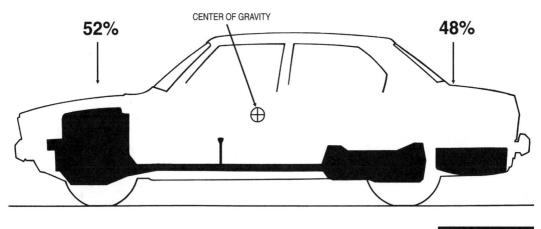

age: frame to pivot-on-axle-housing to frame, or axle to pivot-on-frame to axle. In both, the links constrain all axle movement to the vertical plane.

weather strip The rubber seals around the windows and door openings that seal the passenger compartment from inclement weather and noise. Similar seals are used around the trunk opening and the hood.

wedge-shaped combustion chamber A combustion chamber whose shape in cross section tapers to resemble a wedge. This creates a

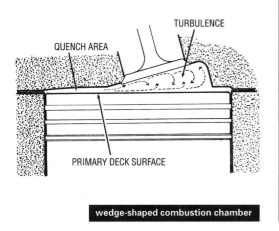

wedge-shaped combustion chamber

large quench area, allowing a high compression ratio in the cylinder for increased power. Also see *quench area.*

weight distribution Proportions of a car's total weight carried by the front and rear wheels; typically expressed as front/rear percentages. An important predictor of a car's handling, which generally improves the closer the weight distribution approaches 50/50.

weight transfer The shifting of a portion of a vehicle's weight forward during braking, rearward during acceleration, and from one side of the car to the other during cornering. In a left-hand corner, for instance, weight would be shifted from the inside (left side) of the car to the outside wheels (right side).

wet liner See *liner.*

wheel The circular, rigid metal frame consisting of a center section and a rim that connects the hub of a vehicle to a tire in a fixed but not permanent way. Also short for *steering wheel.*

wheel alignment See *alignment.*

wheel arch See *wheel well.*

wheel balance Absence of irregularities in a tire/wheel unit's distribution of mass.

W

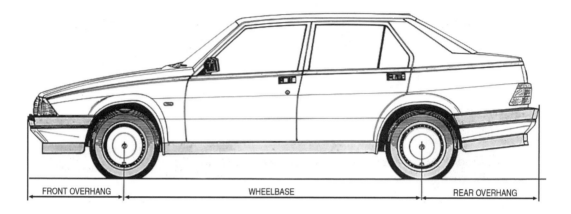

FRONT OVERHANG | WHEELBASE | REAR OVERHANG

Irregularities may cause vibration when rotating; severe irregularities may cause uneven tire wear. Also see *wheel balancing*.

wheel balancing The process in which small weights are attached to the wheel rim to eliminate such out-of-balance conditions as hop and vibration from the wheel/tire assembly. When tires were skinnier, they could be placed on a bubble balancer, which balanced in one plane only while the tire was motionless or static. Today's wider tires, however, can be in balance vertically while out of balance laterally. The most advanced balancing method is off-the-car computerized dynamic balancing in which the tire/wheel assembly spins on a machine and a computer determines exactly how much weight to attach to each rim, and at exactly what points.

wheelbase The longitudinal distance from the center of the front wheel to the center of the rear wheel on the same side of the car. In general, cars with a long wheelbase tend to be more stable but less nimble than those with a shorter wheelbase.

wheel cylinder A small cylinder with two pistons fitted inside a brake drum. Brake fluid from the master cylinder flows through brake lines into the wheel cylinder, pushing the pistons

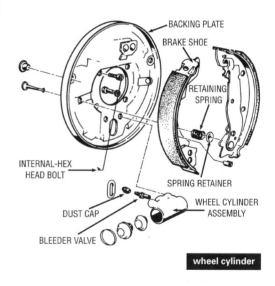

BACKING PLATE
BRAKE SHOE
RETAINING SPRING
INTERNAL-HEX HEAD BOLT
SPRING RETAINER
WHEEL CYLINDER ASSEMBLY
DUST CAP
BLEEDER VALVE

wheel cylinder

apart and forcing the shoes against the rotating brake drum to effect braking action. Also called *brake cylinder*. Also see *brake backing plate*.

wheel hop An undesirable condition in which a wheel (or wheels) moves up and down so violently that it actually leaves the ground. Wheel hop is associated with a variety of suspension problems such as poor torsional axle control, insufficient shock damping, improper shock location, or excessive unsprung weight. Also see *axle windup* and *tramp.*

wheel housing   See *wheel well.*

wheel lift   A condition occurring in cornering, in which a wheel lifts off the road surface.

wheel offset   The lateral distance from a wheel's vertical center plane to its mounting hub. If the wheel's center plane is outboard of its mounting hub, offset is positive; if it's inboard, offset is negative.

wheel patter   Short, relatively fast vertical wheel/tire movements, typically felt as a car crosses transverse ridges or tar strips in the pavement. Also called *bump-thump.* Also see *ride.*

wheel-rim flange   See *flange.*

wheel slip   In cornering, the phenomenon of a tire operating with a slip angle. Also see *slip angle, neutral steer, oversteer,* and *understeer.*

wheelspin   Rotation of a wheel/tire unit at a speed greater than rolling speed, as when a drive wheel spins on ice or snow. Also see *traction control.*

wheel tramp   See *axle windup.*

wheel travel   See *suspension travel.*

wheel well   Opening in a car's fender that partially encloses the wheel. Also called *wheel arch* or *wheel housing.*

windscreen   See *windshield.*

windshield   The front window through which the driver views the road. Called *windscreen* by the British.

windshield wiper   A mechanical arm on which a replaceable rubber blade is attached. The arm sweeps across the windshield or rear window to clear water or snow. Typically, two wipers are mounted at the base of the windshield.

wind tunnel   An indoor test facility in which the airflow characteristics of a body such as a car may be simulated for study and evaluation. For obvious practical reasons, the subject body (either a scale or full-size model) is stationary and the air moves instead. The air stream is generated by a large fan at one end of a carefully designed tunnel-like structure with known airflow properties, thus permitting accurate comparison among different shapes or variations of a single form.

First applied to automobiles in the early thirties, today wind-tunnel testing plays an important part in the automotive design process. It tends to result in reduced body drag, improved fuel economy, and reduced wind noise. Direct comparison of advertised coefficients for different cars is meaningless unless they were obtained under identical test conditions. Particulary for single-seater race cars where the wide tires are out in the air stream, the most accurate measurements of aerodynamic drag, lift, downforce, etc., are obtained when the tunnel has a moving ground plane. The moving ground plane spins the tires at simulated racing speeds, allowing the air flow over and around the the tires to be observed and measured.

wind tunnel

W

wind wander Tendency of a moving car to deviate from a straight course in air currents such as strong head winds, gusty crosswinds, and wake turbulence created by tractor-trailer trucks, and thus requiring steering correction. Generally a function of vehicle weight, weight distribution, height, aerodynamics and, to some extent, the drive system. All other things being equal, rear-engine/rear-drive cars tend to exhibit the most wind wander, front-engine/front-drive and front-engine/four-wheel-drive cars the least. Also see *yaw.*

wind wing See *quarter window.*

wing

wing An aerodynamic device resembling an upside-down airplane wing attached to a car to induce downforce on either the front or rear end. Also see *airfoil, downforce,* and *ground effect.* Also see *lateral support.*

wiring harness Bundled color-coded wires connecting a car's electrical components to their proper electrical circuits.

wishbone See *A-arm.*

W-link A lateral locating device for a live axle; similar to a Panhard rod, but more compact.

wood alcohol See *methanol.*

worm-and-sector steering See *recirculating ball-and-nut steering.*

worm gear Basically an endless screw which, when engaged with a toothed wheel (the worm wheel), forms a device by which the rotary motion of one shaft can be transmitted to another shaft at right angles to it.

worm wheel See *worm gear.*

wrist pin See *piston pin.*

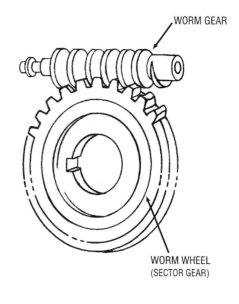

WORM GEAR

WORM WHEEL
(SECTOR GEAR)

worm gear; worm wheel

X-band   A radar frequency used by burglar alarms, automatic door openers, and radar guns.

yaw   Rotation of a body about its vertical axis. Yaw occurs when a car corners or otherwise changes its direction of travel.

yaw moment of inertia   See *moment of inertia.*

yaw response   The lag between the input from the steering wheel and the output in terms of change in angular momentum.

yoke   In general, a control rod. Also a component of universal joints. See *universal joint.*

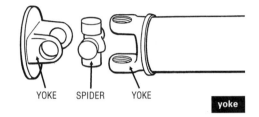

YOKE   SPIDER   YOKE

yoke

Zahnradfabrik Friedrichshafen (ZF)   A well-known German manufacturer of transmissions and transaxles used in many production and racing cars.

Z-bar   A suspension component operating in torsion, much like an anti-roll bar, and com-

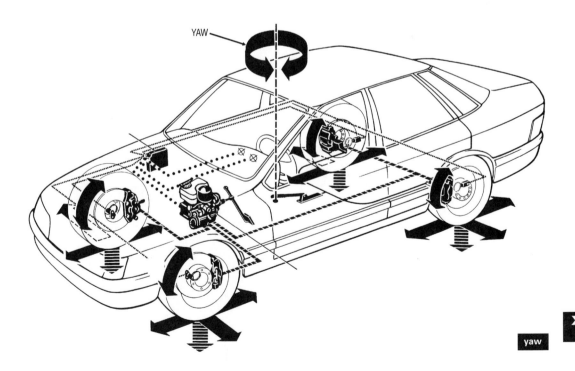

YAW

yaw

monly used in swing-axle suspensions to limit roll stiffness.

Zero emissions vehicle   A vehicle that emits no exhaust pollutants. Currently, only electric vehicles qualify and even they use electricity from generating plants which do pollute the atmosphere.

zero-offset steering   A steering system whose geometry has a zero scrub radius. Such a con-figuration minimizes the steering effects produced during acceleration with front-drive cars or braking on surfaces with varying traction at the different wheels.

ZF   See *Zahnradfabrik Friedrichshafen.*

Zyglow   A type of nondestructive testing used to check nonmagnetic parts for flaws or cracks using a dye penetrant and ultraviolet light. Similar to Magnaflux, which is used for ferrous metals.

ABOUT THE AUTHOR

John Dinkel began his automotive career with Chrysler Corp. in 1967 after earning two engineering degrees from the University of Michigan. Three years later he joined *Car Life* as Engineering Editor, followed by an almost 20-year career with *Road & Track* magazine, first as Engineering Editor, then Editor, and finally Editor-in-Chief. As a member of the SCCA (Sports Car Club of America) Dinkel is a four-time winner of the Nelson Ledges 24-hour endurance race. He was also a regular co-driver in the SCCA's Escort Endurance Series, winning two championships as part of the Bakeracing Corvette team. As an active member of the SAE, Dinkel has served as a chairman, member, and panelist on various committees, and as an author and reviewer of SAE technical papers.

Dinkel is the author of the original *Road & Track Illustrated Auto Dictionary* (1977), and co-author of two books with Jack Yamaguchi, *The Mazda RX-7: Mazda's Legendary Sports Car* and *Miata – Mazda MX-5: Mazda's Affordable Sports Car for the New Millennium.*

During his automotive career Dinkel has worked as an automotive product information specialist for two advertising agencies, Clinton E. Frank and Hill Holliday. More recently he served as the Group Manager for the Automobile Club of Southern California's Member Information and Communication Services, where he was responsible for the club's magazines, maps, and tour books. Currently Dinkel is the Vice President, Editorial Content, for DRIVIN.com, an automotive website. The former Mineola, New York native now lives in Irvine, California with his wife Leslie and kids Meredith and Kevin. In his sparetime he is actively involved in a variety of youth sports programs, plays on an Irvine softball team, and hosts a weekly public service radio show on automobiles, called *Drive Time*, on KUCI.

ART CREDITS

Photos and illustrations courtesy of:

Selected Books and Repair Information From Bentley Publishers

Driving

The Unfair Advantage *Mark Donohue*
ISBN 0-8376-0073-1(hc); 0-8376-0069-3(pb)

Going Faster! Mastering the Art of Race Driving
The Skip Barber Racing School ISBN 0-8376-0227-0

Driving Forces: The Grand Prix Racing World Caught in the Maelstrom of the Third Reich
Peter Stevenson ISBN 0-8376-0217-3

A French Kiss With Death: Steve McQueen and the Making of *Le Mans*
Michael Keyser ISBN 0-8376-0234-3

The Speed Merchants: A Journey Through the World of Motor Racing 1969-1972
Michael Keyser ISBN 0-8376-0232-7

Think To Win: The New Approach to Fast Driving
Don Alexander with foreword by Mark Martin
ISBN 0-8376-0070-7

Sports Car and Competition Driving
Paul Frère with foreword *by Phil Hill*
ISBN 0-8376-0202-5

The Technique of Motor Racing
Piero Taruffi ISBN 0-8376-0228-9

The Racing Driver
Denis Jenkinson ISBN 0-8376-0201-7

Engineering

Supercharged! Design, Testing, and Installation of Supercharger Systems
Corky Bell ISBN 0-8376-0168-1

Maximum Boost: Designing, Testing, and Installing Turbocharger Systems
Corky Bell ISBN 0-8376-0160-6

Bosch Fuel Injection and Engine Management
Charles O. Probst, SAE ISBN 0-8376-0300-5

Race Car Aerodynamics *Joseph Katz*
ISBN 0-8376-0142-8

Scientific Design of Exhaust and Intake Systems
Phillip H. Smith and John C. Morrison
ISBN 0-8376-0309-9

Other Enthusiast Titles

Mercedes-Benz E-Class Owner's Bible™ 1986–1995
Bentley Publishers ISBN 0-8376-0230-0

Civic Duty: The Ultimate Guide to the Honda Civic
Alan Paradise ISBN 0-8376-0215-7

Glory Days: When Horsepower and Passion Ruled Detroit *Jim Wangers*, with
Paul Zazarine ISBN 0-8376-0208-4

Jeep Owner's Bible™
Moses Ludel ISBN 0-8376-0154-1

Harley-Davidson Evolution V-Twin Owner's Bible™ *Moses Ludel* ISBN 0-8376-0146-0

Alfa Romeo Owner's Bible™
Pat Braden ISBN 0-8376-0707-8

Audi

Audi A4 Repair Manual: 1996–2001, 1.8L turbo, 2.8L, including Avant and quattro
Bentley Publishers ISBN 0-8376-0371-4

Audi A4 1996–2001, S4 2000–2001 Official Factory Repair Manual on CD-ROM
Bentley Publishers ISBN 0-8376-0833-3

Audi A6 Sedan 1998–2002, Avant 1999–2002, allroad quattro 2001–2002, S6 Avant 2002 Official Factory Repair Manual on CD-ROM
Bentley Publishers ISBN 0-8376-0836-8

Audi 80, 90, Coupe Quattro Official Factory Repair Manual: 1988–1992 including 80 Quattro, 90 Quattro and 20-valve models
Audi of America ISBN 0-8376-0367-6

BMW

BMW 3 Series Enthusiast's Companion™
Jeremy Walton ISBN 0-8376-0220-3

The BMW Enthusiast's Companion
BMW Car Club of America ISBN 0-8376-0321-8

Unbeatable BMW: Eighty Years of Engineering and Motorsport Success
Jeremy Walton ISBN 0-8376-0206-8

BMW 3 Series (E46) Service Manual: 1999–2001, 323i, 325i, 325xi, 328i, 330i, 330xi Sedan, Coupe, Convertible, Sport Wagon
Bentley Publishers ISBN 0-8376-0320-X

BMW 3 Series (E36) Service Manual: 1992–1998, 318i/is/iC, 323is/iC, 325i/is/iC, 328i/is/iC, M3
Bentley Publishers ISBN 0-8376-0326-9

BMW 3 Series (E30) Service Manual: 1984–1990 318i, 325, 325e(es), 325i(is), and 325i Convertible
Bentley Publishers ISBN 0-8376-0325-0

BMW 5 Series Service Manual: 1989–1995 525i, 530i, 535i, 540i, including Touring
Bentley Publishers ISBN 0-8376-0319-6

BMW 7 Series Service Manual: 1988–1994, 735i, 735iL, 740i, 740iL, 750iL
Bentley Publishers ISBN 0-8376-0328-5

(continued on next page)

Selected Books and Repair Information From Bentley Publishers

(continued)

Chevrolet

Zora Arkus-Duntov: The Legend Behind Corvette
Jerry Burton ISBN 0-8376-0858-9

Corvette from the Inside: The 50-Year Development History
Dave McLellan ISBN 0-8376-0859-7

Corvette Fuel Injection & Electronic Engine Management 1982–2001:
Charles O. Probst, SAE ISBN 0-8376-0861-9

Corvette by the Numbers: The Essential Corvette Parts Reference 1955–1982:
Alan Colvin ISBN 0-8376-0288-2

Chevrolet by the Numbers 1955–1959: The Essential Chevrolet Parts Reference
Alan Colvin ISBN 0-8376-0875-9

Chevrolet by the Numbers 1960–1964: The Essential Chevrolet Parts Reference
Alan Colvin ISBN 0-8376-0936-4

Chevrolet by the Numbers 1965–1969: The Essential Chevrolet Parts Reference
Alan Colvin ISBN 0-8376-0956-9

Chevrolet by the Numbers 1970–1975: The Essential Chevrolet Parts Reference
Alan Colvin ISBN 0-8376-0927-5

Chevrolet and GMC Light Truck Owner's Bible™
Moses Ludel ISBN 0-8376-0157-6

Camaro Exposed: 1967–1969, Designs, Decisions and the Inside View
Paul Zazarine ISBN 0-8376-0876-7

Ford

The Official Ford Mustang 5.0 Technical Reference & Performance Handbook: 1979–1993
Al Kirschenbaum ISBN 0-8376-0210-6

Ford F-Series Pickup Owner's Bible™
Moses Ludel ISBN 0-8376-0152-5

Ford Fuel Injection and Electronic Engine Control: 1988–19893
Charles O. Probst, SAE ISBN 0-8376-0301-3

Ford Fuel Injection and Electronic Engine Control: 1980–1987
Charles O. Probst, SAE ISBN 0-8376-0302-1

Porsche

Porsche Carrera 964 and 965, 1989–1994 Technician's Handbook: Without Guesswork™
Bentley Publishers ISBN 0-8376-0292-0

Porsche 911 Carrera Service Manual: 1984–1989
Bentley Publishers ISBN 0-8376-0291-2

Porsche 911 SC Coupe, Targa, and Cabriolet Service Manual: 1978–1983
Bentley Publishers ISBN 0-8376-0290-4

Volkswagen

Battle for the Beetle
Karl Ludvigsen ISBN 08376-0071-5

Volkswagen Sport Tuning for Street and Competition *Per Schroeder* ISBN 0-8376-0161-4

New Beetle Service Manual: 1998–2002 1.8L turbo, 1.9L TDI diesel, 2.0L gasoline
Bentley Publishers ISBN 0-8376-0376-5

New Beetle 1998–2002 Official Factory Repair Manual on CD-ROM
Bentley Publishers ISBN 0-8376-0838-4

Passat Service Manual: 1998–2002, 1.8L turbo, 2.8L V6, 4.0L W8, including wagon and 4MOTION
Bentley Publishers ISBN 0-8376-0393-5

Passat 1998–2002 Official Factory Repair Manual on CD-ROM *Bentley Publishers* ISBN 0-8376-0837-6

Jetta, Golf, GTI Service Manual: 1999–2002 2.0L Gasoline, 1.9L TDI Diesel, 2.8L VR6, 1.8L Turbo
Bentley Publishers ISBN 0-8376-0388-9

New Beetle Service Manual: 1998–1999, 2.0L Gasoline, 1.9L TDI Diesel, 1.8L Turbo
Bentley Publishers ISBN 0-8376-0385-4

Jetta, Golf, GTI, Cabrio Service Manual: 1993–1999, including Jetta$_{III}$ and Golf$_{III}$
Bentley Publishers ISBN 0-8376-0366-8

Eurovan Official Factory Repair Manual: 1992–1999
Volkswagen of America ISBN 0-8376-0335-8

Eurovan 1992–2002 Official Factory Repair Manual on CD-ROM *Bentley Publishers* ISBN 0-8376-0835-X

Jetta, Golf, GTI 1993–1999, Cabrio 1995–2002 Official Factory Repair Manual on CD-ROM
Bentley Publishers ISBN 0-8376-0834-1

Jetta, Golf, GTI Service Manual: 1985–1992 Gasoline, Diesel, and Turbo Diesel, including 16V
Bentley Publishers ISBN 0-8376-0342-0

Super Beetle, Beetle and Karmann Ghia Official Service Manual: Type 1, 1970–1979
Volkswagen of America ISBN 0-8376-0096-0